# HISPANIC
# NATION

Also by Geoffrey Fox

*Welcome to My Contri*
*The Land and People of Venezuela*
*The Land and People of Argentina*
*Gabriel García Márquez's* One Hundred Years of Solitude:
    *A Critical Commentary*
*Working-Class Emigrés from Cuba*

# HISPANIC

## Culture, Politics, and the Constructing of Identity

# NATION

## GEOFFREY FOX

A BIRCH LANE PRESS BOOK
Published by Carol Publishing Group

For my sons, Alex and Joaquín

A Birch Lane Press Book
Published by Carol Publishing Group
Birch Lane Press is a registered trademark of Carol Communications, Inc.

Editorial, sales and distribution, rights and permissions inquiries should be
addressed to Carol Publishing Group, 120 Enterprise Avenue, Secaucus, N.J.
07094

In Canada: Canadian Manda Group, One Atlantic Avenue, Suite 105,
Toronto, Ontario M6K 3E7

Carol Publishing Group books may be purchased in bulk at special discounts
for sales promotion, fund-raising, or educational purposes. Special editions
can be created to specifications. For details, contact: Special Sales
Department, Carol Publishing Group, 120 Enterprise Avenue, Secaucus, N.J.
07094.

Manufactured in the United States
10  9  8  7  6  5  4  3  2  1

**Library of Congress Cataloging-in-Publications Data**

Fox, Geoffrey E.
  Hispanic nation : culture, politics, and the constructing of
identity / Geoffrey Fox.
    p.    cm.
  "A Birch Lane Press book."
  ISBN 1-55972-311-4 (hardcover)
  1. Hispanic Americans—Ethnic identity.  2. Hispanic Americans—
Politics and government.  I. Title.
E184.S75F69   1995
305.868—dc20
                                                    95-4696
                                                    CIP

# Contents

# Acknowledgments

THE IDEAS EXPRESSED HERE were all first tested in discussions with Susana Torre, my partner in this and many other endeavors, who insisted that I write this book. Her encouragement at moments when the writing seemed especially difficult and her unsparing critiques of earlier drafts have been essential to the clarification of those ideas.

Janet Abu-Lughod, Marc Aronson, and Barbara Garson were also very helpful in sharpening this book's focus at an early stage.

I am very grateful to the many people, some of them old friends and others contacted just for this book, who took time from their work as public officials, television and newspaper professionals, creative artists, scholars, and community activists to answer my questions and share their thinking on the emerging Hispanic identity in this country. A few are quoted directly in the pages that follow; all contributed to the development and refinement of the argument. They work in New York, Miami, Atlanta, Chicago, Los Angeles, San Antonio, Washington, Phoenix, Milwaukee, and Grand Rapids and collectively represent almost every ethnic segment of the emerging Hispanic nation. A few are not themselves Hispanic but are very familiar with some of the issues discussed. They include Miguel Algarín, Daniel Alvarez, David Badillo, Luis "Tony" Báez, Sergio Bendixen, Samuel Betances, Frank Bonilla, Fortuna Calvo-Roth, Alice Cardona, Salvador Cervantes, Reinaldo Colón, Dennis De León, Jorge del Pinal, William Díaz, María Elena Diéguez, Angelo Falcón, Enrique Fernández, Ricardo Fernández, Claudio Gaete, Fr. Peter Gavigan, Jorge Gestoso, Gustavo Godoy, Sonia Goldenberg, David González, Fr. Neil Graham, Rep. Luis Gutiérrez (D-Ill.), María Hinojosa, Jaime Inclán, Patricia Janiot, José "Chacha" Jiménez, Howard Jordán, Guillermo Linares, Guillermo Martínez, Heriberto Mateo, Zenaida Méndez,

Luis Miranda, Lana Montalbán, Carlos Montes, Héctor Morales, Iris Morales, Fernando Moreno, Sergio Muñoz, Louis Núñez, Celeste Olalquiaga, Víctor Ortiz, Rep. Ed Pastor (D-Ariz.), Suni Paz, Fernando Pérez, Rubén Quiroz, Jorge Ramos, Benjamín Reyes, Luis O. Reyes, Stephen Rivera, José Luis Rodríguez, Albor Ruiz, William Salgado, María Elena Salinas, Ray Santiesteban, Jacob S. Siegel, Anthony Stevens-Arroyo, Lee Stewart, Judge Frank Torres, María de los Angeles Torres, Cecilia Vaisman, Marta Varela, Arturo Vázquez, Sara E. Vidal, and Blanca Rosa Vilches.

I am also grateful to Robert Brischetto, Miguel Algarín, Eduardo Márceles Daconte, Jorge Ramos, and Blanca Rosa Vilches, who read and commented on portions of the draft.

Finally, I extend a special note of appreciation to two people who accompanied me on earlier stages of the journey and helped me understand many of the subtler aspects of Hispanic life in the United States. They are Sylvia Herrera López, attorney and formerly director of Aspira of Illinois, who is the mother of Alex and Joaquín, and the anthropologist Mirtha Quintanales Font. I hope that they, and all the people mentioned here, will take this as another contribution to dialogues begun long ago and as an invitation to continue them.

# 1

# Imagining a Nation

WHEN MY SON ALEX first came to the United States from Puerto Rico at the age of seven, he brought a book which would come to have special importance to him. *Pedrito Qué-Soy-Yo* (Peter What-Am-I) was about a little animal who was looking for his own kind. He asked the ducks if he was one of them, but the ducks said, "No, you're too furry." He asked the beavers, but they said, "No, beavers don't have bills like yours, or webbed feet," and so on. Pedrito, dejected and alone, just kept waddling on.

In Evanston, Illinois, in the 1960s, nobody else we knew had a kitchen smelling of culantro and comino, nobody else gestured as vigorously as we did or stood as close to others when they talked, embraced friends as we did when they met, or spoke Spanish— habits that were spontaneous to my Puerto Rican wife and that I, although originally a midwesterner, had also picked up in Latin America. Most puzzling of all to Alex, the Evanstonians he met insisted on dividing all people into "blacks" and "whites," and Alex, with his large, dark eyes and long black lashes, thick, wavy black hair, and tawny skin, was both and therefore neither.

Looking for his kind, at first Alex tried to be "black," which was a new idea to him. He had known dark-skinned people in Puerto Rico whose lighter-skinned relatives would sometimes call them *negro* (black) as a term of affection, but Alex had never before seen blacks treated as a distinct cultural and status group, with their own behavior rules. Alex soon discovered that playing with "black" kids (many of them no darker than he) and bringing them home and visiting their homes was to shun and be shunned

1

by most of the white kids—who were usually no lighter than his own baby brother. Playing with white kids meant shunning the darker ones. Alex had been thrown into a society whose rules he could not obey, and this made him confused, angry, and for a while, withdrawn.

Color wasn't the only conundrum. He was also being treated as a foreigner, even though Puerto Ricans have been U.S. citizens since 1917. The school principal demanded U.S. Health Department certification before admitting him, and his homeroom teacher asked him how close Puerto Rico was to Madagascar (not very).

Pedrito in the story finally found his kind. He was, he discovered, an *ornitorrinco* (platypus), and there were lots of others like him. And a few years later, when we moved to Chicago, with its large Puerto Rican and Mexican communities, Alex discovered that he could be "Latino."

The "knowledge of fundamental belonging—that is, to be French, American, Mexican, English, is...one of the deepest needs of persons," wrote Virgil Elizondo, a Mexican-American priest and liberation theologian. "When this need is met, it is not even thought about as a need; but when it is missing, it is so confusing and painful that we find it difficult to even conceptualize it or speak about it."[1]

Elizondo was writing about what he called "the 'unfinished' identity" of the *mestizo*, which in Mexico is a person of mixed Indian and Spanish ancestry. But his observation on the need for a resolution of the conflict holds for all people who are between any two cultures. Among them are some 25 million people in the United States who trace their origins to somewhere in the Spanish-speaking world.

In a similar vein, James Baldwin wrote, "I have not written about being a Negro at such length because I expect that to be my only subject, but only because it was the gate I had to unlock before I could hope to write about anything else."[2] But, as Baldwin well knew, the quest for identity is not just a matter of finding the key to one's own personal gate. Like Pedrito the platypus, we hope to find others of our kind once we get that gate opened. Even more than platypuses, we humans need a community to confirm, and help shape, our identity. Unlike platypuses, however, we can take part in defining who our kind are, that is, which community we want to associate with, because human identity is not determined solely, or even mainly, by inherited characteristics.

This is true even for African Americans, the people whose self-definition is the most restricted by conventional attitudes in this country toward skin color, hair texture, and other "African" inherited traits. Ghanaian scholar Kwame Anthony Appiah has argued that identity for African Americans is not really centered on such physical traits. More important is "something that goes with" African descent, at least as it is understood in America: "the experience of a life as a member of a group of people who experience themselves as—and are held by others to be—a community in virtue of their mutual recognition—and their recognition by others—as people of a common descent."[3] In other words, physical characteristics are useful signs of membership, but what matters most is the sense of community. This is why someone who is physically "black" may not be accepted as "really black" if he or she does not share the values, speech patterns, and other habits of this supposed community.

Descent has even less to do with the identity of the people we call, and who sometimes call themselves, Hispanics or Latinos. This is mainly because they don't have a common biological descent. "Hispanics," the Census Bureau reminds us whenever it uses the term, "can be of any race." They can also be of any religion and any citizenship status, from undocumented to U.S. citizen by birth, and may have any of over twenty distinct national histories. They do not even all share the same first language. The effective definition of Hispanic in contemporary American ethnospeak is any person who either speaks Spanish as a first language or had some ancestor who did, even if this person speaks only English. Others whose ancestors may never have really mastered Spanish but who had Spanish surnames imposed on them by their conquerors—Mayans, Quechuas, Filipinos, and so on—are often given, and sometimes willingly assume, the label "Hispanic."

These diverse people are a community only to the extent and only in the ways that they imagine themselves to be. And the only sort of community they can imagine themselves to be is that vague sort we call a "people" or a "nation."

## Identity, Community, and Nation

In a provocative little book based mainly on his experiences in Indonesia, political anthropologist Benedict Anderson defines "nation" as "an imagined political community—and imagined as both inherently limited and sovereign."[4] It is imagined, he explains, as bound by language and traditions and endowed with certain political rights. The members do not all know one another personally and may, in fact, have very little in common beyond the language and a few of their traditions, and even these traditions may be recent inventions.[5] Yet they feel affiliated to one another and to some larger collective entity and may even, as with the Serbs of Bosnia and Croatia, go to war against their real geographic neighbors to promote their imaginary, national fellowship.

This way of imagining one's relationship to unknown others, Anderson argues, was virtually unknown before the seventeenth century. Earlier imagined communities had been based on a shared faith, such as the fellowship of Christians, or a myth of common ancestry, but not on language. Most communities were not imagined so much as experienced; that is, one's community was simply made up of people one saw and dealt with almost every day. According to Anderson, the concept of a community of all those who spoke the same language came as a result of "an explosive...interaction between a system of production and productive relations (capitalism), a technology of communications (print), and the fatality of human diversity."[6]

Beginning in the sixteenth and seventeenth centuries, the economies of European societies grew rapidly (agricultural revolution, population growth, improvements in navigation and banking practices); this growth led to incursions into Africa, Asia, and the Americas as well as large-scale internal migration, colonization, and the forced transport of slaves. Thus, for millions of people the home village ceased to be the relevant community, and they had to look for other bases for alliances and solidarity. Meanwhile, the new technology of the printing press was establishing a common lore among those who read the same language, proffering a new possible basis for community. Finally, there was the "fatality of human diversity," which meant that those who did not read the same language were excluded from the imagined community.

Today a similarly explosive interaction is igniting nationalist movements around the world, and again the detonators include rapid economic changes and new communications technology. These same factors, which in places as dissimilar as Bosnia, Rwanda, Sri Lanka, and Chiapas are sparking bloody nationalistic revolts, in the United States are contributing to the (so far) more peaceable creation of the new national identity of Hispanics.

More specifically, deindustrialization, unemployment, and a drop in real per capita incomes in Latin America over the past twenty to twenty-five years, caused by the precipitous decline in the values of traditional exports and other shifts in the global economy, plus the attendant political and civil strife in the region, have driven recent migration to the United States. Once here, people from more than twenty Spanish-speaking countries and hundreds of regions that previously had little contact end up crowded into the same neighborhoods and begin creating communities based on their shared language and shared new experiences in this country. These personal contacts enhance the importance of Spanish as a group identifier and bond across national differences, as Ecuadorian and Puerto Rican mothers band together for better day care in the Bronx or Salvadoran and Mexican and Peruvian youth form a soccer league in New Jersey or California. Such contacts predispose people to a feeling of kinship with other Spanish speakers they have never seen: an imagined community.

Imagining the new community is made easier by the new communications technologies, including television and the post-television media, such as the Internet and on-line computer services. Television has already proved more powerful than was the printing press for diffusing the images of an imagined community. All viewers of nationally broadcast Spanish-language television become parts of a united audience, learning of the same events and hearing their language spoken in relatively homogeneous accents, not easily identifiable as Puerto Rican or Mexican or Argentine or Cuban, but simply as Hispanic. And on television the imagined community also has faces, making it more like one's real, day-to-day community.

One of the most popular Spanish-language dictionaries, *Pequeño Larousse Ilustrado,* defines "nation" as a "natural society of men among whom the unity of territory, origin, history, language, and culture inclines toward a community of life and creates the consciousness of a common destiny."[7]

Like nationalists everywhere, the promoters of the imagined community of Hispanics—let's call them pan-Hispanicists—speak as though this community were a "natural society," as though it existed previous to and independent of any conscious intervention by them. They may be partly right. Spanish speakers and their desdendants from places as widely separated as Chile and Mexico often feel a *simpatía,* a recognition of themselves in the other, that they do not have with non-Hispanics. But for this vague mutual recognition to translate into community rather than warfare, as with those most intimate enemies the Serbs and Bosnians, or into competition, as between Dominican and Puerto Rican grocery-store owners in parts of New York, common institutions and a shared ideology have to be created.

The promoters of Hispanic unity need a history which emphasizes the common events and "forgets" the dissimilar or conflictive ones. "The essence of a nation," French philosopher Ernest Renan observed, "is that all the individuals have much in common, and also that they have forgotten many things."[8] This is why Hispanics in the U.S. put such stress—far more than do people in Latin America—on the mythical date of origin: *El Día de la Raza,* (The Day of the Race), October 12, 1492, when Christopher Columbus landed in the Antilles and, so the story goes, began the mixing of Europeans, indigenous Americans, and Africans to create a new, hybrid people. Pan-Hispanicists may also refer to the common political and cultural history of more than three hundred years of Spanish colonialism. What you will not hear much about from them are the slaughters of indigenous peoples as part of the conquest or the later wars between Chile, Peru, and Bolivia, between Paraguay and Argentina, Uruguay and Brazil, between Paraguay and Bolivia, or among the five Central American republics, most recently Honduras and El Salvador, in 1969. The *imagined* community, unlike its real components, is unitary and harmonious.

"Unity of language," the next element in the Larousse definition of a nation, is the most important constituent of the Hispanic nation. The language is a mark of membership. It is also a source of pride, because it connects U.S. Hispanics—even those who barely speak and read it—to a prestigious literary tradition that runs from Cervantes through the Nobel Prize winners Gabriela Mistral, Miguel Angel Asturias, Pablo Neruda, Gabriel García Márquez, and Camilo José Cela. And it is, of course, a practical tool for building institutions, being a required skill in many U.S.-based organizations that in one way or another serve a large and growing Spanish-speaking clientele, from community-based service organizations to ad agencies to the whole Spanish-language media industry. Today Americans of Spanish-speaking ancestry who do not speak the language often try to learn it, and most want their children to learn it, too. The growth of Spanish-language television makes this much easier, since they can learn by watching soap operas and other entertainment. It also tends to standardize the emerging North American dialect of Spanish and increases its usefulness.

U.S. Hispanics are not—most of them, anyway—laying claim to a united territory. It may therefore be objected that Hispanics cannot become a "nation" because they have neither a flag nor a land to fly it over. And if they did, where would it be? A secessionist chunk of the American Southwest? East Harlem? Miami?

But today, thanks mostly to television, this lack of territorial specificity is no obstacle to a sense of nationhood. As one of the most insightful media analysts has observed, "The relationship between group identity and group territory is tied to the traditional relationship between place and information access....By severing the traditional link between physical location and social situation,...electronic media may begin to blur previously distinct group identities by allowing people to 'escape' informationally from place-defined groups...."[9]

By the same token, the media also permit people to "enter" a group informationally, facilitating the formation of new group identities. Today television and the newer communications technologies create a virtual Hispanic-land which is as seductive and convincing as the fabled Cipangu on the maps of Columbus. Viewers of Spanish-language television news and entertainment see one continuous Hispanic territory that stretches across the United States and all the way to Spain and the nineteen Spanish-speaking countries of Ibero-America. This vast imagined homeland may well be sufficient to anchor the imagined community.

As Guillermo Gómez-Peña's hybrid multiculti character El Johnny tries to explain to the ethnopolice in the performance poem "Califas,"

> it's confusing
> we know
> our nation extends
> from the tip of Patagonia
> to the peak of your tortured imagination.[10]

## Birth of a "Meme": The Hispanic Nation

The idea that the Spanish-speaking peoples of America possess a common purpose and destiny is an example of what British zoologist Richard Dawkins has called a "meme"—a word he derived from "mimeme" or "mimesis," meaning imitation. A meme is any replicable unit of consciousness which, like a gene in biology, propagates itself by invading a receptive host, and from there other hosts, regardless of its effects on those hosts.

Memes can be "tunes, ideas, catchphrases, clothes fashions, ways of making pots or of building arches." In the same way a virus parasitizes a host cell, memes can parasitize a brain, taking over part of its functions in order to propagate themselves "by leaping from brain to brain."[11]

The meme of pan-Hispanic cultural and political community originated as a by-product of Spanish imperialism, itself the result of a fusion of linguistic nationalism, kingly arrogance, and missionary zeal in the court of Fernando and Isabel in 1492. In that year the Catholic monarchs expelled the Jews from their newly united and newly Christian kingdom, published the first grammar of the Castilian language (what we call Spanish), and sent Christopher Columbus off with three ships to look for India.

The overwhelming success of the Spanish conquest of America soon made the court's missionary zeal superfluous, except perhaps in the borderlands. Even lackadaisical, venal, and uninspired bureaucrats were able to manage the enterprise once indigenous resistance had been crushed. During the next three hundred years and more of Spanish colonial rule, the complex imperialist ideology gradually crumbled into its component pieces of linguistic nationalism, monarchism, and religious zeal, as the ideas of imperial and ecclesiastical hierarchy became less essential for maintaining a cultural unity that was no longer seriously challenged. Thus, it was the meme of cultural unity, purged of the icons of church and monarchy, that leaped into the brains of some of the Spanish Americans or "Creoles" in Mexico City, Caracas, Buenos Aires, Santiago de Chile, and other cities when they declared independence from Spain in 1810. One of the brains most thoroughly parasitized was Simón Bolívar's. This new meme linked itself to other tunes and catchphrases and fashions already bouncing around there to help form an elaborate fantasy of a pan-American republic that would stretch from the Strait of Magellan to the Strait of Juan de Fuca (where Vancouver is today). Thanks to other memes picked up in his readings and travels, Bolívar envisioned this republic as ruled by a Greco-Roman parliament with its capital in Panama, the geographic center of his imaginary Hispanic nation.[12]

That idea was never seriously put into effect, but the meme lived on. Its later hosts and propagators have included (among others) the Chilean Francisco Bilbao (who coined the term "Latin America"), the Puerto Rican Eugenio María de Hostos, the Uruguayan José E. Rodó, and the Cuban José Martí in the nineteenth century, and the Peruvians Víctor Haya de la Torre and José Carlos Mariátegui and the Argentine Ernesto "Che" Guevara in the twentieth. All their attempts to make pan-Hispanic political-cultural unity a reality failed, but the meme survived and even now is leaping nimbly from brain to brain, transmitted by books and television and, more recently, the Internet.[13]

However, the meme of Hispanic-American, or "Latino," unity in the United States, while related to and probably descended from the one in Latin America, is significantly different in both form and consequences. For one thing, the Hispanic-American intellectuals promoting it have less influence over their coethnics than do intellectuals in Latin America, partly because intellectuals in general are less influential here and mostly because there are so many other influences on the thinking of Hispanics in the United States. The promoters of Hispanic unity must compete against narrower loyalties, such as Cuban or Honduran nationalism, and against the power of U.S. institutions, which pull people into other kinds of communities (as college students, workers, Democratic or Republican voters, and so on). Also, Hispanic intellectuals in the United States have usually received their education in English, so their knowledge of Bolívar, Eugenio María de Hostos, and José Martí and others may often be rather patchy.

More important, the classic Latin American pan-Hispanicists, whatever their other differences, all conceived of Latin American unity as outside of and *in opposition to* the power of the United States. The U.S. Hispanics in almost all cases are trying to *become part* of that power, to "get a piece of the action." And there are other ways that they are inextricably tied to U.S. institutions. For example, it would be unwise to trample the U.S. flag when thousands of Hispanic Americans are prepared to die for it or to rail against Anglo-Saxon values when only the First Amendment stands between you and a lynching. Broadly speaking, then, U.S. Hispanic politics are not separatist but are firmly entrenched in U.S. political institutions and cannot be understood outside of them. The major exceptions would be those Hispanics who are committed, above all, to independence for Puerto Rico, to the secession of "Aztlán" (the Chicano Southwest), or to the overthrow of communism in Cuba—three very different agendas. But as exceptions these cases are dubious, because people's motives are almost always somewhat mixed. In practice even Puerto Rican *independentistas*, Chicano secessionists and Cuban *exiliados* take a keen interest in local U.S. power and privileges and are quick to avail themselves of constitutional protections.

For these and probably other reasons, in this country the old meme of Latin American unity links up with either or both of the meme clusters that have been most recurrent in U.S. history. The first of these, known in Ben Franklin's day as "trade" and today as "marketing," has as its contemporary symbols the graph and the spreadsheet, in place of the more typical Latin American images of the poet's quill or the rebel's raised machete. Magazines such as *Hispanic* or *Hispanic Business* and the producers of Spanish-language television are forever talking about the numbers of Hispanic dollars, Hispanic votes, Hispanic audience, and so on— in short, of Hispanic *market* strength. This is a concept quite foreign to Bolívar or José Martí.

The second *yanqui* meme cluster, which is every bit as old as the first, does have something in common with the raised-machete icon south of the border. A raised fist is its most frequent symbol here, its catchphrase is "Give me liberty or give me death!" or "Don't tread on me!" These memes cluster to form a concept of personal liberty combined with solidarity for the other "little guys," which together amount to a radical, almost anarchic version of democracy. This cluster was present at Lexington and Concord and in Shay's Rebellion and has popped up repeatedly in both left and right outlaw movements, from Quantrill's raiders to the "participatory democracy" of the 1960s Students for Democratic Society (SDS), and on to the populist campaigns of gun owners and environmental protectionists of today. The memes can parasitize equally a left- or right-thinking brain; either way, they tend to propagate some form of radical populist action. This cluster's tendency toward anarchy makes it fit poorly with imported, more authoritarian doctrines which may be superficially similar. It has made American Fascists too unruly to accept German or even Italian discipline and led American Communists to pursue erratic and idiosyncratic courses that were the exasperation of Moscow.

Among Hispanics, this anarchic-democratic meme cluster spreads most rapidly through the brains of those who have the most experience in this country, inspiring a whole series of radical movements—Brown Berets, Young Lords, and others—that may mimic, but can never replicate, the far more hierarchical radical movements in Latin America.

These two meme clusters of marketing and democratic anarchism can easily cohabit in the same brain, as we see when a politician spouts radical rhetoric but keeps his eye on the poll numbers. No incompatibility is too great for the human mind. Nevertheless, these two meme clusters do tend in different directions, marketing toward the "Right" (tactically) and anarcho-democracy toward the "Left." Here I am referring primarily to *tactical* differences, allowing the possibility that the "Right" tactics of cooperation and negotiation may be associated with a vision of social transformation that is ultimately more radical than that of the "Left" tactic of confrontation.

The "Right" vision accepts the power structure as more or less permanent but dynamic and fluid and responsive to group pressure. Its goal is to join the structure and to use it to benefit one's group, and to do that one needs to assemble as large a group as possible. The Hispanic "Left" sees the power structure as a fortress of whites designed to keep out all people of color, including themselves, and yielding only to force.

## The Name of the Nation: "Hispanics" Versus "Latinos" and Others

Differences of political vision may help explain why so much passion is invested in a terminological debate that is mystifying to outsiders: whether the people we are talking about should be called Latinos or Hispanics.

Today this may seem as pointless as the famous dispute in Jonathan Swift's *Gulliver's Travels* between the "big enders" and the "little enders," who went to war over the proper way to crack an egg. Outside of academic and "activist" circles, it is of concern to a tiny portion of the people referred to, most of whom are indifferent as to which generic term is used and use the two interchangeably. In any case, almost all prefer to be called by their more specific nationality or background: Mexican, Puerto Rican, Cuban, or whatever.[14] But in its origins, like Swift's egg question, the "Hispanic"-"Latino" dispute was about something that seemed to matter. The two terms then represented different strategic and class visions.

What I have referred to as the "Right," or less confrontational and more market-minded wing of the panethnic movement, needed a name that would bring the most people together and would not frighten those already in power so much that they would bar access. Leaders of this tendency have described their constituency at various times as "Latin American" and "Spanish," before settling around 1980 on "Hispanic." The word, from Latin *Hispanicus*, literally means "of Spain." Most people use the term to mean nothing more than "people of Spanish-speaking heritage," regarding it as politically and racially neutral.

The essence of the "Left's" vision of itself is permanent opposition to the imagined power structure. Rebels always want a fighting name for themselves, a name that conveys their challenge. The clearest instance of a defiant, intentionally insolent self-naming by Hispanics was the adoption by some young Mexican Americans twenty-five years ago of the slang word *chicano* when other Mexican Americans considered it offensive or vulgar. *Los Angeles Times* journalist Rubén Salazar put the case most clearly in one of his last columns: "A Chicano is a Mexican-American with a non-Anglo image of himself."[15] This naming was a great success, but Chicanos are only one segment of the larger ethnic community. Permanent oppositionists, tactically on the "Left" and a larger group than the Chicano community, have convinced themselves that "Latino" is the more defiant name.[16]

Today "Chicano" (capitalized in English but not in Spanish) has become such a familiar term, just another synonym for Mexican American, that it has lost its punch. In contrast, "Latino" never had much of a punch. It is not an old in-group slang word or a former term of abuse, as *chicano* had been. At most, it mildly offends some Hispanics, who regard it as a bad dialect joke, neither real Spanish (in Spanish, the *latinos* are another people all together) nor real English.

In fact, "Latino" is simply a truncated form of a nineteenth-century romantic nationalist idea that has its origins in the French Second Empire of Napoleon III. The phrase "Latin America" has been traced to an 1856 speech by the Chilean author Francisco Bilbao and around the same time (and apparently independently) an essay by the Uruguayan José María Torres Caicedo, both of whom were then in exile in Paris. The phrase accomplished a number of things simultaneously: It dramatized the distinction between what had hitherto been known as Spanish America and what Bilbao, Torres Caicedo, and their friends called Anglo-Saxon America, interpreting the division as a conflict between two types of souls (the Latins being the more soulful, naturally). Second, by replacing "Spanish" with "Latin," they could ignore their historical connection to Spain, a country they had still not forgiven for its colonial past and which had lost all its prestige along with its empire. More important, the phrase implied a connection to France, the acknowledged leader of the Latin world. Finally, like its predecessor "Spanish America," the phrase "Latin America" continued to suppress any hint of their countries' embarrassing indigenous or African heritages.[17]

The phrase *Amérique latine* was picked up by the *Revue des Deux Mondes* and other propaganda organs of the Emperor Napoleon III, who must have been pleased to have so many new subjects attributed to him. To show his appreciation, Napoleon III sent an expeditionary army under his cousin Maximilian to invade Mexico in 1863. This caused Bilbao to drop the term, but it was too late; the catchphrase Latin America had already parasitized other brains, and today we hardly know how to speak of the region without it. (The Mexicans, unimpressed, routed the French troops and shot Maximilian four years later.)

Most contemporary Latinos, however, probably know little or nothing about the Latin imperialism of Napoleon III. Those who make an issue of the word say they dislike the term Hispanic because it reminds them of Spain, which they refuse to forgive for the conquest 450 years ago and they prefer not to be reminded that that is where many of their ancestors came from. (As Renan said, to make a nation, we have to forget many things.) Sometimes people will say they prefer "Latino" because it joins them to other Western Hemisphere speakers of Latin-based languages, such as Brazilians and Haitians, although, oddly, they never seem to include the French-speaking Québecois and Cajuns, and they explicitly exclude Italian Americans. More strangely yet, some say they prefer "Latino" to "Hispanic" to emphasize their non-European heritages. This assertion is nonsensical, unless one believes that the Latini were an indigenous tribe of Mexico rather than of Italy.

But all of this is really beside the point. The main objection to "Hispanic" is that it comes as a ready-made term, already loaded with cultural associations. This is why "Latino" is favored by some intellectuals and others who consider themselves progressive. They reject "Hispanic" in order to disorient those who use it, as though to say, "You think you know who we are because you have a name for us, but you're wrong!"

Any name tends to freeze the meanings of something which is in reality a process, a rapidly evolving complex of understandings and relationships. Should "Latinos" displace "Hispanics" as the most widely accepted term, it, too, would be attacked by people who don't want their identities frozen. Most probably, though, "Latino" and "Hispanic" will continue to be used almost interchangeably by most people.

For now, the word "Hispanic" seems to be prevailing. It is firmly established in editorial usage in English and also comes more easily to newer immigrants, who tend to call themselves *hispanos*. Many professional organizations and publications use "Hispanic" in their names, and the word is usually favored by those who do much of their thinking in Spanish and anyone who is applying for a grant. A few years ago Puerto Rican political analyst Angelo Falcón used to say, "A Hispanic is a Latino yuppie," and to some extent that is still true, although Falcón now rejects the whole dispute as unnecessarily divisive. A book in which he and several Mexican American scholars collaborated alternates the terms "Hispanic" and "Latino" systematically to avoid the issue.[18]

More important than the dispute is the vast area of agreement. Both terms implicitly acknowledge the Spanish language, one more directly ("Hispanic") and the other obliquely (as a "Latin" language), as the criterion defining a people believed to have other important things in common. In this book I use "Hispanic" because it comes closest to my meaning: the use of a specifically Spanish-language heritage (not just any "Latin" language) to define a new community. How this idea was born and how it is being developed are the central concerns of this book.

## Unconscious Conspiracies

All around the planet and at all hours of the day, people going about their private affairs are heedlessly reshaping the world. Whether turning rain forests into deserts or spreading AIDS or radiation poisoning, altering national boundaries, or creating new languages, customs, and institutions, the participants rarely give thought to their net effect—like ants hustling grains of sand for an architecture they can't conceive, or even more like ocean waves, oblivious to their effects on the contours of the land.

The creation of a new ethnic force of Spanish-speaking people in North America is such a phenomenon, a great collective construction with no master architect. People from different homelands and different classes, pursuing their own particular, individual goals, often form tactical alliances. And from these alliances grow institutions—political coalitions, drug gangs, television networks, artistic and theatrical and literary and musical buddy networks, to name only a few types. And from the alliances and institutions, which create common interests, and from the experience of interaction facilitated by the common language and other cultural understandings a degree of fellow feeling arises.

## Who Shall I Be Today?

For human beings, unlike *ornitorrincos*, the answer to "What am I?" is always provisional and negotiable. There is no such thing as an *authentic* identity, ethnic or otherwise. There are only the identities that we make up, or that others make up and impose on us, and the one that sticks evolves in an ongoing process of assertion and reaction. Identities are subject to change and must be actively defended if they are to be preserved. So I dress and walk and talk in certain ways to persuade others and practice mental routines, such as prayer, meditation, positive thinking, or fantasy, to persuade myself. But some people have much more room for negotiation than others.

A person born in Texas of parents who came from Mexico has a great many potential ethnic affiliations. He may or may not think of himself first as a Mexican, a Mexican American, a Chicano, a Latino, a Hispanic, a Texan, an American, or something else. Each of these implies a somewhat different set of loyalties and thereby, as Georg Simmel put it, "circumscribes" him a little differently.[19] And each implies a somewhat different way of thinking about himself.

Each change in these claims—say, demanding to be considered "Latino" or "Hispanic" rather than "Chicano"—implies renegotiation. That is, the person tries to get others to see him as he, at least for the moment, has chosen to see himself. If he fails, that is, if they continue to treat him in the old way, he will find it harder to sustain the new self-concept. For the people in these dialogues, and for all those who at least at times think of themselves as Hispanics or Latinos, claims to ethnic-group membership are subject to subtle modification and continuous review.

In a Korean grocery store in Lower Manhattan, a young woman cashier of Korean parentage speaks American-accented English with a customer, calls out something in Korean in response to her bosses, and turns to chatter in Spanish with the Mexican employees who are carting in the vegetables; born in

Argentina and now an American college student, she is Hispanic, American, or Korean, as needed.

For most of the people who claim it, the "Hispanic" affiliation is only one of several available options. They may choose instead to emphasize their specific country of birth or ancestry, identifying themselves as Ecuadoran or Puerto Rican. They may also have alternative non-Hispanic identities, like the Argentine-Korean-American college student or my two Puerto Rican-born sons. Alex, the elder, who married another kind of "Latina" (an Italian-American), finds it useful at times to make people aware he is Puerto Rican. The rest of the time he lets them assume what they will—Italian, Jewish, Asian Indian, American black. His younger brother, who is fairer, asserts his dual ethnicity by attaching, Puerto Rican style, his mother's Spanish surname to my German-derived one, signing himself "Joaquín Fox-Herrera." When he was an apprentice carpenter in Chicago, though, he became the good ol' boy "Jack Fox."

Of course, this is true for other people besides Hispanics. As the historian of American ethnic consciousness Lawrence Fuchs has pointed out, people from Barbados can "decide whether to call themselves Barbadians, West Indians, African-Americans, or blacks, or, in a few cases depending on color, to pass as white", a Jew may "choose to be a Hasidic Jew, a Reform Jew, or not a Jew at all; a Mexican-origin American [may] label herself Hispanic, Latina, Chicana, Mexican, Mexican-American, or just plain American," and so on, or any of these people "could use each of these identities at different times depending upon the setting."[20]

Of all these groups, those labeled "Hispanics" probably face the fewest outside obstacles to their shifting from one identity to another or from one way of expressing the identity to another. The result of having this flexibility is that although there are still virulent anti-Hispanic stereotypes floating around, even practiced bigots cannot always tell which ones to apply or to whom to apply them. In comparison, few African Americans or Asian Americans can escape their respective stereotypes so easily, no matter how culturally assimilated they are—unless, of course, they acquire the language and other traits to pass as Hispanics.

Not everyone who might claim Hispanic identity will do so, or do so consistently, and the Hispanic nation will probably never capture the loyalties of all the people labeled as Hispanics by outsiders. But it doesn't need to. It has already taken hold in the imaginations of enough people in enough different communities that it is changing their self-perceptions and electoral and cultural behaviors.

# 2

# Counting

"THEY COME HERE, they have their babies, and after that they become citizens and all those children use those social services," a supporter of California's "Save Our State" (S.O.S.) ballot proposal complained to a reporter after showing her the town's immigrant neighborhood and "ranting about an imagined 'stench of urine.'"[1]

S.O.S., or Proposition 187, was approved, 59 percent to 41 percent, by California voters in November 1994. It is intended to deny undocumented immigrants any form of California public welfare, including nonemergency medical and prenatal care and public schooling. Even as these provisions are being challenged in the courts, there are proposals from Republicans for even more drastic legislation on the national level, to deny such services even to *legal* immigrants who have not become U.S. citizens. The arguments are, first, that fewer people would then migrate, and second, that the state could divert money to other uses by not providing certain services to noncitizens. Both arguments are weak. The forces driving Mexicans, Central Americans, and other unauthorized persons to enter California (or any part of the United States) are far more compelling than visions of a life of ease on the American dole. And the available evidence indicates that immigrants in general, documented or undocumented, create more wealth than they consume and contribute far more in taxes than they cost—although, under our present system, the federal government gets the contributions (through wage deductions for income tax and social security), while the public costs are borne mainly by the state and local governments. This is why four states—Califor-

19

nia, Florida, Arizona, and Texas—have sued the federal government to recover the costs of educating, housing, hospitalizing, and jailing undocumented immigrants.

At the start of the campaign in California, polls indicated that a majority of Hispanic voters favored the measure. Believing that this was because they did not understand its full consequences, the Spanish-language media—especially the two television networks and Los Angeles's *La Opinión*—conducted an intensive public-education campaign against it, stressing that even citizens and legal residents might be denied services because they *appear* to be foreign. Then, too, in many families of voters there are other members who are undocumented immigrants. In the end, Hispanics voted overwhelmingly against it.

The reason for the proposition's popularity was mainly that at the time of the vote, California's economy was in recession. Undocumented immigrants are easy to blame because they are highly visible and because they are nearly powerless to protest. The Mexicans have "a secret plan to take back the southwestern United States," said one Southern California schoolteacher, taking seriously the outbursts of certain Mexican-American romantics threatening to reconquer the ancient lands said to have belonged to the Aztec kingdom of Aztlán.[2] In fact, "The Spiritual Plan of Aztlán" has been far from secret; it has been broadcast in literary journals and anthologies across the land ever since the Chicano poet Alurista proclaimed it at a Denver rally in 1969.[3] And one should never underestimate the political potential of committed poets.

According to one S.O.S. leaflet, "Blurring...the division of our culture from others...or blurring the use of English as our national language to satisfy—in the name of diversity—the current babble of tongues in use today in our classrooms and in the work place has led to the current chaos we see about us."[4]

Fears of "being overrun by Latinos," as S.O.S. backers put it,[5] are based more on personal encounters and the hype of radio talk shows than on statistical evidence. But to those already inclined to react this way, the census figures appear alarming. According to the U.S. Bureau of the Census, there are already 25.1 million persons of Hispanic or Spanish origin in the United States, comprising 9.7 percent of our total population. Furthermore, because of continuing immigration and higher birthrates than most other groups, their numbers are growing rapidly. By 2010, Hispanics are expected to be 13.5 percent, edging out blacks as our largest racial or ethnic minority, and by 2020 they will be 15.7 percent—51.2 million out of the projected total U.S. population in that year of 326 million. By 2020, in four states Hispanics will be well over 30 percent of the population, and in one—New Mexico, where they are already 40 percent—they will be a large majority.[6]

The impact is especially strong in our largest cities, where Hispanics have been settling as non-Hispanic whites and middle-class blacks move to the suburbs. In three cities, Miami, El Paso, and Santa Ana, California, Hispanics are already an absolute majority. Elsewhere they are becoming the largest minority; they now outnumber blacks in Los Angeles, Phoenix, Houston, and San Antonio and are rapidly closing the small gap in New York, where Hispanics constituted 23.8 percent of the population counted in the 1990 census and blacks were 25.6 percent.

This progressive "Latinization" of the urban population is seen as threatening by some blacks in these areas.[7] One California businessman with political aspirations has written of "the rise of xenophobia" in black neighborhoods and has described the 1992 Los Angeles riots as "anti-immigrant pogroms more than anything else."[8]

Understandably, the reactions of Hispanic political analysts are just the opposite. Juan Andrade, director of the Midwest-Northeast Voter Registration Education Project, an organization devoted to getting out the Hispanic vote, seems to be rubbing his hands as he predicts that a Hispanic governor or U.S. senator will be elected in the next few years in California, Texas, New Mexico, Arizona, Colorado, or Florida, or possibly in more than one; that the Hispanic Caucus in the U.S. House of Representatives "will at least double, and possibly triple, by 2020," and that at least 10 percent of local elected officials across the land will be Hispanics, as compared with 1 percent at present.[9]

But to Americans like those backing California's Proposition 187, what these figures forecast is a growing burden of unassimilated, welfare-dependent baby producers with alien values, extracting ever more wealth from the hard working "native" Americans. In 1990, a national poll found that Americans "perceive Latinos as second only to blacks in terms of being lazy rather than hard-

working and as living off welfare rather than being self-supporting." They also consider them the least patriotic group in the
country.[10] Instead of seeing millions of savvy new citizens voting
"Hispanic," uplifting themselves, and contributing to a rainbow
polity, they see an invasion of more and more of Latin America's
huge social problems, including drugs, violence, ignorance, and
poverty, threatening to drag the whole country down to third world
levels. As more and more Californians are learning to say, *¡Basta
ya!* (Enough already!)

Which vision is right? In their extreme forms, probably
neither. Both drastically oversimplify the processes by which two
culturally distinct populations—in this case, Anglos and Hispanics—change as they adapt to one another. Moreover, both
visions—one out of paranoia, the other out of excessive optimism—ignore the deep differences concealed within the census's
metanational category "Hispanics."

## Who Gets Counted and How?

Who are those "persons of Spanish-Hispanic origin" the census
claims to have found in the United States?

The short answer is, some 25 million people who don't know
or care much about one other, don't think or talk alike, and have
not until recently thought of themselves as having any common
interests.

One could therefore argue that the generic "Latino" or
"Hispanic" category is a statistical fiction, that there are only
Mexicans, Puerto Ricans, Cubans, Dominicans, Ecuadorans, and
so on, with different customs, different problems, and different
aspirations. Indeed, a nationwide survey of stateside Mexicans,
Puerto Ricans, and Cubans found that most much prefer to be
known as such rather than by the more generic "Latino" or
"Hispanic."[11] Earl Shorris writes in and about his own book *Latinos*
that despite the title he chose, "the theory of it is that there are no
Latinos, only diverse peoples struggling to remain who they are
while becoming something else."[12]

But then, the same could be said of anybody whose social
context is in flux (and whose is not?). What this book is about is
the "something else" that some of the Spanish-background people

are becoming, specifically how the statistical fiction is being turned into a social reality. The logical starting point is to deconstruct the statistic by examining the assumptions of those doing the counting. Chief among these are the assumptions about "race" as an indicator of culture.

Census classifications of ethnic and racial groups have always had more to do with the cultural attitudes of the people doing the counting than with those of the people being counted. Thus, for the census of 1920, enumerators were instructed that "a person of mixed White and Negro blood was to be returned as Negro, no matter how small the percentage of Negro blood....A person of mixed White and Indian blood was to be returned as Indian."[13] Such people thus had a racial identity thrust upon them—regardless of how they saw themselves or were seen by others in their communities.[14]

This practice is so familiar to Americans that it may take an effort to see how arbitrary and bizarre it seems to people from other cultures, including those to our south.

"We are unique in this country in the way we describe and define race and ascribe to it characteristics that other cultures view very differently," says Cong. Thomas C. Sawyer (D-Ohio), who chaired the House Subcommittee on Census, Statistics, and Postal Personnel, which has to decide on which racial categories are used in the census.[15]

Here people are considered black if they have even the faintest African traits—"one drop of blood"—evident in skin color or hair or facial structure, for example, or even if they do not have such traits but claim to be, or are regarded by others as, black. The label white is reserved exclusively for supposedly pure Euro-Americans.

In contrast, in most of Latin America and most other parts of the world, there are intermediate categories, and "skin color is an individual variable—not a group marker—so that within the same family one sibling might be considered white and another black."[16] More likely, each sibling would be called by some more nuanced term. People in Puerto Rico or South America or Mexico can be *more or less* white, black, or Amerindian. For example, a *trigueño*, or "wheat-colored" person, is generally lighter-skinned than a *moreno* (from the word for Moor); a *zambo* in several Latin

American countries is a mix of Amerindian and African and may be quite dark, with straight hair; an *aindiado*, or "Indianized" person, is perceived as mainly white but with some Indian features, such as straight black hair or high cheekbones; an *achinado*, or "Chinese-looking" person, has slanted eyes, regardless of whether derived from African or Indian rather than Asian ancestors. Each of these and dozens of other racial descriptions (*café con leche* or "café au lait," for example) have status implications, the most African looking generally (but not always) being the most stigmatized. But the opposite is also true: Status differences have color implications, or to be more precise, affect perceptions of color.

In Anglo America, people sometimes speak of "soul," meaning a special cultural authenticity or depth of feeling, as a black trait, as though race determined culture. In most of Latin America people speak as though culture determined race. Thus, a person who is called *negro* or *prieto* when he is poor and uneducated will almost always be described by some more flattering term, such as *trigueño*, if he rises in status. And all these classifications are subject to interpretation and negotiation.

These same and other mixes of skin-color, hair-texture, and bone-structure traits occur in the native population of the United States. Here, however, those who possess them have all learned to think of themselves as blacks. Frequently they become annoyed with Latin Americans for insisting on subtler distinctions, thinking they are denying their African heritage. To the Latin American, it is the mixed-heritage persons who insist on calling themselves black who are denying the real complexity of their ancestries.

It was not until the 1960 census that people were allowed to specify their own "race." However, if their self-descriptions did not match the preexisting categories, the census reclassified them. Thus "Puerto Ricans" and "Mexicans" were reclassified as white unless they were obviously (in the eyes of the enumerator) Negro, Indian, or some other race.[17]

In 1970, the bureau began to create the classification it would later call Hispanic by gathering data on all those who met any of four criteria: Spanish surname, Hispanic origin, Spanish heritage, or mother tongue. This was done on a 5 percent sample, from which national totals were extrapolated.

"Spanish surname worked pretty well in the Southwest, but not in the Northeast," according to Jorge del Pinal, who at the time of the interview was chief of the bureau's ethnic and Hispanic statistics branch. The problem in the Northeast was that there were so many Italians whose surnames were indistinguishable from Spanish. In this way, the sample may have *overcounted* Hispanics. On the other hand, the "Spanish surname" criterion must also have *undercounted* by missing a lot of the people the Bureau intended to count. Migrations, intermarriages, stage names, etc., have left many Latin Americans with non-Spanish surnames, as a short list of a few of Latin America's most prominent people will demonstrate: Puerto Rican physician and former surgeon general of the United States Antonia Novello (the surname is Italian); Panamanian singer and politician Rubén Blades (his is English); Cuban painter Wifredo Lam (Chinese); Peruvian president Alberto Fujimori (Japanese); Argentine author Rodolfo Walsh, Chilean independence hero Bernardo O'Higgins (both, of course, Irish). And from their stage names no census taker could guess that, as is the case, Martin Sheen, Anthony Quinn, Rita Hayworth, and Gilbert Roland were all of Mexican origin.

Only with the 1980 census were enumerators instructed *not* to enter race by observation but to rely instead on the subject's self-identification. To the immense frustration of U.S. Census Bureau editors and data users, 46 percent of all Hispanics rejected all the multiple choices and listed themselves as "other." And almost all those who chose "other"—96 percent—were Hispanic immigrants. The frustration does not stem merely from a compulsive desire for categorical neatness. Insertion of the wild card "other" in the data makes it impossible to compare the results with other surveys, for example, on health, that are broken down into our traditional race groupings.

It was also for the census of 1980 that the bureau introduced "Spanish-Hispanic origin" as a label for a quasi-ethnic group. That year, and again in 1990, people were asked, "Is this person of Spanish-Hispanic origin or descent?" and presented the following options:

- No (not Spanish-Hispanic);
- Yes, Mexican, Mexican American, Chicano;

- Yes, Puerto Rican;
- Yes, Cuban;
- Yes, other Spanish-Hispanic.

"Other" meant coming from any other Spanish-speaking nationality (Ecuadoran, Uruguayan, etc.) whose numbers were too small to warrant naming on the form. All those who said "Yes" to any part of that question were classified as persons of Spanish-Hispanic origin or descent.

By this two-step method, people are first asked to pick their own national or ethnic origin on the basis of which the bureau reclassifies them into the metanationality "Spanish-Hispanic." It was by such a double somersault that the census found 14.6 million people to classify as "Hispanics" in 1980 and 22,354,000 in 1990, about 9 percent of the total U.S. population of 248,710,000. This indicated a 53 percent increase of the Hispanic origin population in a ten-year period in which the total U.S. population had grown only 9.8 percent. (Comparisons with 1970 and any earlier census cannot be made reliably because of the change in categories.)

## The Politics of Labeling

Given the ambiguities of such a metanational category, unrecognized by most of the people put into it, the obvious question is: Why create it in the first place? From a scientific point of view, we do not learn anything more by saying there are 22 million Hispanics than by saying there are 13.4 million Mexicans and Mexican Americans, 2.6 million Puerto Ricans, a million Cubans, 565,000 Salvadorans, and so on.

One reason is to make it easier for government agencies by grouping people into the categories that are written into the law. Another is for the convenience of social scientists who need consistent categories in order to compare findings on the same population at two different times.[18] But which categories are "recognizable" by social scientists and legislators and vary with shifts in public anxieties and prejudices.

These shifts have been especially great in the treatment of Mexicans and their descendants. In 1930 they were counted as "other nonwhite," a vague and inaccurate label contaminated by cultural prejudice: Anybody known to be Mexican or Mexican American was presumed nonwhite, regardless of actual ancestry. (Many Mexican Americans are, or appear to be, of unmixed European descent.) Ten years later they were counted as a linguistic category, "persons of Spanish mother tongue"—which would not include all Mexican Americans, nor would it distinguish those included from other Spanish-speaking nationalities. In 1950 and 1960, in five states with high Mexican populations in the Southwest, Mexicans had suddenly become "white persons of Spanish surname." In 1970 a new category was created, "persons of both Spanish surname and Spanish mother tongue."[19]

Such shifting definitions make a mess of longitudinal research, for the researcher can't tell to what extent the census counted the same people, or the same kinds of people, in 1930 or 1940 as in 1950 or 1970. Thus, it is impossible to say with any accuracy whether and by how much the group's income, education levels, fertility, or anything else has changed over the years.

The changing census definitions are clearly related to shifts in the nation's political mood rather than to scientific considerations. In the 1920s, when the census of 1930 was being prepared, a major political concern was to preserve the country's old Anglo-Saxon "stock" against a flood of supposedly inferior breeds. In this context, the only important thing to know about Mexicans was that they were nonwhite (and thus part of the perceived problem rather than part of the solution).

The next decade, 1930–1940, saw intense mobilization and agitation by sectors of the population that had not previously been empowered: the organization of the CIO, marches of the unemployed, volunteers to combat fascism in Spain, big copper strikes by Mexican-American workers in Arizona. It was also the period of Roosevelt's "Good Neighbor Policy" toward Latin America, which made at least some Americans more aware and appreciative of the cultural complexity of Latin America. So in 1940 census takers and users were more interested in cultural data, represented by "mother tongue," than in specifying just how European, or white, a group's ancestors were. If we were going to have to deal with people of many cultures, it was important to know what languages they spoke.

Perhaps these concerns seemed less urgent in 1950 and 1960.

(The triumph of the Cuban Revolution [January 1, 1960] occurred too late to affect the wording of census items.) In any case, the language question did not reemerge until 1970, after Chicanos, Puerto Ricans, and Cubans—in very different ways, to be sure—had become more vociferous and the United States was once again conspicuously involved in Latin America.

The late 1960s and the 1970s saw the militance of the Brown Berets, the formation of a "Raza Unida" party, the Tierra Amarilla land-grant revolt, plus agitation by Puerto Rican radicals, such as the Young Lords, Puerto Rican Socialist party (PSP) cadres, and others. Many of the young radicals saw themselves as responding to Che Guevara's call for unity of all of Latin America, "from the Río Bravo to Tierra del Fuego."

The young radicals' sense of solidarity may have been little more than heartfelt rhetoric. It certainly did not correspond to any widespread or deep-rooted sense of ethnic identity among most of the people being called "Hispanic." But the notion of a cultural and possibly even a political unity among all Latinos was in the air when the Census Bureau created the overarching category "Spanish-Hispanic origin."

According to Census Bureau folklore—that is, this is what Jorge del Pinal was told by people who had been there at the time—the man who invented the category was Jacob Siegel, a former senior statistician for demographic analysis who is now retired from the bureau. Siegel, who remains active as a professor at local universities in Washington, D.C., is not sure of his authorship: "I certainly supported the term, still feel it was the right term," he said. "I certainly was involved in discussions of terminology," but the person responsible for any final decision would have been Tobia Bressler, then (in 1969) head of what was then called the ethnic origin statistics branch.

"I was looking for a term which was not value-laden, which was not a term that implied a specific way of measuring this population," such as mother tongue or particular national origin, said Siegel. "Next, we wanted a term which would be meaningful to the educated public that might use the data, and we wanted a term which technically conformed to the group you're measuring." Thus, they could not use "Iberian" (favored by some international organizations for the peoples and cultures of Spain and Portugal) because they did not want to include Brazilians.

"Every group"—not just the "Hispanics"—"was pushing to get the maximum number. Not the *true* number, of course, but the maximum number. So there was a combination of people who were of Puerto Rican origin in the Northeast part of the country, people whose mother tongue was Spanish, and Spanish surname in the Southwest." All of them wanted such a count. "We needed a term that was comprehensive, that didn't apply to any one of these groups, that was value free, that didn't imply a favoritism with respect to any particular group."[20]

And once the category had been created, government funding patterns, market forces, and the political ambitions of some newly labeled Hispanics all conspired to confirm the group's reality.

## Undercounting

Cities and states seeking their shares of monies designated for minority communities by civil rights legislation had millions of dollars at stake in the census count. So did politicians, of whatever ethnicity, especially after it was decided that redistricting was to be based on ethnic distribution. Community boosters wanted to make grand claims, and Spanish-language broadcasters and publishers were eager to sell advertising to one big market. All these forces agreed on two things: First, it served their purposes to simplify the figures by minimizing differences among the component groups so as to speak about a single Hispanic, Spanish, or Latino population. Second, they needed that population to be as big as possible. Thus, every possible person of Hispanic-Spanish origin should be counted.

However, counting the poor and people who are distrustful of authority is especially difficult, for reasons ranging from the census taker's hesitation to spend too much time in certain neighborhoods, to the cleverness of census avoiders, to the scarcity of reliable records in the phone book and on voter registration rolls. For all these reasons and more, the census missed many people who belonged in its new category.

New York City claimed losses of over $50 million a year in

federal aid because of undercounting in 1980 of its black and Latino populations. Prior to the census of 1990, a subcommittee of the California state senate estimated that the state would lose $683 million in the next ten years if the 1990 undercount were as serious as that of 1980 and that the impact would be especially great in Los Angeles. Accordingly, the city of Los Angeles waged a masssive outreach campaign to get people to respond to the census.

State and local governments are not the only ones with a financial interest in boosting the numbers. Spokespeople of the groups most likely to be undercounted also want to demonstrate the presence of as many of "their" people as possible in order to get funding for their agencies and for local grants.[21]

Businesses catering to the ethnic market also have a financial interest in the count. Thus, the motives of the Spanish-language television network Univisión, in collaborating with the U.S. Bureau of the Census in 1990 to bring up the count, through public-service announcements and phone banks, was not entirely disinterested. The network formed focus groups and advised the bureau on the best way to reach the Spanish speaking and also explained the census procedures to viewers urging them to cooperate. As serious as the undercounting of Hispanics was in 1990, it probably would have been worse without this help. Network executives did this because they had no doubt that it was in the interests of Hispanics to be counted—the more there were, the more attention they would get.[22] And obviously a bigger count was in the interests of the network—the bigger the Hispanic population, the bigger Univisión's potential audience and the more attractive its air time to advertisers.

Nevertheless, despite the efforts of Univisión, the Los Angeles City Council, and numerous other government, commercial, and social service entities, Hispanics were undercounted in 1990 by an estimated 5 percent, according to the bureau.

Considering the size of the survey and the problems accompanying any survey research, let alone something as complicated as this, that seems like a small error. As Del Pinal of the Census Bureau points out, it is much smaller than the errors considered acceptable in surveys carried out by other institutions. However, this is the U. S. census, and small errors have large consequences, especially for governments that use minority population figures to seek funding for civil rights and development programs.

The bureau estimates its undercount by reinterviewing in selected neighborhoods to see what percentage of the people they find in the reinterviews match the names for those same addresses on the nationwide census. But, as Del Pinal points out, the reinterviews are plagued by the same difficulties as the original count, such as a landlord's hiding illegal tenants or suspicious people giving evasive or mistaken answers. There is also a certain confusion regarding surnames of Spanish-speaking people, who may be known by their father's or mother's surname or both, and, of course (as with other groups), married women may assume or drop their husband's surname. For such reasons, the mismatches may be exaggerated—for example, the person who showed up as Elpidio G. Durán on the original census form may be the same as the Elpidio Guerrero the reinterviewers locate the second time. Such false negatives, or false mismatches, would tend to exaggerate the bureau's estimate of its own undercount. That is, the real error may be smaller than 5 percent.[23]

Although admitting to the error, the Census Bureau under the Bush administration refused to adjust the figures, even in the face of lawsuits by several cities. The problem was not just the loss of federal funding but also of political clout, that is, votes. Reapportionment of congressional districts, based on population counts, affect the number of congressional seats available in a region and a state, and as the Voting Rights Act was interpreted, the new district boundaries had to be drawn so as to maximize the opportunities for members of the stipulated "disadvantaged minorities"—including Hispanics—to elect one of their own.

In preparation for the decennial census of 2000, the bureau has begun studying how to revise its data-collection methods. Since 1960 it has mailed out forms instead of going door to door. But the increasing numbers of people with limited English and possibly a decreasing trust in the government on the part of low-income blacks and other minorities has led to decreasing returns of mailed questionnaires. When questionnaires have not been returned, enumerators have gone out to the households, and if they got no response, they would ask neighbors, landlords, or anybody who happened to be around about the people living in the house or apartment. It is easy to see how errors would get introduced.[24]

The Census Bureau, as Espiritu points out, is susceptible "to ethnic pressure partly because it needs the assistance of the minority communities to improve its coverage of the population." And there were powerful incentives for leaders both from within and outside the designated ethnic minority to maximize the count. While Mexican Americans, Puerto Ricans, Cubans, and others were still very interested in having the highest counts of their own specific groups, they were eager to be grouped together to get the largest possible numbers for purposes of congressional redistricting and for the allotment of federal funds.

### Imagining "Hispanics"

All of this business about counting is not to imply that the category "persons of Spanish-Hispanic origin or descent" is without meaning. It does have a meaning, but one that is being socially constructed by people with a stake in creating a self-conscious ethnic group, whereas before there was none. The 25-million figure, and the projections of 40.5 million by 2010 and 51.2 million by 2020, can be taken as the outer limit, the most extreme definition of the population that could *potentially* become part of a self-conscious nationwide Hispanic community. It is from this population pool that those who are trying to mobilize people on the basis of their "Hispanicness" or "Latinoness" will draw recruits to the Hispanic nation.

But in terms of the way the word Hispanic is understood by most English-speaking Americans, the census figures are a gross exaggeration. This is because the census's category is vastly broader than any of the common stereotypes.

Many, probably most, Anglo Americans understand "Hispanic" as a synonym for "Spanish speaking," but the census category is about "origin or descent," not current language use, and it includes many people who speak mostly or exclusively English.

For many other Americans, the word Hispanic implies particular racial traits. Thus, in New York or Los Angeles or many other cities, the police will describe a perpetrator or victim as Hispanic based only on his or her appearance. This generally means someone who is too dark to be white, too light to be black, and who has no easily identifiable Asian traits. As a consequence, an Afghan, Asian Indian, American Indian, English-speaking West Indian, southern Italian, or Arab is frequently taken for Hispanic, whereas a Spanish-speaking blond Mexican or Chinese Peruvian is not.

To the most paranoid Americans, though, Hispanics are imagined as a combination of these things: dark-skinned, foreign in speech and manner, and mostly unable or unwilling to adapt to U.S. laws, culture, and norms of hygiene. When such Americans read the census figures, they feel confirmed in their impression that the country is being invaded by millions of unassimilated and unassimilable foreigners from the south and are encouraged in such nativist movements as "U.S. English."

In fact, however, the 25 million includes people of every race and of every degree of assimilation into the majority culture of the United States, including millions who speak only English and whose Hispanic-Spanish heritage is scarcely a memory.

## The Hispanic Market

Whether you are marketing a product, promoting a candidate, or offering social services to new immigrants, it is not enough to know that your target audience is Hispanic. One of the first things you will need to know is national origin—because what works in one sector of the population may not work at all in another and may even be offensive.

The most recently available census report classifies as Mexican 14,628,000 of the 22,750,000 Hispanics here, or 64.3 percent[25] of the total U.S. Hispanic population nationwide. Puerto Ricans account for just over 12 percent, Cubans about 5 percent, with all the other nationalities distributed among the remaining 22 percent. Locally, these proportions may be very different. For example, Mexicans are over 90 percent of all Hispanics in Texas, but only 4.3 percent in Connecticut, where nearly 70 percent of Hispanics are Puerto Ricans.

From the point of view of a newly arriving Spanish speaker who must depend on other Spanish speakers and their institutions for help in settling in, the American West and Southwest continue to be mainly Mexican turf, with an increasing presence from the five countries of Central America, especially El Salvador. The northeastern seaboard (New York, Connecticut, Philadelphia, Boston) belongs to the Puerto Ricans, with a Dominican challenge in northern Manhattan. Miami is still Cuban, although Central Americans and South Americans are staking claims in certain neighborhoods and industries; there is another, smaller Cuban stronghold, in Union City, New Jersey, which is shared with the Puerto Ricans. These are the groups who appear to control (if one is dealing in an exclusively Spanish speaking world) access to jobs and housing in each area and who dominate its Spanish-language media and other cultural and social institutions. The Midwest, in such cities as Chicago and Milwaukee, is a kind of hybrid: Although Mexicans are a majority of the Hispanics, Puerto Ricans are present in sufficient numbers and are sufficiently well organized, to demand their share of whatever opportunities are available for Hispanics.

But such a breakdown is inadequate for the serious marketer. The more than 13 million Mexicans in the 1990 census are further divided culturally. Besides recent immigrants from Mexico, second- and third-generation U.S.-born people who still feel close to Mexico and people who might describe themselves as Chicanos or Mexican Americans but who know little and care less about the ancestral homeland, there are many whose families never were in present-day Mexico. These are descendants of some of the earliest Spanish-speaking settlers of Texas, New Mexico, and other parts of the Southwest, and though their ancestors may have been nominally citizens of Mexico before that territory became part of the United States, they deny any cultural connection to more recent immigrants.

Nor are the Cuban Americans of Miami, Puerto Ricans, or any of the other Hispanic concentrations culturally homogeneous. Besides class, color, and religious differences within each group, different waves of immigration have had different historical experiences. Thus, Cuban families that settled in Tampa in the 1890s may have little sympathy for the much larger group that arrived after 1960, and those who came in the 1960s may scorn the generally poorer, and darker, migrants who arrived in the Mariel boatlift in 1980.

Gustavo Godoy, a Cuban who had worked in both English- and Spanish-language television in Miami, was hired in 1986 to run a Spanish-language station in Phoenix, Arizona, where the market was almost exclusively Mexican and Mexican American. It occurred to him that something similar to Miami's popular Calle Ocho (Eighth Street) festival, a kind of Latin carnival in the heart of the Miami Cuban community, would be a big hit in Phoenix as well.

He proposed combining the street festival with a film festival, with prize-winning movies from Mexico, and presenting a gigantic *paella*. This rice-and-seafood dish from Spain is also very popular with Cubans. Godoy had lined up sponsors, "including people who had *never* advertised in Spanish," and also had the backing of the mayor of Phoenix.

"And everything was set up; everything was in order. Then the Mexican American Chamber of Commerce, of which I was a member, and the only member who spoke Spanish was me, suddenly vetoed the project. And I said, Why?

"They said because the event was too *gachupín*. I said, What's gachupín? And they say, Gachupín? *Spanish*. My God, what does that have to do with anything? They say, it's that the Spaniards destroyed our culture, destroyed our race, destroyed our nation."

*Gachupín* (from an old Spanish word meaning roughly "thingamajig") was how Mexicans insulted Spaniards during their war of independence in the 1810s, with their war cry *"Viva Nuestra Señora de Guadalupe y mueran los gachupines"*—("Long live the Virgin of Guadalupe and death to the *gachupines*.") The other members of Phoenix's Mexican American Chamber of Commerce may not have known much Spanish, but that was the one word they did remember—and that almost everybody else has forgotten.

"For me, this was a *shock*," Godoy concluded.[26] He had discovered the pitfalls of a generic Hispanic campaign, where what's good for the Cubans is considered good for the Mexicans, and so on—a mistake he would be careful to avoid in the future.

Anyone involved in Hispanic marketing has stories like Godoy's. An advertising campaign based on enchiladas and Mayan effigies would work equally poorly among the Cubans of Miami or Union City, New Jersey, or the Puerto Ricans of New York or northwest Chicago. When I was living in Puerto Rico in the mid-

1960s, there was a fleet-footed Dominican baseball player nick-named "El Bicho" ("the Bug") Perdomo whose team came to play in Puerto Rico. He was rebaptized by Puerto Rican sportscasters as "El Pájaro" ("the Bird") because *bicho* in Puerto Rico is a vulgar term for penis. As the sportscasters were undoubtedly aware, *pájaro* has the same connotations in the Dominican Republic, so the poor player could never be sure whether he was being applauded or insulted.

## Counting the Spanish-Speaking

To understand how important a presence Spanish has today and how important it will be in the future, we need to know not just that there were 17.3 million Spanish speakers reported in the 1990 U.S. census but how many are also competent in English and how many Spanish speakers, of whatever level of bilingualism, we are likely to have if present rates of immigration continue.

The truth is that this is very hard to estimate because the numbers keep changing. People who speak Spanish are con-tinually learning English, and some of them even give up using Spanish altogether, changing from being monolingual Spanish speakers to bilingual Spanish and English speakers to mono-lingual English speakers. Meanwhile, new monolingual Spanish speakers are arriving every day. Thus, any estimates must take into account the rates at which monolingual Spanish speakers are immigrating to the United States, plus the numbers born here for whom Spanish is the mother tongue (literally, the language of their mothers), offset by the numbers in both groups who learn English so thoroughly that they cease speaking Spanish.

Prior to the release of the 1990 census figures, the most thorough analysis of this question used the 1976 Survey of Income and Education, which included especially detailed questions not only about the individual's mother tongue but also about what second language he or she used and how frequently. Assuming that the switching from Spanish to English would continue to occur at the same rate among newer immigrants and that immigra-tion and fertility rates would also remain roughly constant, re-searcher Calvin Veltman was able to project the numbers of Spanish speakers in the United States through the year 2001.[27]

In 1976, 8.57 million people in the United States spoke Spanish regularly. Of these, 43.5 percent spoke English more often and more easily than Spanish, 37.6 percent spoke more Spanish than English, and 18.9 percent spoke only Spanish.

By Veltman's assumptions, by 2001 we can expect there to be 16.6 million regular speakers of Spanish in the United States, of whom 18.4 percent, or about 3 million, will speak only Spanish. This increase will be due almost entirely to immigration and is the *net* increase after taking into account that between 1990 and 2001, 4.5 million of those who started out as Spanish speakers will have ceased being so; that is, they will have learned and adopted English as their only tongue.

In short, while it appears inevitable the numbers of Spanish speakers in the United States will continue to increase, this is not because they are refusing to learn English. There is a generational shift from Spanish to English, and among the grandchildren of Spanish-speaking immigrants, "only 4 percent will prefer Spanish to English as their principal language of use when they become adults."[28]

However, the 1990 census found almost 4 million more Spanish speakers than Veltman anticipated. This suggests that people who come here speaking Spanish are not abandoning it nearly as fast as they used to. They may, and most of them certainly do, also speak English, but they have not adopted it as their *only* tongue. What appears to be happening is that with the numbers of Spanish speakers growing so rapidly because of immigration and the greater availability of communications in Spanish, far more than 20 percent of the grandchildren of immigrants are choosing to speak Spanish.

According to the 1990 census, the United States has 17.3 million Spanish speakers, more than ten times as many as the next largest groups, French speakers (1.7 million), German (1.5 million), Italian (1.3 million), and Chinese (1.25 million). This wide use should be recognized by making Spanish a sort of second official language, granting it "most favored language status," argues Columbia University education professor Josué González. "Why make it just a second language?" Ed Gómez, president of KABQ-FM, a Spanish-language radio station in Albuquerque, asked. "It should be just as equal as English."[29]

So far, there is not much momentum for this idea, but it could come, if only as a counterweight to the ravings of the "Official English" people who want to outlaw use of non-English languages, at least in government documents. As historian Arthur Schlesinger Jr. has rightly pointed out, English doesn't need such help, and the insistence on such legislation "will only increase racial discrimination and resentment."[30]

Opponents sometimes argue that bilingualism is a concern just of the Hispanic educational and political elites, who have built what Schlesinger calls a "bilingual empire." In reality, bilingualism is a demand not only of the elites but also of the *pueblo*, ordinary Spanish speakers who do not have a professional stake in the matter. It is a demand they express every day, on the shop floor and on the streets and sometimes in the law courts, when they insist on being allowed to communicate in their own language.

The most common argument against bilingualism is that the United States must have a common language to hold such a heterogeneous nation together.[31] However, there is no reason to expect that acknowledging and accommodating de jure what is already de facto America's second language will "fragment" America any further. On the contrary, making information on citizenship, laws, customs, and social issues available in a language spoken by at least 17.3 million of our people is essential for keeping us together.

The debate over bilingual education, however, is often a conversation among elites, who sometimes seem to be talking past each other. As Thomas Weyr, author of a previous book on Hispanics, has put it, "Common sense is rarely part of the debate and too often ideology takes over." It is only common sense, Weyr thinks, to use Spanish "as a classroom aid," but it should be kept free of "the rhetoric of cultural and linguistic maintenance and the myths of Aztlán"—the supposed Aztec kingdom in the ancient Southwest—and the equally mythical notions of a "mainstream" into which everybody should be channeled.[32] But for many non-elite Hispanics, cultural and linguistic maintenance (if not the "myths of Aztlán") are important goals, which can be combined with learning the new culture and language.

"It would be crazy to deny our children the benefits of English," a Cuban teacher told Spanish journalist Alberto Moncada. English, she and almost everyone else in the world acknowledges, is "not only the language of advertising and of achievement in America, but also of international trade and the new technologies." The refusal of some Hispanics to speak English, she thinks, "arises, very often, as a refuge against the arrogance, the scorn of the Anglos."[33]

The retention of Spanish is in part a defensive strategy against assaults to one's dignity, whether called "arrogance," "scorn," or "discrimination." It is also "a way to preserve linguistic and cultural identity."[34]

But at the same time it is an assertive, proactive strategy. Hispanic Americans may seek to retain Spanish not only to preserve their traditions and identity but also for the eminently practical, unsentimental purpose of communicating with the immense Spanish-speaking world beyond our borders and within them. Spanish-English bilinguals enjoy a decisive competitive advantage over their monolingual compatriots not only in international activities but also in the many jobs dealing with our increasingly diverse domestic population.

There is still another reason for U.S. Hispanics to cling to and renew their Spanish-speaking skills. These skills are necessary to building the larger community, the Hispanic nation, as the vehicle for achieving collective power. A common language has been a major factor in creating solidarity among groups as diverse as Mexicans, Cubans, Puerto Ricans, and all the others. The uniting of all these groups should not be seen as a threat to the eventual integration of America but as a step toward it. It is the vehicle that permits them to participate in the polity, which is the essential premise of our democracy.[35]

All these psychological factors—defense against Anglo arrogance, a new pride in a linguistic tradition, the emerging solidarity of diverse people—help explain why Hispanics are clinging to their ancestral language generation after generation, unlike most other minority-language groups in the United States.[36] But there is also an additional factor, not psychological but environmental, which may be a more powerful explanation. That is the success of the modern Spanish-language mass media.

# 3

# The Image Machine

IN THE SPANISH-LANGUAGE MEDIA in the United States, some of the most heavily advertised products are methods for learning English. One such product, an audiotape system whose ads were aired frequently on Spanish TV in the early 1990s, was aptly called *La Maquina del Lenguaje* (the Language Machine).

Meanwhile, those watching such ads are plugged into a nationwide machine that continually updates their Spanish, encourages them to think of themselves as "Hispanic," and creates glamorous job opportunities for some of those who do. This is the U.S. Spanish-language media complex, an array of television, newspapers, radio, and book and magazine publishers, a $450-million-a-year industry reaching every Spanish-speaking neighborhood in the United States. It is an enormously complicated contraption, with parts moving in seemingly contrary directions, but it works. Since community must exist in its members' imagination before it can become a political or social force, the image machine is helping to produce the Hispanic nation.

No other minority now or in the history of the United States has had as extensive an apparatus for maintaining its language and propagating its myths. A hundred years ago the German speakers probably came closest, with their many schools and libraries and their extensive German-language press.[1] Today many linguistic minorities have publications—in New York City, there are four Chinese-language daily newspapers, two of them claiming circulation of 80,000[2]—and several also have a few hours a week of local radio and television programming. But only in Spanish is there a nationwide system of television, broadcasting most hours of the day every day and producing and reproducing similar images to all speakers of the language. And this makes all the difference, creating a common set of images that influence even the non-TV media.

Forerunners of the Hispanic image machine go back at least to the mid-1800s, when the formerly Mexican citizens of the Southwest published newspapers in towns across the region.[3] At about the same time, expatriates from Spanish America in New York, Boston, and Tampa were publishing journals and newspapers on cultural and political themes.[4] But those communities could not long sustain a major Spanish-language press for any of three reasons: They were not densely enough populated (in most of the Southwest), were not stable enough (in the case of the exiles of the Northeast), or were not receiving enough new Spanish speakers to replace those who died or were assimilated into the English-language culture (e.g., in Tampa).

Thus, the first components of the modern image machine did not appear until the early twentieth century, when newspapers were created to serve the dense and growing populations of Mexicans in Los Angeles and of Puerto Ricans in New York—*La Opinión* in Los Angeles and what would become *El Diario/La Prensa* in New York.[5]

A third Spanish media center arose in South Florida with astonishing rapidity after 1959. Cubans fleeing the revolution brought with them their communications and business skills to reestablish prerevolutionary Cuban publications and radio stations, sometimes preserving the old names or variations thereof. The old *Diario de la Marina* newspaper was rebaptized with the more ambitious name of *El Diario las Américas*, but Miami's Radio QBA (pronounced "Cuba") kept its Havana call letters.

Until the end of the 1960s these three Spanish media markets had little contact with one another, separated by geography, dialect, and radically different social and political concerns. The Cubans seemed to care about nothing but overthrowing the revolution in Cuba, the Puerto Ricans debated their island's political status (as commonwealth, republic, or state) and discussed life in their New York barrios, while the Mexicans were concerned about immigration law, anti-Mexican discrimination, and other local problems. But then, around 1970, two factors began breaking down this parochialism, leading to a connecting of the parts and the creation of new, multimarket media and a nation-wide image machine.

The first factor was demographic. Increasing immigration from other countries of Latin America made the traditional big-three Spanish markets larger and more diverse and also created new Spanish-speaking markets outside these three areas. Editors and producers now had to take into account a much wider range of Spanish-American nationalities and concerns or risk losing their audience to new rival media. Thus, the traditionally Puerto Rican–oriented *El Diario/La Prensa* had to cover the affairs of New York's Dominicans, Colombians, Ecuadorans, and Mexicans; *La Opinión* had to cover Los Angeles's many Central Americans; and *El Diario las Américas* had to cover Miami's several South and Central American communities. An influx of Mexicans and Central Americans made San Antonio a Spanish-speaking town again, and places like Chicago, Washington, D.C.; Philadelphia; and San Francisco became attractive multiethnic Spanish media markets.

The second factor has been technical and entrepreneurial, the growth of nationwide Spanish-language television. By redefin-ing and remaking the audience, it is television that holds the national Hispanic image machine together.

## The World According to Television

Spanish speakers are the only linguistic minority in the United States to have any nationwide television network, and they have *two*, not counting the several cable channels and a few unaffiliated local stations. The two broadcast networks, Univisión and Tele-mundo, are each available to over 90 percent of Spanish-speaking households, from the Bronx to San Diego, Denver to Miami, on UHF or cable. Major cable services include Galavision and the Spanish-language service of Cable News Network, Noticiero CNN Internacional.

The first Spanish speakers in the United States able to watch television in their own language at home were in San Antonio, where a non-Hispanic entrepreneur, René Anselmo, started trans-mitting in Spanish on KWEX-TV in 1961. Soon other cities were connected by satellite to Anselmo's Spanish International Network, or SIN, including New York, where the SIN affiliate began broad-casting in 1969. By 1976, SIN had a network of eleven "markets," as media people call their audiences: New York, Miami, San Antonio, Corpus Christi, Los Angeles, San Francisco, Fresno, Hartford, Sacramento, Albuquerque, and Phoenix. In 1987 it changed its name to Univisión. The network has had a succession of owners but has continued to grow and now has over five hundred affiliates and reaches over 90 percent of Hispanic households in the United States.

The competing network, Telemundo, began with one station in Los Angeles in 1986 and has since grown so that it now reaches nearly as many areas as Univisión. Today viewers in most of the country have at least two Spanish-language TV programs to choose from at almost every hour of the day. Many also receive Spanish programming on MTV, ESPN, and CNN and in the larger cities can get programming from Colombia, Peru, and other countries on cable. On the two broadcast networks alone, Univi-sión and Telemundo, offerings include Hollywood movies dubbed in Spanish, circuslike variety shows, sentimental serials called *telenovelas*, music videos, raunchy comedy, and spiritist sessions with becaped and bejeweled astrologers. However, where the stations make the most direct claim to telling viewers how things really are is in their news programs, especially the half-hour news-of-the-world programs broadcast during prime time.

CNN anchor Jorge Gestoso uses the sign-off *"Y así es como está el mundo,"* a translation of Walter Cronkite's famous signature line on CBS, "And that's the way the world is." Implicitly, all international news anchors are making that same ambitious claim, to have summed up every noteworthy event in the world in twenty-three minutes (after allowing time for ads). They must convert the chaotic events of each day into an immediately comprehensible, coherent narrative intelligible to a vast audience of very dissimilar people. By their selection of information, their editing and presen-tation, newscasters confect a particular version of events. Their narratives, or "stories," must be presented as chapters of the master narrative, the one titled "That's the Way the World Is."

What is interesting about the Spanish-language *noticieros* (newscasts) is how their version differs from those on the English-language stations.

Political scientist and media critic Michael Parenti has

summed up the grand themes of the master narrative of the major U.S. English-language newscasts as "American Policy as Virtuous," "The Nonexistence of Imperialism," the existence of "Moderate Authoritarian Regimes," and "Power-Hungry Leftists Who Do No Good."[6]

The *noticieros* do not directly challenge these assumptions, but they do treat events from an angle so different that it tends to undermine them. In particular, the *noticieros* focus much more closely and sympathetically on the sufferings of the poor in Latin America. And they interview respectfully, and in their own language, dissident voices among politicians and social critics in Latin America and in the barrios of the United States.

In the Spanish-language newscasts, the master narrative has a different set of heroes and somewhat different themes. Here the protagonists are the countries of Latin America and their leaders, along with *el pueblo*—the common folk—of Hispanic United States. The main theme is the common bond among all Spanish-speakers and their incessant struggle for *un mundo mejor* (a better world) and "justice" from the "Anglo Saxons"—meaning anybody white who speaks English.

News from Latin America often comes earlier in the program and is given more extensive treatment than other events that may lead the news on the other channels, and the issues and individuals of Latin America are considered with far greater respect. For example, Univisión and Telemundo were the *only* U.S. networks to send reporters to cover the 1991 summit meeting of Ibero-American presidents (those of all the Spanish- and Portuguese-speaking countries in America and Europe) in Guadalajara; viewers of the other channels were probably unaware that such a major event was even occurring. Both *noticieros* frequently secure exclusive interviews with Latin American presidents and other leaders, and Univisión—with its greater resources—was especially aggressive in covering both sides of the war in El Salvador, discontent in Panama since the American invasion, and other stories that were virtually ignored on the English-language networks.

Even more prominent attention is given to Hispanics in the United States. Person-in-the-barrio interviews, stories on neighborhood programs and cultural events, and interviews with Hispanic politicians and community workers, professionals, and artists appear on almost every broadcast. And, as if this were not sufficient, both newscasts devote a segment each week to a portrait of some noteworthy *hispano*—a government official (e.g., the Puerto Rican–born U.S. surgeon general under Bush, Dr. Antonia Novello), a professional (Argentine-born architect César Pelli, Bolivian-born math teacher Jaime Escalante), entrepreneurs, athletes, and so on. All are held up as models of both personal accomplishment and service to the community—meaning the emergent Hispanic community.

The Spanish newscasts often have a different "take" on events that are widely reported elsewhere. For example, neither of the two networks was as completely swept up in the cheering for the Persian Gulf War as were the English-language media, mainly because significant sectors of their audience opposed it. Articulate opponents, such as Cong. José Serrano (D-N.Y.), who objected to the war as an unnecessary and unwarranted risk to the lives of American troops, many of whom were Hispanics, were treated respectfully and given prime time to express their views.

During this episode, Univisión was able to use its resources to create one of the most effective images of Hispanic unity and the collective struggle for *un mundo mejor*: Correspondents taped greetings from Spanish-speaking U.S. troops in the Gulf to their loved ones at home, which were broadcast during the commercial breaks in the news. The sight of these shy young men and women of different accents and colors but dressed all alike in desert camouflage, struggling to express themselves in Spanish to their mothers or spouses or children, made a powerful image of pan-Hispanic unity in diversity. These shots simultaneously flattered the audience, presented ideals for it to live up to, and defended its reputation to outsiders. Anyone wanting to make the point of the wholesomeness and patriotism of Hispanic Americans had only to point to these scenes.

From the constant repetition of images like these, whether in the Persian Gulf or in U.S. barrios or in the reports from Latin America, a viewer might imagine that the Hispanic nation is already a reality. However, the television professionals are not themselves convinced.

CNN anchor Gestoso is pessimistic about any possible political unity among Hispanics, which he sees as *muy verde aún* (still far from ripe). He speaks of jealousies and distrust among *hispanos* of diverse origins, and among some—especially people of Mexican heritage in Los Angeles—a "confusion of identity. They've been in this country for twenty years but they still feel themselves Mexicans and they feel themselves Americans and they don't define themselves as one or the other." Also, because "in many cases the cultural level is very low, they don't have a clear awareness of the vehicle that political participation could be for achieving their goals."

The newscast, he says, should be "the mirror of our community," reflecting the concerns "of the average Hispanic." But who or what is that? His only answer is that, besides language, the main thing that his viewers have in common is precisely what makes it so hard for Hispanics to unite for any practical purpose: the "arrogance" that all Hispanics "inherited from the Spaniards" and that they "drink with our mothers' milk. That is, we imbibe it from our parents."

Gestoso's counterpart in Univisión, anchorman Jorge Ramos, also believes that narrower identities—Mexican, Puerto Rican, etc.—still take precedence for most viewers. Even among people who use the word, he says, *"Nadie realmente se siente hispano."* ("Nobody really feels Hispanic.") The only things that unite all the varied groups in his audience, he believes, are the language and the fact that "we all come from Latin America, with the desire to do something different that we couldn't do in our own countries."

As for the vaunted Hispanic "family values" that politicians attribute to Hispanics, it has become clear at least to Ramos that families are disintegrating among Hispanics as fast as among other sectors of the population. Maybe, he thinks, unity among Hispanics will one day be possible, but *"muchas veces esas uniones son ficticias"* ("often the proclamations of unity are fictitious").

One of the most influential figures in shaping Spanish TV news in the early years was Cuban-born Gustavo Godoy. He ran Univisión's news department until 1986, when, after a dispute with the network's Mexican owners, he offered his services to the upstart rival, Telemundo, which was just getting organized. As coordinator of local news broadcasts throughout the Telemundo network in the early 1990s, he produced "packages"—two- or three-minute news videos on topics of general interest—to be shown simultaneously to Mexicans in Los Angeles, Cubans in Miami, Puerto Ricans in New York, and all the other, smaller groups. To appeal to them all, he "created a structure" of Hispanic diversity in each segment. Thus, "when we did a series on AIDS, well, we focused on finding a patient who was Cuban, a doctor who was Mexican, the nurse should be Puerto Rican, in short, *para darle cabida para todos* (making room for everybody). We did a series on the economy, so the banker was Mexican, the economic adviser Cuban, the adviser from a company was Puerto Rican, to integrate all the different elements."

Thus is the Hispanic nation manufactured—first by "creating a structure" that will "make room for everybody" and then by attending to each of "the different elements" attracted to this structure. The imagistic integration comes about not because of any nationalist sentiment on the part of professionals like Godoy, Ramos, and Gestoso, but just because the very nature of the industry demands the consolidation of its market.

Telemundo ended its association with CNN in May 1993 to develop its own network news with anchor Raúl Peimbert, a Mexican, and several veteran correspondents lured from Univisión. The CNN Spanish news show continues to be produced at CNN headquarters in Atlanta, for audiences in Latin America, but is also received by cable subscribers in the United States and broadcast on an independent station in Los Angeles. Thus, viewers in most parts of the United States today have a choice of at least two, and in some places three, U.S.-produced national and international newscasts in Spanish.

Of course, news is not the only way that television shapes the Hispanic-American collective consciousness. The variety programs, talk shows, and *novelas* all serve to reinforce certain values such as family loyalty and to create the illusion of a common televised territory of all Spanish speakers.

The longtime top-rated Spanish-language television program is *Sábado Gigante*, Univisión's Saturday variety show hosted by the Chilean Mario Kreuzberger, who uses the stage name Don Francisco. Produced on alternate weeks in Santiago, Chile, and Miami, it appears not only on the Univisión stations throughout the United States but also (on broadcast or cable) in almost every country of Latin America. The guests that Don Francisco invites to play silly games come from all over the Spanish-speaking world and are of all colors, shapes, accents, and probably (although these topics are not addressed) political and religious beliefs. The jovial, pudgy host portrays a Hispanic world made up of an immense and surprising variety of generous individuals who, despite their obvious differences, have no deep conflicts and are happy to applaud one another. And—despite Shining Path, narcoterrorism, strikes, protests, guerrilla wars and racial strife throughout his listening area—for two hours every Saturday he makes that vision seem true, in this most benign version of the great Hispanic nation.

After Don Francisco, the most popular entertainment programs are the *telenovelas*. English-language television doesn't have anything quite like them. They are closer in dramatic structure to series like *Dallas* and *Twin Peaks* than to American daytime soap operas in that they always come to a dramatic conclusion after anywhere from 120 to 400 episodes. (Daytime American soaps drag on for years; as one story line concludes, another is beginning.) There are usually four or five *novelas* appearing daily on each channel, two or three in the afternoon, with the most popular ones reserved for prime time, after the evening news.

To attract male viewers (who are often 30–40 percent or more of the audience), the *novelas* tend to be more violent and more sexually explicit than their U.S. counterparts. Although most are imports from Mexico or Venezuela, where production costs are lower than in the United States, they are made with an eye to the U.S. market, a major source of revenue to the Latin American producers. For this reason a recent Mexican production shown on Telemundo, with Mexican stars, supposedly takes place among Cuban Americans in Miami. In another concession to the U.S. market, Venezuelan *novelas* have included courtroom scenes, familiar to Americans but unknown in Venezuela, which does not have a jury system.

The *novelas'* complex, highly emotional episodes are cathartic even for viewers from other cultures—a Mexican novela, *Los ricos también lloran* (The Rich Also Weep) has been a huge hit in Russia, and Venezuelan *novelas* are popular in China and Italy, among other places. For their Hispanic audiences in the United States, *telenovelas* offer not only catharsis and companionship but also, especially for recent immigrants, continuity with their home cultures. Not only are they in a familiar language; they refer to familiar dilemmas and types of relationships. The *novelas* also offer a readily comprehended narrative structure in which the wicked are ultimately punished, the virtuous rewarded, and the viewer can easily tell who is which; such a morally orderly universe can offer comfort to people in a confusing new land.

And there are the talk shows, with formats similar to Oprah's or Donahue's. The most successful of these are Univisión's *Cristina* (Cristina Saralegui) and its Telemundo clone *Cara a Cara* (Face-to-Face), hosted by María Laria. While their main function seems to be to build ratings by being outrageous, they do perform a sort of public service. These programs may be the only places that Spanish speakers new to this country can hear frank (if often absurd) discussions of sexual and other problems that may be bothering them. Still raunchier comedy shows, with no redeeming public purpose beyond laughter, are saved for late night.

**The Daily Press**

After television, the Spanish-language medium with most at stake in developing a common Hispanic consciousness is the metropolitan newspaper. Six large-circulation Spanish dailies are published in the United States, two on the West Coast, two in the New York area, and two in the Southeast. San Francisco, Chicago, San Antonio, and most other major centers of Spanish speakers have at least one, and often several, weekly papers in Spanish or in Spanish and English, and many English-language newspapers carry bilingual or Spanish magazine inserts.*

The largest Spanish-language daily today is *La Opinión*, with a circulation of 120,000. It has been on the newsstands since 1926 in Los Angeles, where it competes with the West Coast edition of *Noticias del Mundo* as well as papers from Mexico and Central America.

The Spanish press in the Northeast grew along with the

---

* *El Daily News*, a separately edited and separately sold bilingual product of the *New York Daily News*, was launched in 1995 and found "more than enough demand, both from readers and advertisers," according to Albor Ruiz, its editor. He attributes the bilingual paper's collapse six months later to a dispute between the parent company and the Drivers Union, which crippled distribution.

Puerto Rican population after the island became a U.S. territory in 1898. *La Prensa* (the Press), founded as a weekly by a Puerto Rican–born Spaniard in New York in 1913, became (as it billed itself) "the only Spanish and Hispanic American daily in the United States" in 1918. By 1948 the market was big enough to support the rival and much more populist *El Diario de Nueva York*, with its more assertive slogan "Champion of the Hispanics."[7] Merged in 1961, *El Diario/La Prensa* today has a circulation of over sixty thousand, making it the largest Spanish publisher in the New York region's crowded market.[8] In the New York metropolitan area, readers of Spanish have a choice of twenty-two newspapers, mostly weeklies, but including another daily, *Noticias del Mundo* (News of the World). In Spanish-speaking neighborhoods of New York, New Haven, and other cities, newsstands also carry dailies flown in from Puerto Rico, Colombia, and other countries and dozens of local and regional weeklies and biweeklies in Spanish.

The extremely conservative old Cuban daily now called *El Diario las Américas* is published in Miami. The much larger and more professional *El Nuevo Herald* began as a small Spanish-language insert of the *Miami Herald* but has grown to be a semi-independent newspaper with its own editorial board and staff. *El Nuevo Herald* often carries stories that do not appear in the English-language *Herald*, especially on Latin American and Cuban events, and tends to be more conservative politically than its English cousin. Its circulation is reported to be 107,000 weekdays, 125,000 Sundays.[9]

Like television, the metropolitan newspaper must appeal to a heterogeneous audience, and nowhere is it more heterogeneous than in New York. Fernando Moreno, a Spaniard who was editor in chief of *El Diario/La Prensa* in the early 1990s, notes "that a few years ago, it was easier to put out a paper in Spanish, because there were just two large communities, the Puerto Ricans and the Cubans. Whereas these days we have people from all the countries of Latin America."

To reach them all the paper pursues two strategies, sometimes at the same time. The first is to treat them all as *hispanos*, as television news does, especially on the editorial and "hard"-news front pages dealing with regional and national events that will affect all the Spanish speaking. Here the words *hispano* and *latino* are used interchangeably to describe individuals who, later in the story, may be identified by the country they come from.

The second strategy is one that television can scarcely afford. Because print space is cheaper than airtime, the paper can devote segments to each ethnic community. To cover them all, Moreno says, the *Diario* would need "three times" its usual sixty-four to seventy-two pages, many of which are taken up by wire-service news, nonnews features (comics, recipes, horoscope, crossword, etc.), and sports and ads. The larger groups, such as Puerto Ricans, Cubans, Dominicans, and Colombians, each have their own regular columnists, and the next-largest tier—including Hondurans, Ecuadorans, Mexicans, and Salvadorans—are covered frequently, if not daily. An international news section called "*Nuestros Países*" (Our Countries), based mainly on wire services, presents the most detailed country-by-country reports on major events in Latin America available in the New York area.

There are about 220 full-time Spanish-language radio stations across the country, plus others that take paid programming in Spanish.[10] In New York and Los Angeles, Spanish stations achieve ratings equal to or higher than their English-language competitors.[11] At the beginning of 1991, CBS inaugurated its Hispanic Radio Network, providing some forty of these stations with Spanish-language coverage of sports and other events. Radio, though, tends to be more narrow-cast, with programming aimed at quite specific market segments, and does not generally have as important an integrative role as television and the general-circulation press. To the extent that it brings its listeners into contact with other segments of the Spanish-speaking audience, however, it, too, contributes to constructing the Hispanic nation. Thus, people from other walks of life who happen to tune into the United Farmworkers Radio Campesina, broadcast from El Mirage, Arizona, because they like the music, will in between music selections hear the voices of many Mexican farmworkers calling in greetings, complaints, or requests. Similarly, outsiders can stumble onto the Junta Patriótica Cubana's very narrow concerns on Radio WADO in New York on Sunday mornings, or any of the various faith healers scattered about the dial, and thus get a sense of how great and diverse the Hispanic world really is.

Spanish-language books published in the United States range

from astrology and other occult sciences to history and self-help to Spanish and Latin American classics and a growing body of fiction and poetry written in Spanish in the United States. These, which will be discussed in a later chapter, also contribute to expanding a common Hispanic consciousness, if only among the most literate segment of the Hispanic nation.

## The Imagined Audience

Anyone sending messages must imagine the audience in order to shape messages to produce the desired effect (perhaps arousal, understanding, stupefaction, rage, or laughter). Editors and broadcast producers need working images of the educational level, linguistic sophistication, taboos, and tastes of each audience they address. These are internal or *in-house* images, guiding professional practice, and are adjusted when they no longer work or as new information comes in regarding audience composition and preferences.

Communicators also commonly hold a second set of images of their audience, not as they think it is but as they choose to portray it. These are external or *projected* images deliberately constructed for show—most often to flatter the audience or to excite it, sometimes to reform it, and occasionally to protect it.

For example, in television commercials Hispanics are shown as having intense family loyalty, industriousness, and frugality. Whether they are preparing Goya or General Mills products in the kitchen, purchasing a Nissan Sentra, considering a diarrhea remedy, or selecting a long-distance telephone service, they are thinking first of their spouses, offspring, and parents, some or all of whom appear in the ad. They are also hard workers, eager for success, especially those looking for English-language aids such as the Máquina del Lenguaje. And, of course, they demand value for their money.

At the other extreme, the talk shows present incest and adultery, violence, and all manner of quirks and addictions as more or less ordinary events among Hispanics, and the late-night burlesques amount to crude but occasionally witty satires of the frugal-industrious-loyal families of the ads. In the same vein but usually without the satire, the *telenovelas* are full of violent, sex- or money- or power-crazed Hispanics. So are the pages of *Impacto*, *El Especial* and the many other garishly colored, boldly headlined Spanish-language periodicals.

The in-house images in the media are often quite contrary to the projected ones. If the editors of *Impacto* or *El Especial* really believed Hispanics were as sex crazed and violent as their magazines imply, they wouldn't expect them to sit still long enough to read the articles. If advertisers thought Hispanics were as smart as they are portrayed in some commercials, they wouldn't promise miracles from such products as Miracolo Reducing Cream—"Lose fat without exercise! Without dieting!"

Where the tension between in-house and projected images is most apparent is in the production of "news," as was apparent in Jorge Ramos's and Jorge Gestoso's comments on the fictitiousness of Hispanic unity. And here we can see most plainly why the Hispanic media cannot *not* contribute to building the Hispanic national myth—whether media personnel believe in it or not. Whereas many media professionals see the majority of their audience as fragmented, often quarrelsome, and with pathetically poor resources for solving their problems, they project images of Hispanic unity, cooperation, and growing power. And these professionals just may be helping make their images come true.

The reason the Hispanic media portray Hispanics as all one huge, more or less harmonious family is not, clearly, because people in the industry believe that they are; on the whole, media professionals do not believe anything like that. It is not even that the professionals wish they were. The reason is that the networks and newspapers are commercial enterprises and the chief concern of their managers (if they are to survive) has to be the bottom line. The main function of the news department from the network's point of view is not to establish one or another ideological portrayal of Hispanics or of anybody. Nor is it really to help listeners make more informed decisions, although these may indeed be the main concerns of many of the reporters and of anchors working in them.

The real function of the news, as with any program, is to deliver an audience so as to be able to sell advertising time at the highest possible price. This is the imperative that determines what gets covered and how. In the case of Spanish-language television, it is an imperative that forces the networks to promote a concept of *hispanidad*.

Thus, when Guillermo Martínez, at the time Univisión's vice president of news and sports, was asked during the 1992 Democratic convention in New York to comment on the importance of his station's news coverage, what he spoke about most enthusiastically was not the long, exclusive interview that anchorman Jorge Ramos had gotten the night before with Bill Clinton (a major achievement for a Spanish-language station) or any other news story, but the ratings. In fact, his ratings were impressive: much higher than those of Telemundo-CNN in every market and higher even than those of CBS, ABC, and NBC news in Miami.

Martínez nevertheless insisted that he was not a salesman but a newsman. "I am nothing more than a journalist, but also nothing less than a journalist," he is fond of saying. But he could not avoid paying attention to ratings, because his job depended on them. His counterparts at Telemundo and CNN are equally concerned with them. And it is just such commercial considerations that make them and everybody else in the industry, from Gustavo Godoy and Fernando Moreno to Don Francisco and the writers of *telenovelas*, appeal to the widest possible Hispanic audience. And, regardless of the intentions of the media entrepreneurs, a common audience of passive receptors of images may be a step on the way to creating a single people—active proponents of the Hispanic nation.

### Whose Media Are They?

Back in Texas in the 1850s, or even in Los Angeles and New York or Tampa in the 1920s, Spanish-language media were owned and run by people from the same community that they served. Today, however, both television networks, four of the five daily newspapers, and most of the radio stations are owned by public and private U.S. companies.[12]

To be specific, the East and West Coast editions of *Noticias del Mundo* are owned by Reverend Moon's Unification Church, and *El Nuevo Herald* is owned by the *Miami Herald*. In 1990, the Lozano family, founders and owners of *La Opinión*, sold a 50 percent interest to Times Mirror, Inc., owners of the *Los Angeles Times*. *El Diario/La Prensa* now belongs to a partnership of Hispanic and non-Hispanic owners that includes its publisher, Carlos Ramírez. Only *Diario Las Américas* is wholly U.S. Hispanic owned, by its founding family, the Aguirres.

The largest television network, Univisión, was begun in 1961 by a non-Hispanic entrepreneur, René Anselmo. In 1987, SIN (as it was then known) was purchased by Emilio Azcárraga, the owner of Mexico's Televisa and reputedly the richest man in Latin America. He changed the company's name to Univisión and began using it as an additional outlet for the many programs Televisa was producing in Mexico. The Mexicanization of the programming provoked protests in Miami and New York, where viewers quickly tired of singers with big hats and endless movies in Mexican accents and slang. On a more positive note, the network tripled its news programming by adding late-night and weekend newscasts to the nightly newscasts it had broadcast since 1981. In any case, in 1988 the Federal Communications Commission (FCC) forced Azcárraga to sell the company on the grounds that a foreign national should not have a majority share of such an important media enterprise. It was purchased by Hallmark.

In 1992, Hallmark sold Univisión to a group headed by the "Anglo" entrepreneur A. Jerrold Perenchio, with Televisa and the Venezuelan media conglomerate Venevisión as minority partners, and today Televisa is once again the majority owner.[12a]

The second network, Telemundo, continues to be owned by the non-Hispanic entrepreneurs who created it in 1986, starting with a single station in Los Angeles. Henry Silverman, one of those entrepreneurs, succinctly explained his motivation for moving into the Spanish-speaking market: "It'll be like Star Wars!" he was quoted as saying in early 1987. "We're going to make tremendous amounts of money."[13]

So far, both networks have been *losing* tremendous amounts of money: Telemundo reported losses of $20.4 million for the first half of 1992 (an improvement over the previous year), and it was Univisión's losses that made Hallmark decide to sell it to the Mexican-Venezuelan-American consortium in that year.[14] Despite past losses, Univisión insists it is here to stay, now backed by investors with deep pockets and an expectation of future profits.

Many Hispanics see danger in the fact that Anglo-owned corporations control so much of the information reaching their communities.[15] But to suggest that Hispanic owners could make the media better serve Hispanic communities is to underestimate the constraints under which all commercial media in this country operate. It is also to romanticize the benefits of Hispanic ownership. Frequently, Hispanic owners have used the media to express their own idiosyncratic, often very unrepresentative opinions and to promote their own chosen causes and candidates, which is why Manuel Galván, a past president of the National Association of Hispanic Journalists, says that "Spanish-language media's biggest obstacle to success" is "credibility."

Galván recalls that when Chicago's first black mayor, Harold Washington—who was elected with broad Mexican-American, Puerto Rican, and Cuban support and who had gone to great lengths to include Hispanics in the city administration—"was honored at a community forum together with the Nicaraguan minister of culture, a conservative Spanish newspaper ran a banner headline in red, reading: 'The Mayor, a Communist.'" Such exaggeration undermines the credibility of the whole publication.[16]

Censorship by a Hispanic owner, the Mexican TV magnate Emilio Azcárraga, was what caused Gustavo Godoy to resign as news director of Univisión in 1986. When reporters he had sent to cover elections in Mexico reported massive fraud by the governing party, the PRI (Partido Revolucionario Institucional), the response was what he called "the coming of the troops of Montezuma": Azcárraga, the owner of Televisa, and therefore of Univisión, and a close ally of the PRI, sent his own man, Jacobo Zabludovsky, to Hialeah to take charge of the news. For Godoy this was "a very disagreeable experience." He resigned, as did thirty of his staff, who then became the nucleus of the news department of the new rival network Telemundo, which was just getting organized.

Such blatant censorship by owners, though, is exceptional in the television networks and the major dailies. In practice, pressures to present a particular political or cultural view are more likely to come from organized Hispanic groups than from stockholders. For example, protests by Puerto Rican organizations forced Univisión to remove Carlos Alberto Montaner, a Cuban prominent in exile politics, from the public affairs program *Portada*. Offended by Montaner's remarks implying that Puerto Rican women were bearing illegitimate children in order to stay on welfare, Puerto Ricans protested to the other media and picketed the station's offices in New York for more than two months. Blanca Rosa Vilches, New York City correspondent for Univision, recalls that during that period she was unable to get interviews with Puerto Rican organizations on other issues, such as AIDS. "It was a kind of boycott of Univisión."

The network defended Montaner, but when the protests continued even after he apologized for the "misunderstanding," he was dropped (or resigned) from the program.

From another quarter, intransigently anti-Castro Cuban organizations have repeatedly attempted to intimidate *El Nuevo Herald* and its owner, the *Miami Herald*, for not taking a harder anti-Castro line, using demonstrations, diatribes on radio stations and other media, and always the implicit threat of violence. While these efforts seem not to have had a great effect on editorial policy at *El Nuevo Herald*, they may have had some impact at Univisión, which conspicuously ignored a report by Americas Watch on right-wing Cuban intimidation in Miami. Telemundo, *El Diario/La Prensa*, and *El Nuevo Herald* gave it extensive coverage.

It seems obvious that for the Hispanic media to be effective they should be run by people who share their audience's language and culture. But Hispanic ownership is no guarantee of editorial impartiality or of responsiveness to the problems of the poorest Hispanics, as viewers of largely Hispanic-owned Univisión discovered. Nor does the ethnicity of the stockholders and board members make much difference in the large social impact of these media, which is the creation of a single nationwide U.S. Hispanic audience.

## Media Clout

The Hispanic media have been gaining more respect in recent years; politicians and advertisers recognize that the population they reach has become too large and too highly organized to ignore.[17] As recently as 1988 the Spanish TV networks could scarcely get five minutes with the presidential candidates. In 1992 both Bill Clinton and George Bush sat through half-hour exclusive interviews, waiting more or less patiently as questions and answers were translated. When Fernando Moreno began working at

*El Diario* seventeen years ago, it was hard for him or his colleagues to get into a mayoral press conference; in the 1990s, New York mayor David Dinkins was apt to drop in at the paper's office, and the paper has even established a respectful relationship with Dinkins's pugnacious successor, Mayor Rudolph Giuliani.

The media not only have respect but, at least in limited ways, a degree of influence. They can mobilize their audience. Moreno maintains that *"El Diario* created Herman Badillo," the first Puerto Rican ever elected to the U.S. Congress. "It invented him.... Well, I don't want to take anything away from Badillo. But *El Diario* promoted him."

The television networks do not openly endorse candidates, but they do carry political advertising by candidates and generally encourage viewers to vote. They also seek to mobilize in other ways: telethons for disaster victims (hurricanes in Puerto Rico or Florida, earthquakes in Costa Rica and Colombia), and, as already mentioned, they have encouraged people to cooperate with the census. They also use both news stories and public service announcements to urge better health practices and warn against fraud to which immigrants may be especially vulnerable (phony lawyers promising citizenship papers and so on).

Except for the telethons, which have raised substantial sums, it is hard to measure the effectiveness of any of these campaigns. At the least, they create images of Hispanics as active participants in American political and social life.

## The Media and the Spanish language

The media, and most particularly television, help to preserve and reproduce Spanish in the United States, providing an easy way to practice listening to it and, for those who appreciate the newscasts, *telenovelas*, or other programming, or the articles and features and word games in the newspapers, a reward for learning it.

But they do not preserve the language unchanged. Two powerful forces are at work, altering and reshaping the Spanish used in the media. One is the mutual influence of professionals with twenty or more different accents working in the same newsroom or story conference. Eventually, they all begin to sound alike. The other force is the constant input from the surrounding

English-language culture, tending to make their Spanish more and more like English in word order, grammar, and vocabulary and less and less like what was spoken in the home country.

Jorge Ramos, the Univisión anchor, notes that because they all come from different places, "our correspondents little by little have been losing their accents. Including me. In the ten years I've been in the United States, I have been losing my Mexican accent and acquiring a sort of neutral accent."

TV Spanish strives to be "neutral"—without a marked regional accent, "simple," and "correct," abiding by the rules in standard dictionaries. But English influences are unavoidable. Ramos says, "We keep finding how difficult it is to express certain ideas in Spanish. Sometimes we use the word in English, followed by the translation into Spanish. For example, how do you translate *caucus*?"

In fact, that's not impossible—"caucus" can be rendered as *junta*, for example, if it's a one-time meeting, or a *comité político* if it's an ongoing interest group—but there is no single word with precisely the same range of meanings as the English. Also, in a hectic *sala de redacción*, or as they really say, "newsroom," the translation may not come to mind as easily as the English term, so a "caucus" gets called a *caucus*—only the pronunciation is Spanish.

What makes it harder to keep the language straight is that almost everything spoken off-camera is in English. Editorial meetings, rehashing the previous night's program, and planning the next one are all in English because the news directors, even if "Hispanics," seldom speak Spanish fluently. Even the instructions coming through an anchor's headphone are usually in English. This can be very confusing to a journalist like Patricia Janiot, the CNN coanchor, who was trained and began her career in her native Colombia.

"I couldn't understand how the editorial meetings could be in English, to produce in Spanish....There were lots of people, including producers, who didn't know Spanish well. Even directors! For me, that was a surprise," she says. And she is still not used to it.

"We try to use the simplest language possible," says Ramos. "I don't think we're reflecting the Spanish being spoken in the

United States. I think that most of the people who work in the communications media tend to have a somewhat higher education than the rest of the Hispanics in the country."

Evidence of the discrepancy is apparent almost every night in the newscast itself. One of the most common scenes is the bidialectal interview: the reporter speaking a careful, idiomatic, but rather simple Spanish, the interviewee answering in a complex, fluid, and expressive Spanglish. Blanca Rosa Vilches, a Peruvian who had her own news show in Lima before she began covering New York City for Univisión, has finally given up trying to get people she interviews on the street in New York to say *edificio* instead of *bildin* (building). "That business of Spanglish"—she sighs—"I think that's what we struggle against most. But it's impossible."

"You have to keep in mind that we're not living in a vacuum," says Ramos. "We aren't isolated. And we are totally permeable to the influences of English. And something we talk about a lot, and that we complain about a lot, is that we are continually losing more of our Spanish in the United States.... What happens to us is a little like what happens to Hispanic children who are born into Hispanic families. Television and the school are much stronger influences than their own parents."

Such excuses are unacceptable to Madrid-born Fernando Pérez, media critic for *El Diario/La Prensa* and an unrelenting adversary of Anglicisms and other *disparates*—a wonderfully explosive word covering both solecisms and balderdash. Once, he recalls, *un amable colega* (an esteemed colleague) in another Spanish-language periodical criticized him for being too harsh because "here we are in the United States and that's why Spanish is spoken the way it is and we just have to get used to it." Pérez replied, "All right, *you* get used to it and write it however you like,"[18] but as far as he was concerned, the "disastrous editing" of the newscasts on both channels "has no name," meaning it was beneath contempt. Its opposite, he said, does have a name, however, "and its name is GRAMMAR."[19]

Not that Pérez's own paper is exactly above reproach. The former editor in chief of *El Diario/La Prensa*, Fernando Moreno, who, as it happens, is also a Spaniard (though born in Tangiers), readily acknowledged his paper's Spanglish problem. "As you can see here," he said, pointing to an article on that day's page 3 by a Peruvian columnist, *"una nota en un español impecable*... (a piece in impeccable Spanish), and next to it"—pointing to another article by a New York–raised Puerto Rican—"something in—I don't know what, *sanscrito a lo mejor"*—(Sanskrit, maybe).

He explained that he could easily have limited himself to hiring people with perfect Spanish, but then he would not get people who grew up here and can really cover the city. So he sacrifices linguistic correctness for reportorial insight. In some of these articles Anglicisms abound, the subjunctive is a mystery seldom invoked, and even genders get confused, making the result a little comical and occasionally indecipherable. The paper's other reporters, with a better knowledge of Spanish, hardly have time, or the inclination, to rewrite everything.

On the whole, though, the Spanish of *El Diario* has been improving—that is, growing closer to standard Spanish—in the past few years. It seems that the U.S. Hispanics are learning from their foreign-born colleagues faster than those colleagues are getting corrupted by Spanglish.

María Elena Salinas of Univisión thinks that Spanish in the United States is enjoying a renascence due to a resurgent "pride in being Hispanic." She tells of a friend who had never spoken Spanish and felt offended that people expected her to, just "because she looked Hispanic," until "she realized that in order to do business, she had to speak Spanish" and went off and learned it in Mexico. That moment, she suggests, has arrived for many people.

Moreno agrees, and as he sees it, *"Es una gran cosa, es maravilloso.* ("It's a great thing, it's wonderful.") An *hispanidad* of all the nationalities is taking shape here. And that's the mission of *El Diario*....And the Puerto Ricans, or Nuyoricans, as they're called, those who've been here three or four generations, who had abandoned Spanish, *están volviendo a lo hispano* (they're return- ing to things Hispanic) and are using Spanish again, speaking better than their parents." But of course it is "not the same Spanish, not with the same accent." Rather, it has the new, homogenized accent of North America—as heard on TV.

Meanwhile, in some of its entertainment programming Span- ish television has begun experimenting with bilingual and Spanglish formats, which have long been familiar on radio—to the despair of purists like Pérez. On Univisión, Paul Rodríguez, a Mexican-born, Los Angeles-raised comedian, switches back and forth between languages constantly as he interviews Anglo and Hispano guests. And, in the late hours of Saturday, Johny Canales presents his show in fast, slangy Texas Spanglish.

## The Future of the Hispanic Media

Even though large numbers of people are constantly dropping out of the audience and switching to English-language media, media entrepreneurs, advertisers, and media personnel all expect the Spanish-language market to grow hugely in the next few years. The main reason is immigration, which most observers think is unstoppable. A second reason is what is perceived as an increased reluctance among Spanish speakers to give up their language, in part because of the availability of Spanish media.

Guillermo Martínez is convinced that there will be a Spanish-language audience for a very long time. He recalls that when he was one of the founding editors of *El Miami Herald* in Spanish in 1976, the editor of the parent paper, the *Miami Herald*, John McMullen, announced, "The job that you're doing is very important because it is a job that you're doing for a number of years. Ten or fifteen years from now, when the new generation has been born here, your jobs will be obsolete and everybody will be speaking English once again."

By 1987, John McMullen had retired, but the modest Spanish insert known as *El Herald* had been replaced by "a bigger product, called *El Nuevo Herald*," a full-scale newspaper with its own staff.

"And in 1991, while the *Herald* was firing and dismissing employees, *El Nuevo Herald* was increasing its staff."[20] Continued immigration not only from Cuba but from all over Latin America has kept the Miami Spanish-language newspaper readership growing.

Important as they are, the Spanish-language media cannot meet the information needs of all the people in the United States whom the census labels Hispanic, especially since nearly half of them speak English mostly or exclusively. But the mainstream English-language media do not address their specific concerns as

Hispanic Americans, nor do they respond adequately to their hybrid culture.

This has created market space for Hispanic-targeted English-language periodicals like *Hispanic*, *Hispanic Business*, and the livelier but now defunct *Latino New York*. A monthly newsletter, the *Hispanic Monitor*, flourished briefly (1983–84), and the weekly newsletter *Hispanic Link* has been operating since 1980 and remains an essential resource for journalists and community activists. These, too, are parts of the Hispanic image machine and are likewise constrained by the diversity of their target audience to treat all Hispanics as a single group. If anything, the tendency to homogenization may be stronger in these English-language media, for their readers are less closely tied to a specific foreign homeland.

Their reporters, however, still need to be bilingual; Hispanic readers demand access to what is going on in the Spanish-speaking world. What happens in the editorial offices is often the reverse of what goes on in a Spanish-language TV studio: The internal conversations may be mainly in Spanish, but the product for the public is in English.

These small periodicals survive because mainstream English-language media have been slow to go after their market by hiring Hispanic reporters.[20] But there are exceptions.

María Hinojosa, born in Mexico City in 1961 and brought up and educated in the United States, possesses one of the most familiar Hispanic voices in the English media. She describes herself as "a woman of color" and is fiercely proud of being "Latina"—not "Hispanic," because "I've never been to Spain. I don't speak Spanish like the Spanish from Spain do."

Although the family spoke Spanish at home, when she was in her early teens, she "lost" the language. "I mean, I would speak it, but I had a very thick [American] accent. And it was just more difficult, more uncomfortable. And I made a concerted effort to speak Spanish, to study it, to read in Spanish."

What she says about her own professional aims could be said also by many other Hispanic-identified reporters working in English media: "What I like best is to get out and gather the voices of the people who are rarely heard. Young people, poorer people, people of color, women, I think Latinas. I think there are a lot of issues where Latin American women have stuff to say and they're not being heard. So that's my agenda. It's what I do. But I'd like to be able to do more of it."

## A Job With a Soul?

The Spanish media help develop the Hispanic nation in other ways as well. One of the most important is providing employment to professionals who, either because of a special commitment to their communities of origin or because of discrimination, or both, would not be happy in the English-language media. That is, the media make it possible for these people to make a living as Hispanics.

María Elena Salinas is the only one of the five network anchors who is by origin a U.S. Hispanic. She was born in Los Angeles in 1964 and brought up in that city's Mexican-American neighborhoods. Her family always spoke Spanish, and she kept it up and worked on it and now speaks it quite as well as any of her colleagues, while her native fluency gives her an edge over most of them when conducting interviews in English. If she were to switch to English-language media, she would lose that edge and of course face greater competition. In Spanish, she is at the top of her field and speaks of the "great satisfaction" she derived from her long-standing relationship with her audience.

Spanish TV news directors Gustavo Godoy and Guillermo Martínez both worked in English media (Godoy in television, Martínez on the *Miami Herald*) before going, respectively, to Telemundo and Univisión. For both, the motivation for the switch to Spanish media was a mix of wanting to be a bigger fish in a smaller pond and a desire to serve what they saw as their own community.

Reynaldo Colón, a Bronx-reared Puerto Rican who was briefly the news director on New York's Channel 47, a Telemundo affiliate, also made the switch, for similar reasons. He spent fifteen years at CBS news as a producer for network shows, including *60 Minutes, CBS Morning News,* and *CBS Evening News With Dan Rather.* But he had felt frustrated because "you were always reporting to people who had less experience than you, but because they were in these powerful positions you couldn't really get things done." And he knew he was not going to get promoted to such a "powerful position" because he was Puerto Rican and had not graduated from an Ivy League school.

He pointed to his arm and ran a finger up and down his light brownish skin—Puerto Rican sign language for "color is the issue."

Determined that it should not be an issue at Telemundo, when his light-skinned Argentine anchorwoman resigned, he replaced her with a talented, much darker Dominican woman. This was a significant gesture in an industry where the network (as distinct from local) news anchors (Gestoso, Janiot, Peimbert, Ramos, and Salinas) are all fair-skinned and all but Janiot are blond. However, his attempt to make the newscast more of a "community service" by emphasizing upbeat community news and health and service information failed to boost ratings, and Colón was soon out of a job.

**Keeping the Nation Alive**

As Ana Veciana-Suárez has put it, "What Spanish-language media do well, almost in spite of themselves, is to serve as liaison and window between the different groups that make up Hispanic U.S.A. Primarily because of network television, the Mexican-Americans in the Southwest know more about the Cuban-Americans in the Southeast who, in turn, know more about the Puerto Ricans in the Northeast."[21]

In sum, the Hispanic media contribute to the construction of the Hispanic nation in at least three ways: by establishing the imagery of the imagined community, by providing a livelihood for an important group of professionals as "Hispanics," and possibly, in limited ways, by mobilizing listeners or readers to take joint action. And the Spanish media also contribute in a fourth way, by helping develop the Hispanic nation's continent-wide dialect, peculiarly adapted to its North American environment.

Even so, Hispanics may eventually go the way of their predecessors, the German Americans, who long clung to their language and distinctive customs. As recently as the 1950s, after two wars against Germany and forty years since the end of large-scale German immigration, there were still towns and counties in the United States where a modified form of German was the language of community life.[22] But with the exception of these pockets, by mid-twentieth century the German Americans "would become the only large ethnic group to disappear as a serious ethnic political force," despite the fact that "from the earliest days of the republic through the nineteenth century, no immigrant-ethnic group, including the Irish, had a larger ethnic press."[23]

But the disappearance of Hispanics "as a serious ethnic political force," if it occurs at all, will be many decades into the future, if for no other reason than because of the continuing immigration of Spanish speakers. In the meantime, they will continue to assert their own imagery on other Americans more forcefully than the German Americans ever could, through the greater communications power of the electronic media.

# 4

# The Peoples Within the Image

AS POWERFUL AS THE SPANISH-LANGUAGE IMAGE MACHINE may be, it could not create its portrait of a homogeneous, unified Hispanic community out of nothing. The imagined community takes as its raw material the real, lived experiences of the numerous Hispanic peoples of the United States and their sometimes divergent, sometimes convergent histories.

These histories go back a long way, to more than two centuries before the United States became an independent country. Spanish colonists built the oldest town in this country, San Agustín (today St. Augustine), Florida, in 1565 and established many others well before the signing of the United States' Declaration of Independence in 1776. Hispanic-American historians like to point out that during the war to establish that independence, a Spanish force (with Cuban and Indian troops) under command of the governor of Louisiana, Bernardo de Gálvez (for whom Galveston, Texas, is named), intervened militarily to help the rebels by repelling British incursions up the Mississippi River. Spain also assisted the rebels with weaponry and cash and offered safe haven in its Caribbean ports for American vessels fleeing British warships. Later, distinguished Americans of Spanish descent included the best-remembered Union navy hero in the Civil War, Adm. David Farragut ("Damn the torpedoes! Four bells, Captain Drayton, go ahead!" he ordered at the Battle of Mobile Bay, August 5, 1864).[1]

By the middle of the nineteenth century there were two

radically different cultural systems of Spanish speakers on U.S. soil. One, centered in the old Spanish settlements in the Southwest, was far-flung, agrarian, and conservative. The other, made up of Spanish-speaking expatriates clustered on the Atlantic (Boston, New York) and Gulf (Tampa) coasts, was compact, urban, and progressive. Despite their common language, the two systems had little contact or sense of affinity, less because of the geographic distance than because of differences in social organization and culture.

Both these cultural systems would be transformed by the economic and territorial expansion of Anglo America in the coming decades, although in very different ways. The contrasts in their legacies help explain the differences in outlook that make Hispanic unity problematic today.

## From Spanish Northland to American Southwest

When Mexico declared its independence in 1821, it inherited the viceroyalty of New Spain's northern provinces of Alta ("Upper") California, Texas, and Nuevo México, large territories which today have been divided into the states of California, Nevada, Utah, Colorado, Arizona, New Mexico, Texas, and parts of Wyoming—all of what is today called the U.S. Southwest. However, there were only about sixty thousand Spanish speakers in this area of over 850,000 square miles.[2]

Spanish settlement had begun in 1598 in New Mexico, but those first outposts along the upper Río Grande were destroyed by a revolt of Pueblo Indians in 1680. Over the next century those outposts—Santa Fe, Taos, and others—were reestablished and expanded along with other missions and towns, including Ysleta (site of modern El Paso, Texas) in 1682, San Antonio in 1751, Tucson in 1775, San Diego in 1769, San Francisco in 1776, and the Pueblo de Nuestra Señora de los Angeles del Río de Porciúncula, or simply "Los Angeles," in 1781.

Because of the rugged terrain, the vast distances and the hostility of the "Gentiles" (non-Christianized Indians), settlers in California had little contact with those in Tucson or Texas and even less with those in the mountains of New Mexico. Nor did they hear very often from the viceroy in Mexico City, or from his successors, following Mexican independence. Except for the priests and friars, whose superiors were in central Mexico and whose ultimate terrestrial superior was in Rome, and the few administrators sent out from the capital, residents rarely had political loyalties or awareness much beyond a day's ride from where they lived. In each of the scattered *pueblos*, forts, missions, and ranches, people relied mainly on one another for survival, in close-knit communities where everybody spoke the same language, knew the same stories, and had been married by the same priest. These people surely had many problems to resolve, but "cultural identity" was not among them.

Outwardly, these widely separated settlements had many similarities. Almost all were laid out according to the central plaza and street-grid design commanded by the royal ordinances of 1573 (*Ordenanzas de Población*), and the people in them (or at least those in authority) all spoke Spanish and formally and officially accepted the Roman Catholic religion (whatever their private beliefs). On closer inspection, however, their cultures and economies were markedly varied in several respects: Because those in New Mexico and some in Texas were founded much earlier, in some cases as much as two centuries earlier, than the others, they remembered more ancient traditions and tended to be more conservative in speech and customs. Also, the differences in terrain and location led to the development of different kinds of economies and thus to different class structures. The mountains of New Mexico, for example, supported independent sheep farmers, self-reliant and suspicious of outsiders, whereas San Francisco was a port with traders and longshoremen and other occupations related to sea traffic, men accustomed to dealing with Russians, British, Americans, and other foreigners.

Early expeditions into the Spanish and Mexican northland had consisted of Spaniards, Hispanicized Indians and mixed breeds from central Mexico, and a few Africans, almost all of them men. These intruders often took local indigenous women as mates, produced offspring with a mixed gene-pool and hybrid cultures. Spanish intentions were reshaped by Indian craftsmanship and customs, most obviously in architecture but also in social order and psychology. European building designs, copied from books brought in by the priests, were almost always erected and decorated by indigenous people out of local materials—timber where it was available, inspired improvisations of mud and stone where it was not—and according to their own local aesthetic traditions. The results were strikingly varied: homely but solid mud churches in *pueblos* of New Mexico, for example, lovingly re-shaped year by year, in contrast to the stone-walled, fortified missions near San Antonio, Texas, or the imposing white San Xavier de Bac on a promontory outside Tucson, Arizona, designed by Mexican missionaries in imitation of the monumental mission churches of Querétaro.

In the northern provinces, as throughout the vice royalty, society was divided into elite *criollos* (descendants of Spaniards born in the New World) at the top, followed by *castas* (mixed bloods), who were further divided according to how mixed they were, and unacculturated Indians at the bottom, with very little unity among them. However, the specific character of these relations depended on local conditions and history. The date of settlement made a difference: In the century after 1680 mission-aries and government officials had become progressively less zealous in their respective missions and more corrupt and venal, occasioning more complaints of abuse from Indians and even *criollos*.

Tucson and Tubac in Arizona remained rough frontier towns, at war with Pimas and then Apaches well into the nineteenth century. In Alta California, from San Diego to San Francisco, missionaries more successfully subjugated the local Indians, turning them into a labor force for a flourishing agriculture. Moreover, the towns that grew up around these missions, es-pecially in the north, had far more contact with the outside world; San Francisco was a regular port of call for American, British, and Russian ships, trading manufactured goods for California's hides and timber. New Mexican settlements, especially in the moun-tainous north—Santa Fe and Taos—were not only the oldest but the least connected, geographically and commercially, to the empire. No sooner had the Spanish colonial government, with its onerous trade restrictions, been removed in 1821 than wagoneers opened up what would become famous as the Santa Fe Trail, connecting the province with trading partners in Independence, Missouri.

Geography may not have been the only reason some New Mexico *hispanos* held themselves aloof from Spain. A number of families secretly carried on such forbidden Jewish traditions as lighting candles on Friday evenings and celebrating non-Catholic festivals—including a Feast of St. Esther and one of Jacales, corresponding to Purim and *Succoth*, respectively. Since the expulsion of the Jews from Spain in 1492, such practices had been punishable by death in all Spanish dominions.[3]

These Spanish domains, then, were far from uniform, and they did not respond alike to changes introduced from outside— such as the eighteenth-century imperial administrative reforms, the Mexican war against Spain that began in 1810, or Mexican independence in 1821. For the most part, these events were barely felt in upper New Mexico and were generally absorbed and accommodated with equanimity in California, but they often brought about major shake-ups in parts of Texas, the province most accessible to and most dependent upon central Mexico. Nor did these settlements react uniformly when struck by the greatest force of change yet, Anglo-American expansion.

For a cultural system that had been evolving slowly over 150 years, the collapse was quite sudden. By 1847 most, and by 1853 all, of Mexico's far north had become the United States' Southwest. Two-fifths of Mexico's territory had changed hands.

### El Debacle

The young Mexican Republic's rule was briefest in Texas, where it lasted a scant fourteen years. The first legal settlement of Anglo Americans, three hundred families led by Stephen T. Austin, had been chartered by the Spanish governor of Texas in January 1821, just one month before Gen. Agustín de Iturbide proclaimed Mexico's independence. Nine years later, Anglo Americans already outnumbered Spanish speakers in the province. These first settlers were truly "Anglos," in the sense that not only their language but their ancestry was mostly English. (Later, the word Anglo would be applied to English-speaking European Americans of any ancestry.)

In 1835, the Anglos and their many allies among the *tejanos*— Spanish-speaking Texans—revolted against the rule of Mexican president Antonio López de Santa Anna. Formally, they were not demanding independence but only greater autonomy, along with a return to Mexico's own liberal 1824 constitution, and—what they must have known was the deal breaker—the removal of Santa Anna from power. Santa Anna mobilized a large army against them, but—after the Alamo and the Texans' victory at San Jacinto—in 1836, Texas became an independent republic, governed by English-speaking Protestants.

The same year as Texas's independence, 1836, the Spanish-speaking settlers of Alta California also revolted against Santa Anna. The *criollos* there had already begun referring to themselves as "*californios*," to make the point that they were not "Mexicans." In 1845, they finally succeeded in driving out what would be the last Mexican governor, but their autonomy was not to last long. The very next year, Anglo settlers—who had been moving into California in increasing numbers—revolted against the *californios* as well as Mexico and, led by John Charles Frémont under the "Bear Flag," proclaimed the California Republic. This in turn was nullified in less than a month by Comdr. John Drake Sloat of the U.S. Navy, who captured Monterey, the provincial capital, and claimed the territory for the United States.

In the north, where the Anglos were most numerous, *californios* had little choice but to go along with this new turn of events, but southern *californio* resistance continued for another year. Then, after gold was discovered at Sutter's Mill in 1848, so many Anglos poured into the territory that *californios* were soon a tiny minority in what had been their own land. Two years later, in 1850, California was admitted as a state of the United States of America.

Meanwhile, the annexation of Texas by the United States in 1845 had provoked war with Mexico, leading to the 1846 invasion of Mexico and the latter's complete defeat. There was a clamor in the United States to annex the whole country. Instead, on February 2, 1848, President Polk compelled Mexico to sign the Treaty of Guadalupe Hidalgo, ceding almost all the rest of its northern territories to the United States in exchange for $15 million. As a concession to Mexican sensibilities, the United States granted citizenship to Spaniards and Mexicans residing in those territories. The United States' new acquisitions were rounded off by the purchase negotiated by U.S. minister James Gadsden of the southernmost parts of Arizona and New Mexico in 1853. Between the Texas, California, and Mexican-American wars and the Gadsden Purchase, Mexico had lost two-fifths of its territory (wherein, however, lived only about 1 percent of its population).

The size of this debacle is a source of continuing embarrassment to Mexicans on both sides of the resulting border. How could an army that was five times as large as the U.S. Army, was fighting on its home territory, and was led by some of the same generals who had won a glorious victory against Spain less than fifteen years earlier be so utterly defeated by uncultured *gringos* whose only prior battle experience had been against Indians?

As late as the 1960s, Mexican-American folklorist Américo Paredes was collecting stories handed down by embittered veterans to their grandchildren and now surely being told by their great-great-grandchildren. One commonly invoked explanation is the foolish rigidity of Santa Anna, who refused to permit *guerrilla* tactics that would have taken full advantage of the audacity and ingenuity of the Mexican cowboys under his command.[4]

This is surely a major part of the explanation. Another part, besides the unexpected effectiveness of the U.S. Army in what was a new kind of war for it, was disunity among the Mexicans, who had not managed to substitute the old centralism of the Spanish Empire with a sufficiently forceful centralism of their own. Internal rivalries not only engendered distrust and impeded cooperation, they also prevented widespread acceptance of innovations, whether of tactics or technology. The United States, though only a little older as a nation, was already more cohesive ideologically (everyone saluted the same flag) and enormously more open to new ideas and experimentation.

The dynamism of the northern country is apparent in a list of inventions in this same period. In the United States during those two war years, 1845–47, railroads and steamships were improved and expanded, the first clipper ship was launched, and a rotary press that would revolutionize the newspaper industry was patented. Just the year before, in 1844, Samuel F. B. Morse had transmitted his first telegraph message, and it was a huge government order for revolvers for U.S. troops fighting Mexico that led (or enabled) Samuel Colt to invent mass production.

Mexico, despite having a much older urban tradition than the United States (Tenochtitlán was founded in 1325 and, renamed

Mexico City, had been the capital of New Spain since 1535), lagged way behind it in technical innovation. This was not because the descendants of Mexicas, Mayas, and Spaniards were any less inventive than the Scots, English, and Germans who had settled in the north but because their entire social system was more efficient at suppressing bright new ideas. This was especially true during Spanish colonial days, when the Inquisition used torture and executions to punish innovators. In the years since independence, political turbulence and the semianarchy of rival caudillos had a similar effect.

The concept of a common Mexican nationality was still a very vague thing, even in the central part of the country around the capital. Thus, leaders in the war of independence had rallied their forces around the banner of the Virgin of Guadalupe rather than the new national flag.[5] To most people in the provinces of Texas, New Mexico, Arizona, and California, and even in Sonora and Chihuahua, "Mexico" was the name of a valley far to the south, not of their home territory. Now Santa Anna's arbitrary and despotic rule made it even less likely that the northern provincials would feel great loyalty to Mexico. It was because of this that so many *tejanos* joined the Anglo-led 1835 revolt in Texas and *californios* revolted even without Anglo encouragement. Mexican generals felt so little commitment to the national cause that they would "steal" one another's troops to bolster their own forces. Furthermore, their military supply systems were corrupt and chaotic, in contrast to the greater efficiency and discipline of the American effort.[6]

In any case, Mexican rule—that is, under the independent Republic of Mexico—lasted less than a generation in Texas, and not much more than a generation in Tucson (in the last area to be ceded to the United States as part of the Gadsden Purchase of 1853), and had been scarcely felt in remote areas like northern New Mexico. The changes of sovereignty happened so quickly that the northern provincials had scarcely had time to acquire a new identity as "Mexicans" even if they had wanted to.

Because a common Mexican national identity never had had a chance to flourish in this area, it would be exceedingly difficult in later years to develop a common Mexican-American identity, especially as the peoples of Mexico's former northern provinces were joined by newer immigrants from the south.

## North of the Big River

After the war, a stretch of the river known in the north as the Grande, or Big, and in Mexico as the Bravo, or Turbulent, became part of an international boundary. The Río Grande begins its 1,885-mile course in the San Juan mountains of southwestern Colorado and flows southward through the middle of New Mexico, past Albuquerque, to El Paso, Texas, and Ciudad Juárez, on the Mexican side. There and until it empties into the Gulf of Mexico at Brownsville, Texas, and Matamoros, Mexico, it is the line separating two countries.

Around the Big Bend and farther south, the river is deep, swift, and dangerous.[7] But the turbulence of the river has another, metaphorical meaning. Crossing it plunges Mexicans into a cultural whirlpool, a disorienting and often destructive struggle against powerful currents as incomprehensible as the forces of the river.

Nevertheless, it continued to be crossed regularly by people visiting families, trading goods, or fleeing the police on one side or another, even after the river became an international border. The rest of the border, from El Paso to Tijuana on the Pacific Ocean, is artificial, a series of straight lines drawn on a map. Nevertheless, in the popular imagination, the Big River stands for the entire U.S.-Mexican border, and illegal immigrants have long been derisively called wetbacks even when they crossed dry land farther west.

After Santa Anna was out of power (1855) and the far more popular Benito Juárez, leader of Mexico's Liberal party, was in, Mexicans north of the river began to take more interest in events to the south of it. And when Juárez took up arms against the French, who had occupied Mexico and installed the Austrian prince Maximilian as emperor in 1862, his representatives found many supporters among the Mexicans on the U.S. side. Some of them even joined Juárez's forces or fought under the northern Gen. Juan Nepomuceno Cortina. In 1859, Cortina had crossed the Big River into Brownsville, briefly raised the Mexican flag, and later supported Juárez against the French.

But not all Mexicans of the north were so friendly to those from the south, especially as more of the latter crossed over to escape the turmoil of civil war. The old settlers with property regarded the newcomers as inferiors, those without property were likely to see them as competitors for jobs. The attitude of superiority and distance—*categoría y distancia*, as people used to say—was more marked among the *hispanos* of New Mexico than among the *tejanos* and *californios*, who were more likely to have family and business dealings on the other side, but was shared by all three.[8]

In 1867, the year Benito Juárez defeated the French (with the aid of some Mexican Americans and hundreds of American Civil War veteran mercenaries), gold was discovered in Arizona. In the next few years mining of gold and other metals—silver, copper, zinc—increased rapidly in the territory, worked by Mexicans from both sides of the border. Then, as the U.S. economy began to surge in the 1880s, many more Mexicans entered the country to work in slaughterhouses and on railroads and construction projects, moving through the Southwest and all the way to Kansas City, Chicago, and Milwaukee. The numbers of Mexicans in the United States increased ninefold from 1880 to 1920, while the U.S. population as a whole merely doubled.[9]

Besides those who came seeking work, thousands crossed the river as refugees from violence in the last years of the nineteenth century. Among these were the Yaquis, indigenous people who had risen against the dictatorship of Porfirio Díaz in 1885 in an attempt to hold on to their lands and continued fighting for the next twenty years. Some of the refugees settled in Arizona in a village they called Guadalupe, today completely surrounded by the city of Phoenix, Arizona. The fifty-four hundred inhabitants of this self-governing little cluster of houses are generally thought of as "Mexicans," and while they may not object to the label, their identity and their relation to Mexico are quite a bit more complex. Today, Yaqui, English, and Spanish are all spoken here.[10]

The low-paid Mexican laborers were frequently involved in strikes, in many cases instigated by the outlawed Partido Liberal Mexicano (PLM; Mexican Liberal party) that was working toward the overthrow of longtime Mexican president Porfirio Díaz. The PLM organized strikes among Mexican workers on both sides of the border, where workers were facing the same corporations. In 1903, it pulled off a strike of sugar-beet-field workers in Ventura, California. In 1906 the PLM organized the big strike against the copper mines of the U.S.-owned corporation Anaconda, in Cananea in northern Mexico, which was quelled when the company called in U.S. troops. That same year, the PLM issued a program in St. Louis, Missouri, defending the rights of Mexican workers, including the right to repatriation at the expense of the future revolutionary government they hoped to install. The next year, the PLM set up a U.S. affiliate, the Unión de Obreros Libres (Union of Free Laborers), in Morenci, Arizona.[11]

On October 5, 1910, the signal for insurrection against dictator Porfirio Díaz was given in San Antonio, Texas. There Francisco I. Madero, fleeing Díaz's hired assassins, had found safe haven and issued his revolutionary manifesto, the "Plan de San Luis Potosí." Shortly thereafter, Díaz was forced from power, then Madero was assassinated, and full-scale civil war broke out in Mexico. It raged until 1917, and aftershocks, including local insurrections, assassinations, and a savage but low-intensity religious war, would continue into the 1930s. The most direct incursion into the United States occurred in March 1916, when the Chihuahua-based guerrilla chieftain Pancho Villa led a raid into Columbus, New Mexico. This provoked President Woodrow Wilson to order Gen. John Pershing into Mexico at the head of an expeditionary force that engaged in a fruitless chase of Villa.

The revolution affected Mexican Americans in contradictory ways. Some were radicalized as emissaries of the various revolutionary factions circulated in their communities in Los Angeles and other U.S. cities, promoting their causes and soliciting funds. In rural Texas, Mexican-American small owners were inspired to carry out their own revolution with armed attacks on Anglo ranchers and merchants. This Plan de San Diego rebellion of 1915–17 was finally quelled by a massive deployment of U.S. Army troops and Texas Rangers. But there was also a conservative effect: The violence in the south was driving a stream of individuals and families across the border who had been traumatized by the violence and wanted nothing to do with revolution or populist appeals of any sort. They introduced a new, deeply conservative strain into Mexican-American life.

Armed uprisings like the Plan de San Diego rebellion were exceptional and atavistic in the southwestern United States, where the political economy based on *charros*, or cowboys—really

peasants on horseback—was rapidly being supplanted by capitalist agriculture and mining. The most typical forms of political
action by Mexicans over the next thirty years would be labor
agitation, including strikes and occupations of mines and lobbying
by civic organizations in defense of civil rights.

Mexicans and Mexican Americans had to cope with two
contradictory types of Anglo behavior toward them. One was the
attempts to recruit them to work in the mines, fields, and factories,
especially in boom times, including luring workers from south of
the border. This was because Mexicans were the handiest source
of cheap labor in the Southwest, especially after the U.S. immigration act of 1882 excluded entry of Chinese.

The other, contradictory behavior was harassment by Anglos,
especially in economically slack times, when many Anglos were
having a hard time making a living. Agitators fanned intense anti-
Mexican sentiment on the part of some white Americans, particularly those who didn't own industries to staff. Gunmen like
Billy the Kid (William Bonney) or O. Henry's fictional "Cisco Kid"
murdered Mexicans on sight for amusement and (in their own
minds) as a public service, and gun battles between Mexicans and
los rinches—the Texas Rangers—have entered the folklore of both
Anglo and Mexican Texans.

Among the white elite, racism might take the more benign
form of paternalism, as exemplified in Helen Hunt Jackson's
romantic novel Ramona (1884) or the "Old Spanish Days" festivals,
when local dignitaries disported themselves in the imagined style
of Mexican "grandees" of colonial times. These virtuous and noble
Mexicans were always imagined as belonging to the distant past
and having little connection to the dark and scruffy peasants who
repaired the ditches or gathered the cattle on the big estates or kept
to themselves in their Mexican towns outside the white
settlements.

For Mexicans, therefore, the United States was alternately
welcoming and threatening: Anglos needed Mexicans but didn't
really want them around. Government measures encouraging
Mexicans to enter the country to labor were hedged with restrictions and tended to be followed by punitive measures colored by
racism. This contradiction is evident in U.S. policies in the era of
World War I and afterward.

In 1917, after entering what was then known as the Great European War and in anticipation of greater labor needs for the war effort, the U.S. government lifted all barriers to Mexican immigration except an eight-dollar-a-head tax and a literacy test. For many, these were stiff requirements, but (as the U.S. government well knew) not enough to deter those seeking jobs up north.[12]

Meanwhile, Mexican Americans who wanted to join the army to fight in the war were generally prevented from doing so unless they could pass for "white" (non-Mexican), because the army was still segregated. One young Texan, Richard Cantú, who enlisted under his mother's surname as Richard Barkely, was killed in action and awarded the Congressional Medal of Honor for heroism. The family did not reveal the Mexican ancestry of Richard Cantú Barkely until many years after his death.[13]

But as the postwar recession began in the 1920s, new laws were passed to deny the immigrants public medical assistance, and other legislation was proposed to restrict further entry. In this same period, the Ku Klux Klan became active in the Southwest.

The major response of Mexican Americans to such renewed hostility was to organize, as they had been doing at least since 1894, when the mutual-aid and cultural society Alianza Hispano-Americana was founded in Arizona. In 1921, veterans who, unlike Cantú Barkely, had been unable or unwilling to pass for Anglo formed an association they called Sons of America.

Both Mexican Americans and newer Mexican immigrants also turned again to a more openly combative form of organization that was very familiar to them: the labor union. Many Mexican immigrants, agitated by radicals in their homeland and having fewer economic options and less exposure to Anglo-American ideology than long-established Mexican Americans, flocked to the most radical unions, including the anarchist-led Industrial Workers of the World. They participated in the fierce strikes in the mines, sugar-beet fields, and other work sites that turned much of the West into a battleground during the 1920s, even in the face of deadly force by company goons and National Guard troops. The interpersonal bonds between union comrades were forged of both class and ethnic loyalties, since the class enemy, the bosses, were (almost always) non-Mexicans. In the late 1920s and throughout the thirties, Mexicans and Mexican Americans would also be prominent in organizing drives of the Congress of Industrial Organizations (CIO) in the radical years before its merger with the American Federation of Labor (AFL).

The *hispanos* of New Mexico continued to pursue their own idiosyncratic and very exceptional course. In contrast to every other territory of what had once been northern New Spain, the old *hispano* elite of New Mexico had come to a more or less cordial power-sharing arrangement with the Anglos in which each group respected the traditions and rights of the other. In 1912 the territory became the first and only one to be admitted to the Union as a bilingual state. Not only were legislative sessions conducted in Spanish and English, but public education in the child's home language, whether Spanish or English, was guaranteed by the state constitution. This was at a time when, in Texas and Arizona, children were punished for speaking Spanish in school. And while Anglos in Texas, Colorado, Arizona, and California were doing everything they could to attack the Mexicans in their midst, voters in New Mexico—where Spanish monolingualism was no impediment to voting—elected one *hispano* governor after another: Ezequiel C. de Baca in 1914, Octaviano A. Larrazola in 1916.

After the United States entered World War II, the government entered an agreement with Mexico to establish the *bracero* program, whereby farmhands (*braceros*) from Mexico were admitted as seasonal contract labor; at the end of the season they were required to return to Mexico. Thus, the labor needs of employers could be satisfied without having to grant the laborers the rights to remain in the country or to form unions.

Around the same time, the other impulse governing Anglo policy toward Mexicans—race-based antagonism—made itself dramatically apparent. In 1943, in the wake of a sensational trial of young Mexican-American men accused of a murder in Sleepy Lagoon, near Los Angeles, "zoot-suit riots" broke out in Los Angeles, San Diego, and Oakland, California.

The zoot suit was the stylish outfit of the pachucos, Mexican-American kids who had grown up in the cities without much education or much hope for their future and whose main preoccupation was showing off to one another. One of the ways of doing this was by wearing outlandish clothing, described in José Antonio Villarreal's novel *Pocho*:

The black motif was predominant. The tight-fitting cuffs on trouserlegs that billowed at the knees made Richard think of some longforgotten pasha in the faraway past, and the fingertip coat and highly lustrous shoes gave the wearer, when walking, the appearance of a strutting cock. Their hair was long and swept up to meet in the back, forming a ducktail....

The girls were characterized by the extreme shortness of their skirts, which stopped well above the knees. Their jackets, too, were fingertip in length, coming to within an inch of the skirt hem. Their hair reached below the shoulder in the back, and it was usually worn piled in front to form a huge pompadour.[14]

Such defiance of convention—nobody else was wearing clothes like that at the time—aroused the ire of Anglos who were not well disposed toward Mexican-Americans in any case. The 1942 Sleepy Lagoon case had been exploited by the press to exaggerate the pachucos' danger to society. Then, in 1943, after a series of less serious skirmishes, American soldiers and sailors on furlough went on a rampage, attacking zoot suiters and young Mexican Americans generally. The police did not interfere with the white assailants but did arrest a number of Mexican Americans for instigating a riot—at a time when great numbers of Mexican-American youth were joining the army, navy, air force, and marines to fight fascism, to demonstrate patriotism, and to get some kind of job. Many of them did not come back.[15]

After the war, Mexican Americans in the labor movement had to contend with a new enemy; strong antiunion repression in the guise of anticommunism. Militant Mexican-American union workers were thus doubly harassed, as members of a despised race and as suspected Communists.

One of the most militant Mexican-American unions of the 1940s and 1950s was the independent (not AFL or CIO-affiliated) International Union of Mine, Mill and Smelter Workers, based in Denver. In 1949, with the assistance of other, larger left-wing unions, including the United Electrical Workers and the Meatpackers, it created a broad-based organization to give a "new voice" to Mexican-American and Mexican workers, the Asociación Nacional México-Americana (ANMA). The union is best remembered today thanks to the movie *Salt of the Earth*, about an episode in the bitter 1950–52 strike of Local 890 in Bayard, New Mexico, against Empire Zinc. After months of strike and facing an injunction against picketing, the miners reluctantly agreed to let their womenfolk go on the picket line, facing the police and arrest. They finally won their strike in 1952.[16]

Both the ANMA and the union were harassed mercilessly by the House Un-American Activities Committee (HUAC) and through other anti-Communist pressures, including raids on membership from the much larger United Steelworkers Union (USW), which was then under very conservative leadership. The ANMA disappeared, and the Mine, Mill and Smelter Workers finally allowed itself to be absorbed into the USW after a new and more flexible president, I. W. Abel, had assumed office in the larger union. Maclodio Barrazas, one of the principal leaders of Mine, Mill and Smelter, was given charge of organizing the many Spanish-speaking workers in the industry.[17] He and other veterans continued working through the 1960s and 1970s, passing on their organizational experience to younger generations in the copper-mining districts of Arizona and elsewhere, working in new kinds of unions and in the huge growth of community organization that took off with the War on Poverty.

The old-fashioned strategies that had built unions like the Mine, Mill and Smelters and the many fraternal organizations like the Alianza Hispano-Americana, the Sons of America, and their successors, consisted mainly of patient, endless, face-to-face meetings, sometimes with a single worker or resident at a time, sometimes with little groups, and a heavy emphasis on shared cultural values. These values included an appeal to the code of virility, or "*machismo*," to stay in the fight. Alternatively, when the men realized they couldn't resolve a problem on their own, they invoked the ancient image of the steadfast and loyal Mexican woman or even the more modern and more threatening image of the *soldaderas*. These were the women of the Mexican Revolution who, according to numerous ballads, or *corridos*, and a famous photo (a fiercely scowling young woman descends from a train, bandoleers draped across her bosom and rifle grasped firmly in her small hand), accompanied their menfolk into battle. Organizers also relied heavily on the ritual bonds of *compadrazgo* and *comadrazgo*—the semisacred tie between the parent and godparent of a child—to guarantee loyalty when things got tough.

Except perhaps for the *soldadera* image, with its patronizing attitude toward women—"You're so cute when you have a dagger in your teeth"—these approaches would stand Mexican-Americans in good stead as they faced the new challenges of the 1960s and 1970s and continue to be fundamental in building strong organizations. But important as they are, such strategies would no longer be sufficient either in labor or community organizing. The world was changing, more rapidly than ever, because of new communications technology and upheavals in other parts of the world, creating both dangers and opportunities previously unknown. And as they began to have more contact with the rest of the world, Mexican-American organizers started to seek allies. A logical place to look was among peoples who shared their language and some of their same history and who knew about *compadrazgo* and the power of religious symbols.

### The Two Wings of a Bird: Cubans and Puerto Ricans

Puerto Ricans and Cubans, the second- and third-largest Spanish-speaking nationalities in the United States, started out in this country with parallel histories. The two islands of Puerto Rico and Cuba, similar in climate and with similarly mixed Spanish and African heritages, were also the last remaining possessions of Spain in the New World after the wars of independence (1810–21). The islands were, as Puerto Rican poet Lola Rodríguez de Tió wrote in her most quoted line, "of one bird the two wings."[18] A lopsided bird, to be sure—Cuba is nearly thirteen times the size of Puerto Rico and had then, as it has now, over three times as many people—but a bird nonetheless, longing to fly free. For the Puerto Ricans and Cubans who found themselves in exile in the United States, freeing the bird from the Spanish cage was a priority objective.

In contrast with the widespread, slow-moving, and mostly rural life of northern New Spain and Mexico in the nineteenth century, life in the Spanish-speaking communities of the East Coast was a whirlwind of plans and plots and grand philosophical theories propounded by exiles from Cuba, Puerto Rico, South America, and Spain. New York was its center, but its vortex reached Spanish-speaking settlements from Key West and Tampa to Philadelphia and Boston.

The United States, and particularly New York, was a popular haven for refugees from the turmoil of Latin America in the nineteenth century, and Cubans and some Puerto Ricans had been settling there and in other eastern United States cities since the 1820s. Not everyone who sought haven was a progressive: The aged Venezuelan general José Antonio Páez, as authoritarian an old codger as one could find, settled in New York to write his memoirs after he was thrown out of power for the last time in 1863. But the general tenor of the Spanish-speaking communities was libertarian, tolerant, and cosmopolitan. After all, it would have been difficult to live in an immigrant neighborhood of a great port city like Boston or New York, where people from so many diverse places interacted with and depended on one another, and not become cosmopolitan.

Cuban immigration was given an unintended boost by rises in U.S. tariffs on cigars in 1857 and later. Cigars were big business in Cuba, and the United States was the chief market. When the tariffs threatened to put small manufacturers out of business and after the failure of a revolt against Spain in 1868, some of the smart ones moved their production to U.S. soil to avoid the tariffs and took their Cuban workers with them. Initially the most popular destination was Key West, but after 1886 most of the industry moved to Tampa, Florida. Other Cubans, Puerto Ricans, and Spaniards all set up cigar factories in New York, where there already was a Spanish-speaking community and, of course, a major market.

Besides cigar rollers and cutters, the expatriates included professionals—doctors, lawyers, teachers—and an assortment of adventurers with less clearly defined trades. And, of course, there were Spanish-speaking landladies and landlords, corset makers and music teachers, grocers and deliverymen. But the people we know the most about were the intellectuals, because they wrote so much about their activities, and the cigar makers, chiefly because the most important chronicler of this subculture, Bernardo Vega, was himself a Puerto Rican cigar maker. As we know from Vega and numerous other sources, the cigar workers' tradition of hiring someone to read aloud while they worked at their nearly silent handicraft kept them up-to-date on the latest political and social issues and much else. Cosmopolitan and voluminously informed, they debated how to throw the monarchy out of Spain, the Spaniards out of Cuba and Puerto Rico, and dictators out of the Spanish-American republics—as well as other cultural and political issues of the day, such as theories of education and new developments in the arts.[19]

But a cigar maker working ten hours a day could hardly devote himself to politics fulltime, as did a number of expatriates who either had family money or other, portable means of support, such as journalism. There seems to have been quite a number of such men (almost always men) who came through New York, often on their way to organizing a conspiracy somewhere else.

The most visible members of this vibrant community, or perhaps only the ones that have been remembered, were highly progressive (a term they themselves would have used), meaning that they advocated "progress" through scientific and technological innovation and the introduction of social reforms to make society more rational. To this purpose they established literary journals, newspapers, cultural clubs, and political associations. They stimulated one another to ever-bolder words and deeds, traveling on missions to cities as distant as Santiago de Chile, even into the backlands of the countries they sought to liberate, by sailing ship and stagecoach and, when necessary, mule.

In 1867 two Puerto Rican revolutionaries, Segundo Ruiz Belvis and Ramón Emeterio Betances, arrived in New York after eluding the Spanish authorities who sought to arrest them, and both were immediately involved in organizing insurrections in Puerto Rico and Cuba. The following year, Ruiz Belvis died suddenly in Chile while on a mission for the conspiracy, but the uprisings went ahead without him. On September 23, 1868, a small group of separatists proclaimed a republic in the town of Lares, in the interior of western Puerto Rico; the insurrection was quickly suppressed and the participants imprisoned, but the *Grito*, or "Outcry," *de Lares* is still commemorated by Puerto Rican separatists. On October 10 of that same year, a similar action in the Cuban town of Yara—the *Grito de Yara*—had greater success, setting off the Ten Years' War for Cuban independence and the abolition of slavery.

The progressives considered Spanish colonialism abhorrent not just because colonialism was an offense against national dignity but because Spain in particular was embarrassingly backward. Three centuries earlier, it had been one of the world's great powers, but now its economy was weak, its technology primitive, and its bureaucracy rigid, inefficient, and arbitrary. American cartoonists portrayed Spain as a touchy, decrepit, and savage old man, an image the exiles—including the radical Spaniards among them—could hardly dispute. (Uncle Sam, in contrast, was always shown as a vigorous and overly generous old man.)[20] The expatriates tended to admire the United States not only for its industrial might but also for its liberal political institutions, especially its Constitution, with its separation of powers and Bill of Rights. Thus, when, in 1869, Americans talked seriously in the press and Congress about buying or otherwise annexing Cuba, some of the exiles were for it, causing great arguments with those advocating outright independence.

The Cuban war that began with the 1868 Grito de Yara finally ground to a halt in February 1878, after both sides were exhausted. The insurgents had achieved neither of their goals, independence or the emancipation of all slaves, but perhaps they had not really lost. Spain soon gave up the struggle to preserve slavery, and abolition came in 1886.

Many of the combatants would return to fight again for independence in the Cuban war of 1895–98. In these years, Santiago Iglesias Pantín, a radical Spaniard who had founded Puerto Rico's Socialist party, and Luis Muñoz Rivera, a leader of the Puerto Rican autonomy movement, were among the political refugees who also found havens in Spanish-speaking New York.

Today the person who is best remembered from that ferment is José Martí, the Cuban author and politician most revered by both pro-revolutionary and counterrevolutionary Cubans today. While he was living in New York, Martí edited journals, wrote poetry and essays, and—with help from his Puerto Rican and other comrades—founded the Partido Revolucionario Cubano in 1892. Three years later he joined an invasion of Cuba to liberate it from Spain and was killed by Spanish troops. At the Fifty-ninth Street entrance to New York City's Central Park stands a large statue depicting him not as his fellow New Yorkers knew him, speaking from behind a podium or writing at a desk, but on horseback just as he receives the impact of the fatal bullet.[21]

Martí's conception of *Nuestra América* (Our America) was a brilliant rhetorical device that wedded social class and nationalist concerns in the most succinct manner imaginable. By "América" he meant the whole Western Hemisphere, and by "Nuestra" he was referring to the shared aspirations of its Spanish-speaking portions. As his essays make clear, the implied "we" of *Nuestra América* were not any and all Spanish speakers of the continent, but workers and tradesmen whose real interests were opposed to royalist bureaucrats or oppressors of any kind. If you sided with the oppressor, then you were not part of "Our" America. This was a formulation that would inspire Cubans again, sixty years after his death, and would be taken up by pro-independence Puerto Ricans as well.

By the middle and late 1890s the radical Cuban and Puerto Rican expatriates, like their countrymen still on the islands, were convinced that they were on the verge of finally ridding their homelands of the doddering Spanish Empire. In Cuba, although the death of Martí had been a blow, the guerrillas (among whom were many Puerto Ricans) were wearing out Spain. The Spanish generals' resort to "reconcentration camps" of civilians, forerunners of Vietnam's "strategic hamlets," the rebels read as signs of desperation. To forestall rebellion in Puerto Rico, Spain in 1897 had granted autonomy to the island, so that Puerto Ricans were for the first time governing themselves. The men in the autonomous government expected that soon they could, if they chose, haul down the Spanish flag.

With Spain nearly out of the picture, the revolutionaries were already thinking about the longer-range enemy of *Nuestra América*: the corporate and government power of Anglo America, the United States. This had been the subject of much of Martí's last writings. The concept of *Nuestra América* would, logically, have to include the Mexicans and Mexican-Americans of the Southwest and Midwest. The radicals of New York and Tampa were not only conscious of this other Hispanic-American world, they were ready to join their two struggles, aware that ultimately they faced the same enemy.

By the 1890s, whatever feudal, aristocratic, and isolationist traditions survived from Spanish colonial days—and there are pockets of such attitudes in the Southwest even today—were of little consequence compared to the far greater force of the proletarianization of Mexicans on both sides of the border and their ever-widening circulation across territory in search of work. The copper and zinc miners of Arizona, Colorado, and southern New Mexico, the San Francisco streetcar workers, the stockyard workers in Kansas City and Chicago, the railroad hands across the west, and other Mexican and Mexican-American workers and their ever more radical trade unions had far more in common with the radical cigar workers and craftsmen of the Eastern Seaboard than had the herders and villagers of a half century earlier.

However, the unanticipated entry of the United States into a war against Spain in 1898 aborted these projects of transcontinental Hispanic unity and would ultimately destroy the expatriate subculture of the East Coast. Spanish rule on the two islands was ended, but in a way quite contrary to the thinking of Martí, Muñoz Rivera, and the other patriots in exile. And the U.S. occupation set in motion processes that would bring a much larger and very different exile population to U.S. shores.

The United States had long coveted Cuba. Serious proposals to buy or seize it from Spain had been debated in Congress and the press at least since 1869. American corporations were already heavily invested there, especially in the sugar industry. The war of independence, Cuba's second in a generation, not only interfered with production, it also damaged consumption on the island, as the middle class was less able to purchase U.S. goods. And there were other, equally compelling reasons for planting the Stars and Stripes on Cuban soil: The war represented the conquest of a new frontier, an opportunity for Teddy Roosevelt and many others to exercise their manly vigor, a long-awaited slap at America's favorite bad guys, the Spaniards, and finally, as publisher William Randolph Hearst observed, it sold newspapers.

The invasions, which cut short aspirations to real independence on either island, were at least in part an unforeseen consequence of the agitation of the Cuban and Puerto Rican expatriates themselves. They had done everything they could to stir up a war of independence on both islands and had succeeded in dramatic fashion in Cuba.

Obviously, the patriots in exile in New York cannot be blamed for what happened. But without their agitation and the homegrown war for independence that they had fomented, the pretext for U.S. intervention might not have seemed so plausible. In 1898, under mysterious and still-unexplained circumstances, a bomb went off below decks on the U.S. battleship *Maine*, which for no very good reason happened to be in Havana Harbor. The explosion killed a number of American seamen. As quick as could be managed, the United States mustered an army—getting Civil War woolens out of storage, awarding contracts for the manufacture of more Spring-field rifles, and recruiting farm boys in town squares across the land to free poor Cuba from what was painted as the Catholic-Spanish tyranny. With the exception of Admiral Dewey's handling of the navy, the whole operation was so chaotic and inept that if the Spaniards in Cuba had not already been practically defeated by the Cuban rebels, the invasions could have been a disaster. As it was, more Americans died of malaria than of Spanish bullets, and the one decisive U.S. military action occurred not in the Caribbean but in distant Manila, where Dewey sunk the Spanish fleet and ended what little will Madrid had left to fight. The United States suddenly found itself in possession of more than even Hearst had imagined: Cuba, Puerto Rico, the Philippines, and Guam.

With the occupation of Cuba and Puerto Rico, the wings of the Antillean bird were not just pinioned but plucked, albeit in somewhat different fashions.

It seems ironic that Puerto Rico, rather than the larger and economically more attractive Cuba, should end up as a colonial possession of the United States. Whereas Cuba became a quasi-independent republic in 1902, Puerto Rico continued to be a federally managed territory until a peculiar, not-quite-colonial, not-quite-free status was invented for it in 1952.

This difference in treatment of the two islands was more or less accidental: Cuba turned out to be too large and complicated to administer easily, and native Cubans were readily located to manage it in a quasi-independent status. Cuba was never supposed to be truly independent: A clause was inserted into its new constitution, the Platt Amendment, guaranteeing the United States the right to intervene militarily whenever it saw the need.

While Puerto Rico had a number of capable men who had already been managing the country as an autonomous province in the final months of Spanish rule, the United States disregarded them and their governing institutions entirely. Perhaps this was because the United States government was less familiar with them than with the Cubans and not sure it could trust them to look out for U.S. interests. So the United States administered the island directly, at first under military rule and then, after 1900, under a civil administration, with a governor and legislature appointed by Washington. Almost immediately American interests began exploring the island for economic opportunities, encroaching on the old *criollo* elite in the sugar, tobacco and coffee industries through more modern and efficient production.

In 1917 the U.S. Congress passed the Jones Act, making Puerto Ricans citizens of the United States and establishing an elected senate, although the governor continued to be federally appointed. Overnight the United States had acquired a new population of Spanish speakers. Among its other consequences, the act made Puerto Ricans eligible for draft into the U.S. Army. Thus, hundreds of Spanish-speaking country boys who had never before traveled anywhere and had no quarrel with anybody in Europe found themselves digging trenches, dodging shells, and discovering new worlds in France; those who were lucky came back more or less whole but far more knowledgeable and sometimes far more radical than when they had left. One returning veteran who would have a profound impact on the development of Puerto Rican identity was the dark-skinned Harvard graduate and U.S. Army lieutenant Pedro Albizu Campos.

Even with their new citizenship, Puerto Ricans continued to be colonial subjects. In their homeland, English speakers from the United States controlled everything. The governor was a stateside American, and the public health, judicial, and education systems were American. Even the Puerto Rican Catholic church came under the jurisdiction of the diocese of Boston. Until the 1940s public schools were required to teach in English, which many of the teachers themselves barely knew. But the dropout rate was so high that most Puerto Ricans neither acquired English fluency nor more than basic literacy in their own language. For the political thinkers who found these conditions intolerable, there were only two possible solutions: statehood or independence. These two options divided the island's political parties, which, although they could not elect a governor, still elected islandwide legislators—whose bills were subject to veto by the appointed governor—and municipal governments. The difference between *independentistas*, or independence advocates, and *estadistas*, which in Puerto Rico does not mean "statesmen" but simply those who favor statehood for the island, was not necessarily a left-right split. Among the *independentistas* were fiery nationalists like Pedro Albizu Campos, who argued that independence was necessary to bring about social justice. But there were others who favored independence because they were extreme conservatives with aristocratic pretensions, who wanted not only to preserve Spanish culture but to restore the pre-1898 class structure. Likewise, Puerto Rican *estadistas* included conservative, privileged families who feared that independence would bring about just the sort of social revolution Albizu Campos was talking about, which they found especially frightening because he and several of his followers were black. Yet among the *estadistas* were also social democrats like Santiago Iglesias Pantín, the Spanish-born labor leader and head of the Puerto Rican Socialist party (PSP), who believed that only statehood would extend American civil liberties to the island's workers.

Meanwhile, the modernization of sugar production by American corporations entailed the consolidation of small holdings into huge, corporate-owned plantations, or *centrales*, whose cane had to be cut and carried and fed into the monstrous sugar mills, much bigger than the island had ever seen. To form these plantations, in the flatlands along the coast, tenant farmers were driven from their tenancies on subsistence plots. They then had to work for the *central*, there being almost no public-works construction and very little other work. Sugarcane cutters were wretchedly paid, had no employment guarantees or benefits, and were usually indebted to their employer, whose company store advanced credit for their minimal necessities. The work was painfully hard and dangerous, but what was worse was that nearly half the year was "dead time," the period between harvests when all but a very few workers were laid off. Little wonder that young families and single individuals fled to the cities or, if they could save for the passage, took ships to the United States.

A very similar process was occurring in Cuba, and again the

main engine of displacement of small farmers was corporate sugar production. And in Cuba as in Puerto Rico, it stirred up diverse forms of resistance. A violent, right-leaning nationalism, based in the lower middle class, rejected everything foreign, including Marxism. Leftist resistance, usually Marxist influenced, emphasized class struggle and *inter*nationalism. This was based in the unions (sugarcane workers, stevedores, tobacco workers, and others) and articulated by radical bourgeois, especially in the University of Havana. In 1933 the Left temporarily gained the ascendancy in a revolution (that also had its rightist participants) that threw out the dictator Gerardo Machado and established a short-lived reformist government under a University of Havana professor, Ramón Grau San Martín. There were even "soviets" proclaimed by Communist-led workers who seized the large sugar plantations by force. In the end, a jovial and astute army sergeant named Fulgencio Batista, suddenly in command of the army, betrayed his nominal chief, Grau San Martín, and seized power for himself. Once in, he allowed the United States to continue to dictate policy.

Cuba's economy was larger and more complex than Puerto Rico's, so its marginal industries—everything from prostitution to numbers running and shoe shining—could absorb a greater part of the underemployed population. That it was formally an independent country yet served the U.S. market (Havana is only ninety miles from Florida, an easy weekend visit) created other opportunities. Liquor sales during the United States' Prohibition and casino gambling were big businesses in which a lad or gal with street smarts but little formal education might make a decent living, might even get a crack at making it big time in the rackets. The presence of so many American pleasure seekers also stimulated the more and the less legitimate entertainment professions, from nightclub musicians and dancers to sex-act performers. This is the world portrayed in Guillermo Cabrera Infante's 1967 novel *Tres tristes tigres* and, in a more subdued version, in Oscar Hijuelos's 1989 novel, *Mambo Kings Play Songs of Love*.[22]

As picturesque and bustling as it was, the Havana demimonde was not for everybody and could not absorb every ambitious unemployed person. Thus, in Cuba as in Puerto Rico, there was substantial migration from farms to towns and from towns to the nearby United States. Although emigration from Cuba and Puerto Rico had the same ultimate causes—the dislocations in the local economy caused by America's agroindustry—probably a higher proportion of the Cuban immigrants had prior urban experience.

Some of the Cubans went to Key West or Tampa, where Cuban communities were long established. But the preferred destination of most was New York City and its environs, where a web of small, unregulated factories in the garment and other industries, and restaurants and other service establishments, offered low-paid work for the unskilled.

Puerto Ricans also gravitated to New York, for the same reasons but in much greater numbers. This was partly because of the fewer economic opportunities in Puerto Rico but mainly because, as U.S. citizens, Puerto Ricans faced no restrictions to entry. Thus it was that Puerto Ricans largely defined the character of the Manhattan neighborhoods where many Cubans also settled: the Lower East Side, the West Side (of *West Side Story* fame), and East Harlem. Soon they would spill into Brooklyn and the South Bronx as well.

Back on the island, intellectuals worried about the transformations at home and about the huge emigration to dark, cold northern cities. Where was Puerto Rican pride? When were Puerto Ricans going to stand up and protest the conditions that were driving them from their Isle of Enchantment? asked the novelists, poets, and playwrights. They quoted the turn-of-the-century exhortation by poet and politician José de Diego:

> Do as the bull when it is penned up,
> Bellow!
> Or like the bull that does not bellow,
> Charge!

The Puerto Rican bull, however, appeared to be asleep, or perhaps sniffing the flowers in the field. Albizu Campos's Nationalist party had a devoted but small following, perhaps because only a small segment of the population had ever developed any very strong sense of nationhood. The island does not seem very big, but even with modern highways and automobiles (and mammoth traffic jams) contacts between people in Jayuya and Cayey, or even

Aguadilla and San Juan, are inconvenient and infrequent. In the earlier decades of this century, people living in one town were even less likely to know or care much about events in the others. Ironically, it was in New York where many of them began to encounter one another and to begin to develop a common "Puerto Rican" identity. Even there, the earliest fraternal organizations were based on people's original hometowns, such as Sons of Jayuya, and so on. It was not until 1958 that an association was created to bring them all together, the Congress of Organizations and Puerto Rican Hometowns, created in 1958, with fifty-seven organization members.

Another reason for the limited appeal of nationalism may have been that people who had never governed themselves were unsure whether they could. Moreover, the Puerto Rican peasant had the reputation of being especially sweet-natured and accommodating, unlikely to protest even if he thought his rights had been violated. This was "the docile Puerto Rican" that the Puerto Rican playwright René Marqués complained about in a famous essay by that title.

By World War II there was already a generation of Puerto Ricans who had grown up in New York and who were as far from docile as they were from being peasants. During the war, Puerto Rican men recruited into the army from the island and from the mainland were assigned to the same units under "white" officers. Frank Bonilla, who was born and raised in New York, and would later become a distinguished sociologist and one of the most prominent defenders of the concept of Puerto Rican studies, was one of those who gained his first personal acquaintance with Puerto Rican island life when his unit, of mixed island and New York Puerto Ricans, was rotated back to the island after the war.[23]

The war interrupted migration—in fact, all nonessential ship traffic—from the islands. Right after the war, migration from Puerto Rico to the United States began again, at a faster pace, stimulated by easier transportation (airplane rather than boat), rising expectations, and a greater awareness of the outside world. By 1948, the Puerto Rican citizens were displaying not docility but an enthusiasm for political change. Having finally won the right to elect their own governor, a great majority rallied behind the candidate expected to bring major social reforms and to take them closer to independence, Luis Muñoz Marín, son of Luis Muñoz Rivera, who had been one of the architects of Puerto Rico's short-lived autonomy in 1897.

Muñoz Marín initiated an ambitious, New Deal–type economic development program called *Manos a la Obra*—something like "Getting Down to Work," rendered into English by the folksier Operation Bootstrap. This was intended to use public spending in Keynesian fashion to stimulate economic development; however, the hour of Keynesianism had passed in Washington, and Muñoz could not get congressional approval for anything more ambitious than a program of tax incentives to lure American investment.

Muñoz also pressed for a new arrangement with Washington which would grant Puerto Rico greater autonomy but without a total divorce from the United States, as an "Associated Free State" (*Estado Libre Asociado* [ELA]) of the United States. To make clear that what he had in mind was a compact between two sovereign states, neither subordinate to the other, he translated the formula by Great Britain's term for its arrangement with Canada, Australia, and other former colonies which were by then independent but still "associated" with Britain: "Commonwealth." For the Nationalists such gestures were not nearly enough. On October 30, 1950, the little party staged an insurrection in municipalities across the island, while in Washington, D.C., on November 1, party members assaulted Blair House, where President Harry Truman was staying. They killed one guard, but two of the assailants were shot, one dead. It was a replay on a wider stage of the 1868 Grito de Lares, equally futile and with equally disastrous results for the insurgents. Federal Bureau of Investigation (FBI) surveillance and harassment of the Nationalists—already intense—was intensified even further.

Given the conservative tenor of the times and the objections in the U.S. Congress, the E.L.A., or Commonwealth, proclaimed in 1952, resulted in much less autonomy than Muñoz had led people to expect.

Muñoz also established an office of the government of Puerto Rico in New York City, which functioned as a virtual consulate, assisting migrants to find work on New Jersey farms and in New York industries, counseling them on their legal and other problems, and promoting U.S. investment in Puerto Rico. Puerto Rican farm laborers, recruited in Puerto Rico under contracts negotiated by the government of Puerto Rico, had a unique status, similar to the Mexican *braceros* in the West. Unlike Mexican *braceros*, however, the Puerto Ricans laboring in the tomato fields of New Jersey were U.S. citizens and thus could not be prevented from staying in or returning to this country as they wished.

The Nationalists struck again, this time in the U.S. House of Representatives, on March 1, 1954, when Lolita Lebrón stood up in the gallery and shouted "¡Viva Puerto Rico libre!" as she and three confederates fired eight shots and wounded five congressmen; each of the assailants subsequently served at least twenty-three years in prison, refusing parole because they refused to recognize U.S. sovereignty over them. On the whole, however, urban Puerto Ricans in the United States were now organizing specifically around their problems as a permanent minority in an English-speaking world. The National Puerto Rican Forum, founded in 1957, was one such U.S.-based organization. Another important organization, founded in New York City in 1958, was the Congress of Organizations and Puerto Rican Hometowns; its very name revealed its continuing nostalgic connection to the island its members had left, and it was not about to come up with new and imaginative solutions for the very different life in that northern city.

Puerto Ricans also settled wherever they found job opportunities in the Midwest, including Lorain, Ohio, where they were recruited to work in the steel industry. They moved in larger numbers to Chicago, Milwaukee, and other cities. Here they encountered Mexicans and Mexican-Americans who had preceded them. Like them, and perhaps in imitation of them, the Puerto Ricans established mutual-aid associations.

The older Mexican-American community and newly arriving Puerto Ricans did not mix easily.[24] Puerto Ricans settled far from the established Mexican neighborhoods, and if their kids met, they were likely to fight. Their music, accents, cuisines, and even physical appearances were, and are, markedly different. And each group imagined it had some sort of social superiority over the other: the Mexicans because they had got there first and were established in business and organizations, the Puerto Ricans because they were "Americans"—U.S. citizens from birth—and simply because they were *not* Mexicans.

Mutual distrust was exacerbated by the Democratic party

running these towns. The pols had utterly ignored the Mexicans, even though some were citizens and thus eligible to vote. Democratic politicians did, however, make some feeble attempts to reach out to Puerto Ricans. This may have been because they simply assumed the Mexicans could not vote or because the Puerto Ricans looked more "white" to them. This difference in treatment was enough to make the Mexicans view the Puerto Ricans as poachers on their political turf rather than as potential allies.

However, the largest number of Puerto Ricans continued to establish themselves in New York City, following a path blazed by their predecessors in colonial days. In the old Italian neighborhood of East Harlem, they eventually outnumbered the older residents by so much that the area came to known simply as "El Barrio," the Puerto Ricans' term for "the neighborhood." The dense network of small factories in New York, and especially the garment industry, became even more polyglot than it had been, with Puerto Rican seamstresses, cutters, and other workers working side by side with Yiddish and Italian speakers.

In the United States, Cubans and Puerto Ricans usually lived in the same neighborhoods, held the same kinds of low-status urban jobs, and commonly intermarried. Employers and landlords generally made no distinction between Cubans and Puerto Ricans, discriminating against them equally, regardless of their citizenship. The rhythm of the smaller-scale Cuban migration was affected by the same economic cycles as the Puerto Rican, but with one additional factor: Cuba, unlike Puerto Rico, was permitted to have its revolutions as long as they did not seriously damage U.S. interests. Political unrest always spurred emigration.

Before the war, the tyrannical rule of Gerardo Machado in the early 1930s and the revolution that overthrew him in 1933 had had this effect. After the war, the return to power of Fulgencio Batista by a coup in 1952, the armed movements in the city and countryside to get rid of him, and the increasing repression of his police forces all stimulated an exodus of mostly middle-class opponents.

In each period of turbulence, Cuba's revolutionary streams had grown a little wider. In the Ten Years' War of 1868–1878, the insurrectionists had been white men of property and black men and women who didn't want to *be* property, united against a colonial system that, in different ways, kept them both subjugated. In 1895–98, the insurgents had included veterans of the earlier war plus many of the now enlarged class of rural poor—so many that the Spanish packed them into "reconcentration camps" to keep them from aiding the combatants. In 1933 key actors included university students and rural and urban workers, who, in combination with rebel junior officers of the army, overthrew the dictator Machado. Their expropriations of sugar plantations and the ambitious reforms of the provisional government of Ramón Grau San Martín were brought to an abrupt end by Fulgencio Batista, a thinly educated but shrewd army sergeant, who assumed the presidency with U.S. backing.

Batista governed either directly or through puppet presidents from 1933 until 1944, when, misjudging the mood of the electorate, he permitted free elections and lost to his erstwhile victim, Grau San Martín. Grau was succeeded four years later by another duly elected president, Carlos Prío Socarras (1948–52). But then, as Cubans were preparing for a third presidential election in 1952, Batista—a candidate with little hope of success—cut the process short by rallying his old supporters to stage a coup, reinstalling himself as president.

President Eisenhower pinned the Medal of Freedom on the chest of President Batista in a much-publicized photo, but his new medal did not prevent him from stamping out freedom and the very lives of his enemies. As the violence intensified in 1956–58, those willing to risk their lives for a vision of a different Cuba again included university students, urban professionals, small-business people, small farmers, and politicians committed to normal democratic process—but not, with few exceptions, organized labor. In one of the ironies of the era, in the 1940s, Batista had signed a pact with the Communists of the Partido Socialista Popular (PSP), whereby he supported wage increases and social security for the Communist-led unions in return for labor peace, and even now the union leadership remained reluctant to oppose him openly.

The intrigues of the Batista era would echo years later in Hispanic politics within the United States. Even today the old feuds continue, less often by gunfire now than by ferocious verbal barrages in the Spanish-language press.

# 5

# Coming Together

WITH SUCH DIVERGENT HISTORIES, it would be hard for all the people who are today called Hispanics to forge a common agenda or even to imagine themselves as one community. But a number of events occurred in the late 1960s and early 1970s that made such an image seem not only possible but necessary.

## The Generation of '69

Except for a few older-timers, like Texas congressmen Henry B. González and Kika de la Garza, the most visible Hispanic leaders of today came of age and acquired their political reflexes in the late 1960s or early 1970s. It was a period of mass civil protests, from Prague to Paris and from Mexico City to Chicago, riots across urban America, revolutionary wars in Southeast Asia, Africa, and Latin America. It was a time when, even more than usual, young men and women everywhere were challenging the traditional politics in their communities and inventing new dreams, slogans, and methods.

The intervening years have been rough on those dreams of love, hedonism, solidarity, and revolution, and many forty- and fifty-somethings have learned to keep them hidden or have abandoned them. Still, they and their youthful deeds are important to the story of the Hispanic nation in two ways. First, they have become part of its myth, a potential source of inspiration to its alienated youth today. Second, this generation developed the arguments which continue to shape ethnic politics in this country.

For the defining of Latino identities, 1969 was an especially intense year—and not just because of Carlos Santana's memorable performance at Woodstock, although that, too, was relevant. In the West and Southwest, young Mexican Americans founded La Raza Unida party and proclaimed their "Spiritual Plan for Aztlán," a mythical homeland to be created by the equally mythical *raza*, or cosmic people. The Brown Berets, Mexican-American radicals from Los Angeles, who had organized only a year earlier, in 1969 faced prosecution for conspiracy.

Meanwhile, a Puerto Rican street gang in Chicago, the Young Lords, was turning itself into a reform lobby with revolutionary slogans and a violent edge, quickly spreading to New York City and beyond. And Cuban Americans, ten years after the triumph of the Cuban revolution, were facing identity crises of their own, for they had to confront the likelihood that they would not be going home anytime soon.

It was in the heat of the battles of this period that today's leaders forged the bonds that still hold together their *viejo compañero* (old comrade) networks. In the case of the Cuban exiles, the battles sometimes included military operations with heavy weapons against targets in Cuba and smaller-scale bloodshed among their own factions. For Puerto Rican and Mexican-American radicals, the battles were usually against police bullets and billy clubs, bulldozers and bureaucrats, strike-breaking goons and U.S. government provocateurs.

The old comrades of '69 have since gone in many directions: Some now head community organizations, some run departments in city, state, or federal government, some are practicing law or running businesses; several have become prominent journalists, and a few seem simply to have lost their way or to be endlessly repeating the poses and slogans of their youth. The leftists among them may no longer keep that once-cherished photo of Che Guevara on the wall, and the illusions of all have become more complicated with experience, but they don't forget. They invoke old ties in pursuit of new projects, sometimes repaying favors or avenging wrongs received decades earlier. And many are trying to make their ideals live on in the youth of today.

It was in this period of a few years on either side of 1969, from 1965 to about 1974, that all three groups—Mexican Americans,

Puerto Ricans, and Cubans—began a painful and intense re-evaluation of their respective histories, seeking to remake themselves consciously as the national communities they had once been unthinkingly.

## Obsessed With Cuba

The triumphal entry of Fidel Castro and his cohorts into Havana on January 3, 1959, sparked a new revolutionary optimism throughout the hemisphere, a literary "boom" in the Spanish-speaking parts of it, and the sudden popularity of berets and beards everywhere. Guerrilla movements on the Cuban model sprouted in Venezuela, Colombia, Peru, and Guatemala. The new literary prizes and publishing outlets of the revolutionary regime attracted attention to, and encouraged writers like Gabriel García Márquez, Mario Vargas Llosa, Mario Benedetti, Julio Cortázar, and many others, giving them a wider audience than any of them could have hoped for otherwise. For the Left and particularly the radical youth in the United States, Cuba became the symbol of resistance to racism, imperialism, the CIA, and consumer culture.

The Cuban revolution redirected the evolution of the Hispanic nation in two ways. First, it enlarged and altered the composition of the Spanish-speaking population by causing thousands, then tens and finally hundreds of thousands of Cuban opponents of Fidel Castro to migrate to the United States. Second, it divided even non-Cuban Hispanics, who were still the great majority, more deeply than any event since the Spanish-American War of 1898. While many younger, urban Mexican Americans and stateside Puerto Ricans embraced the revolution as a metaphor, if not a model, for their own people's liberation, their elders and many rural Latinos saw it, as did most of the Cuban émigrés, as Communist hell.

The first wave of Cuban émigrés arriving in 1959 naturally included many *batistianos*—supporters of the Batista dictatorship—as well as most of Cuba's old bourgeoisie. The latter, often implicated in Batista's shady deals even if they had not been political supporters, were frightened or enraged by the new regime's assaults on property (urban reform, which cut rents in half, and agrarian reform, which expropriated land) and by its bad manners. Eschewing the more liberal Cuban-American community in Tampa, these two rather different but interconnected sectors of the Cuban Right, *batistianos* and bourgeois, settled in Miami, which until then had few Cuban residents.

Soon—in some cases, as early as 1960—they were followed by other émigrés of different politics and more modest wealth, who had not been especially committed to the old regime. Among them were liberals and socialists who had fought in the underground against Batista but had then refused to accept Fidel Castro's leadership. There were others who had not been actively political but, being from the conservative and Catholic middle class, feared Castro's alliance with the Communists. The many professionals and businessmen in these early waves of immigrants had far greater skills, wider contacts (among themselves and in the American business community), and a more aggressive style than other U.S. Latinos for prospering in urban capitalism and quickly set about doing so. Miami became a new center of Cuban banking, Cuban radio, and eventually Cuban television, the Cuban press, and all manner of other businesses, licit and illicit.

These new arrivals differed not only from other U.S. Spanish speakers but also from most Cuban Americans already living here. The Cubans who had settled in northern cities in the forties and fifties were mostly integrated into the struggling working class, most commonly in "Spanish"—usually Puerto Rican—neighborhoods. There they and their neighbors had to confront the class, ethnic, and racial prejudices of white Americans as well as all the usual working-class problems of having to work too hard for too little money. Many of them, especially at the beginning, were sympathetic to the revolution, believing they understood the kinds of injustices in the old Cuba that had provoked it, and a few remain fervent supporters of Fidel Castro's leadership. In New York, pro-Castro Cubans founded a cultural and political club they called Casa de las Américas, named for the revolutionary government's cultural institute in Havana, where they show Cuban films and hold political forums. Even today, pro-Castro Cuban Americans rally to confront their anti-Castro countrymen with shouts and pickets of their own.

Then, from the late 1960s on, after most of the bourgeoisie

and political opponents had already departed, wageworkers, fishermen, and a few small farmers made up the bulk of the flow from Cuba to the United States. By this time, however, Miami's Cuban enclave was firmly established, and the special legislation secured by its lobbying granted them privileges beyond those of any other Spanish-speaking group, including immediate acceptance in this country regardless of how they arrived (there was by now no such thing as "an illegal Cuban immigrant") and financial and other assistance for settlement. These privileges and the constant propaganda barrages from the Cuban media in Miami made it difficult for these fairly humble people to see themselves as similar to Mexicans, Puerto Ricans, or other Spanish-speaking immigrants.

The multiplicity of anti-Castro factions assured that politics in Miami would be turbulent, complicated, and violent right from the start. There were *batistianos* and anti-*batistianos*, who themselves were divided into numerous groups differentiated sometimes by ideology, sometimes just by the personalities of their leaders. The 1952–58 struggle to overthrow Batista had been carried out by numerous "movements," "directorates," "federations," and "parties," some with traditions dating back to the 1930s. Each had its own agenda and dynamics, and when the dictator fell, each claimed a share of the credit and the spoils. But they found themselves excluded from power by Fidel Castro's 26th of July Movement, which had the largest military force and the widest urban underground network.

As Castro's civilian supporters and military intelligence closed off opportunities for antigovernment conspiracy within the island, especially after the failed Bay of Pigs invasion of April 1961,[1] the opposition retreated almost *in toto* to the United States, where they found ready support from agencies of the U.S. government. Weapons, funding, and training were all available to counterrevolutionaries from the Central Intelligence Agency (CIA). The downside was that the CIA controlled every move of the counterrevolution.

"We could not do anything without the CIA being involved. Nothing!" recalls Albor Ruiz. "In Miami nothing was done without the CIA. And if anybody tells you different, he's fooling you. I lived those years. Years beyond measure. If I wasn't in the office in Miami, I was in Marathon Key"—a staging area for attacks on the island—"in the boat base, ready to go to Cuba. I was one of the people of action."

Ruiz is today editor of the op-ed page of the *New York Daily News*. A slightly built man with a quick wit and a courtly manner who is now an outspoken advocate of lifting the U.S. embargo on Cuba, he seems an unlikely counterrevolutionary terrorist.

"Yes, I have a background that I'm not necessarily proud of," he admits with a wince. "But it is real. Part of my life. I at least have the satisfaction that at that moment I thought I was doing what I had to do. Later I realized it wasn't true, but..."

When Fidel entered Havana in January 1959, Ruiz—then eighteen and living in Varadero, eighty-seven miles east of Havana—was exhilarated, especially when the University of Havana, which had been closed by Batista, was reopened. He started at the university but then dropped out a couple of months later when his father was arrested briefly "for aiding someone to flee the country or something like that." Ruiz was soon deeply involved in a Catholic youth organization working against the Castro government, the *Directorio Revolucionario Estudiantil* (Revolutionary Student Directorate), and even though he himself was not Catholic, quickly rose to be the organization's coordinator for his home province of Matanzas.

On April 17, 1961, a force of about fifteen hundred Cuban émigrés assaulted Playa Girón at the entrance to the Bay of Pigs, on the south coast of Matanzas Province. The attackers—recruited, trained, and armed by the CIA and supported by a few U.S. aircraft and ships—were supposed to seize the beachhead and spark a general uprising throughout Cuba. But not only were the invaders routed and hundreds taken prisoner, their action led to a full-scale dragnet by Cuban security which destroyed practically the entire counterrevolutionary underground network. Ruiz narrowly escaped arrest and went into hiding until finally arranging to get on a small boat to Miami in September 1961. His own younger brothers and a sister were able to join him there about a year later.

Regrouped in Miami, the members of the directorate were happy to accept CIA funds, but chafed at CIA control. The CIA wanted them to be a "propagandistic" organization, devoted to distributing counterrevolutionary leaflets and newsletters aimed at university students like themselves. "But what we in the directorate wanted was to go to war!"

So what they did "was to steal all the time from the CIA" by overbilling for the newsletters and other propaganda expenses (in collusion with the printer) and using the surplus to buy weapons on the black market. As he recalls it, they had no trouble deceiving the CIA in this fashion.

"You know that in those days the CIA was handing out lots of money in Miami....There was so much money, so many people, so many things going on, that there really wasn't much control. We had a CIA agent who was a drunk. The guy would come to us, drunk, and start telling us things" about the operations of other groups. "And sometimes I'd tell him, 'Shut up! I don't want to know this....

"We didn't have enough experience to catch on to a whole lot of things, because we really believed that our relation with the CIA was one in which we were using them. Not them using us. There wasn't anybody in the directorate who wanted to work under the orders of the CIA. But it was an inevitable reality. It was the way to obtain resources...."

Ruiz's group would also save most of their CIA-supplied living allowance for black-market purchases of weapons. "So we lived very poorly."

"It was crazy. Under my bed there were cannons and dynamite. Under my bed! With my brothers and sister living in the same house! I'm telling you this now, but it was completely crazy!"

Thus armed, he and his comrades carried out "the famous first attack ever on the Cuban coast," at Havana's Hotel Rosita de Hornedo, in 1962. In a rented yacht, they sailed within cannon shot of the terrace where they knew Soviet technicians dined on Fridays and fired fourteen volleys before turning around and sailing back to Miami.

"Fortunately," he says today, "nobody was killed....But it did make a big impact."

Upon their return, their CIA handlers "wanted to tear our heads off" for the unauthorized mission. "But that would have been a little awkward for them, you know, because we had made fools of them. And that was a great satisfaction for all of us."

It would be almost the last such satisfaction; the CIA kept a closer eye on them after that. Finally, around 1965, Ruiz dropped out of the organization.

"In those last years it had become something else. Because, first, there was a bit of disenchantment, in the sense that nothing was going to happen in Cuba." Second, he had become disgusted with "the number of wretched people" in the counterrevolutionary subculture in Miami—people who did not share his idealistic aims.

"To think that that whole thing, all those people killed...and all that time invested" had been for naught, and that even if they had succeeded in overthrowing Castro, "maybe it would have turned out to the opposite of what we wanted to achieve."

And what was that? Did he and his comrades have a clear idea?

"Sure! Well, not all that clear. The idea I had, and that we all had, was an independent, sovereign country where there would be an honest enough regime for there to be real social justice."

Thus, he acknowledges, there was "an *enormous* contradiction" in collaborating with the intelligence service of a foreign power. "Which we resolved, among ourselves, by thinking that we were the ones using the CIA."

His break with the directorate occasioned "a very great crisis. An existential crisis, a horrible crisis." He now had to face the question, *Y ahora, ¿qué?* (Now what?).

Ruiz was not the only Cuban American asking himself this question in the late 1960s. The conflict with the United States had stimulated a resurgence of Cuban nationalism and, within Cuba, its merger with left-wing thought. This was one of the things that threw into confusion anti-Communist nationalists like Albor Ruiz and made continued collaboration with the CIA intolerable.

Prior to 1959 nationalism in Cuba, understood as special pride in being Cuban and as loyalty to Cuban sovereignty above other loyalties, was a minority sentiment that seldom found expression in the press. Its targets were, first, the United States and those perceived as its Cuban lackeys, and second, the antinationalism of the Cuban Left. Leftists thought of themselves not as nationalists but as internationalists and associated nationalism with reaction and terrorism, as a kind of Creole fascism. (This was also the way the Nationalist party was viewed at the time by liberals and leftists in Puerto Rico.) The secret organization ABC, a survival from the anti-Machado underground, probably best fit the stereotype. It sought no mass support and elaborated no program of government because it expected not to govern, only to overthrow.

In contrast, the Communists in the Partido Socialista Popular (PSP) were so unnationalist that they unquestioningly followed the lead of the Communist Party USA (CPUSA). At one time, in 1944, they were on the brink of dissolving their organization simply because the CPUSA, under Earl Browder, had done so—the Cuban comrades had to be talked out of it by the Soviet party. The other major force on the Left, Fidel Castro's 26th of July Movement, was more ambiguous in this respect, combining nationalist and social-ist appeals, but on the whole it was also more internationalist than nationalist. Several key figures were foreigners, including the revolution's most famous warrior after Fidel, Ernesto Guevara. Guevara's foreignness was in fact the point of his nickname, "Che" (a common epithet for Argentines).

But once a revoluntionary government was in power and facing the hostility of the United States, the leftist ideology of the intellectuals and the spontaneous nationalism of the masses merged. It could hardly have been otherwise. For nationalists, it became clear that the most direct way to defy the United States was to declare one's movement "socialist." For the leftists, defending socialism meant to defy the United States. Crowds in the Plaza de la Revolución and town squares across the country chanted: *"¡Cuba sí, yanqui no!"* Other chants, perhaps less spontaneous but repeated enthusiastically by movement militants, combined na-tionalism and *fidelismo*, as in the famous unanswerable question, *"Fidel, Fidel, ¿qué tiene Fidel / que los yanquis no pueden con él?"*—(Fidel, Fidel, what has he got / that the Yankees can't handle him?) Thus, under Castro, the Cuban Left ceased to oppose or deny nationalism, but instead co-opted it.

The nationalism within the internationalism was expressed in a partisan reading of Cuban history, emphasizing international-ist episodes and individuals such as Martí and Máximo Gómez, the general from the Dominican Republic who led Cuba's 1895–98 fight for independence. As Cuba, a tiny country with few natural resources and almost no industry became a major actor on the world stage through aid to revolutionary struggles in Latin America, its presidency of the Non-Aligned Nations, and, later, its deployment of combat troops in Ethiopia and Angola, its internationalist ventures enhanced nationalist pride within Cuba. The appeal to nationalism, especially the insistence on the revolution's continuity with authentically Cuban traditions, is surely one of the main explanations of how the regime has retained significant—at times massive—popular support even while subjecting its people to the most extraordinary and painful changes.

The combination of nationalism and internationalism also made the Cuban revolution immensely attractive to Mexican Americans and Puerto Ricans, grateful for a heroic model in their own quest for national identity in the United States.

A genuinely nationalist opposition, one subservient neither to the United States nor to Castro's revolutionary internationalism, would surely have been a healthy thing for Cuba. At the least, it could have forced a wider debate of the most consequential decisions of the regime, such as the disastrous campaign to achieve a record sugar harvest in 1970, an almost pointless effort (given the low price of sugar at the time) which failed and set back production in other areas; the commitment of troops to ambiguous struggles in Ethiopia and Angola; the alliance with the Soviet bloc and Cuba's commitments to the Non-Aligned Nations; the erratic policies regarding rationing and free markets, and so on.[2]

Unfortunately for Cuba, such an autonomous opposition never had a chance to flourish either at home or abroad. Within Cuba, except for a lingering insurrection in the Escambray Mountains (which was hardly autonomous, being sustained by the CIA), the opposition was almost extinguished as an organized force by late 1962. Outside of Cuba, the nascent nationalist opposition could hardly resist being swallowed up and distorted by the the CIA, pursuing its own agenda. The need to establish their independence is what drove some Cuban nationalists to ever more dramatic, if politically futile, gestures of violence—such as the bazooka attack on the United Nations in December 1964, when Che Guevara was speaking, or the blowing up of a Cuban airliner transporting the national fencing team. This same need is what drove other nationalists, like Albor Ruiz, to reexamine their whole position regarding the Cuban revolution.

The notorious violence and intolerance of Cuban Miami were characteristics of the antidemocratic, winner-take-all political culture which they shared with their compatriots back on the island. This unwillingess to compromise was one of the things that would retard their alliances with other Hispanic groups in the U.S. Even though Cuban politicians and *guerrilleros* of all persuasions shouted *"¡Libertad!"* at every opportunity, few, if any, respected or even comprehended civil liberties as understood in the U.S. Parliamentary procedure, dispute resolution by majority rule, and guarantees of the right to dissent were regarded as absurd rituals of the gringos, unsuited to the Latin temperament or to Cuba's needs. Democracy in Cuba had been tried, briefly, and deemed a failure. The democratically elected governments of Ramón Grau San Martín (1944–48) and Carlos Prío Socarrás (1948–52) had been so corrupt and ineffective that only a tiny group, gathered around the self-exiled Prío, wanted to return to that model.

A study of the political thinking of recently arrived Cuban émigrés in Chicago in 1969, mostly working-class men, found that virtually all claimed to have left Cuba *"por la libertad"* (for liberty).[3] But when asked about their specific complaints, only three older, rural men offered an answer that would be recognizable to an American libertarian: They wanted to be left alone. They objected that militants of the revolution had badgered them to join work brigades, the militia, a trade union, or some other collective effort.

Far more common were complaints about material shortages—"liberty" to these émigrés meant the right to consume. "Look, in Cuba you only get two pairs of pants and one pair of shoes per year!" bemoaned a former restaurant cook. But the most frequent source of outrage was the loss of social privileges that even some of the working class had enjoyed under the old regime. Foremost among these were gender and racial privileges.

The men denounced the revolution's policy of sending girls to schools with boys, encouraging women to work and participate in the mass organizations and advancing some into (usually minor) leadership positions.

"It's a disaster!" one man exclaimed. "In Cuba, a woman is no longer governed by her husband, she's not governed by her father, you could almost say she governs herself!"[4]

Racial integration, another campaign of the revolutionary government, was also seen as an assault on *libertad*, meaning in this case what might be called the liberty of nonassociation. A former hotel clerk, a man in his late fifties, complained bitterly that he and his wife had given up dancing at their old social club in Oriente Province because blacks were now admitted. Others mentioned their disgust at the presence of blacks on their favorite beaches. Curiously, even the few blacks in the sample (at that time, emigration from Cuba was still almost entirely a white phenomenon, even though whites were less than half the population) were uncomfortable with the new racial etiquette, feeling embarrassed by the frequent references in Cuba to their color.[5]

People are adaptable, and no doubt these men could have adjusted to the more liberal currents in the United States had they remained in Chicago. But soon most had made their way to Cuban Miami, where they thought they wouldn't have to. It was clear that these and other Cuban émigrés would be among the least likely people to get caught up in the radicalism sweeping through other Hispanic sectors at the time.

In their pamphlets and mass media, Cuban émigrés took to calling themselves *exiliados* (exiles) and began to refer to their community as a whole as *el exilio* (the exile). Nobody had been literally expelled or exiled from Cuba—as, for example, opponents of the Chilean government of Augusto Pinochet were to be some years later, when they were hustled in chains to the airport at Pudahuel. On the contrary, the Cubans had left voluntarily, generally against the will of their government. Calling themselves exiles was a way of portraying themselves as victims rather than authors of their emigration and of perpetually reminding themselves that they could not return.

The phrase "*el exilio*" denotes a particular kind of community, an enclave of sojourners rather than immigrants. That is, members of *el exilio* were not here to adapt to their new environment but to hold themselves and their culture intact until their return to Cuba to undo the revolution. Meanwhile, instead of seeking assimilation, Cuban Americans tried to construct an idealized alternative Cuba in South Florida, something like the living theater of Colonial Williamsburg but with the clock stopped at 1959. The quaint traditions of the bourgeoisie were frozen and held up as the ideal for all, complete with *quinceañeras* (elaborate coming-out parties for girls at age fifteen) and civic associations representing townships that no longer exist in the real Cuba. This attitude of nonassimilation was reinforced by constant harangues on Spanish-language radio and in proclamations by the many counterrevolutionary organizations in Dade County and by murders of dissenters.[6]

The enclave strategy was remarkably successful for a long time and is still working for some interest groups in Dade County—for example, those controlling the far-right Cuban-American media, who need a near-captive audience, and those marketing specifically Cuban foods and other products. But by 1968 the contradictory forces within *el exilio* were threatening to tear it apart. Castro was not falling, the exiles' children were Americanizing, and it became clear to more and more Cuban Americans that they needed allies outside the suffocating, xenophobic little world of *el exilio*.

Cuban Americans who sought to break out of the enclave pursued three very different strategies, each with its own consequences for the larger Hispanic nation. One group, probably the largest, sought alliances with the American Right, where they found sympathy for their aggressive views on Cuba.

As one of the rare Democrats among Cuban Americans in Miami told journalist David Rieff, "We in the exile went right because when we arrived in this country, we soon discovered that the liberals and the Left here were pro-Castro. No matter what we told them about abuses at home, they refused to believe us. We were all Batistanos [*sic*], all pigs and fascists. The only people who would listen, at least after 1962, were the Republicans, I'm sorry to say."[7]

In the Miami enclave, the spontaneous anxiety of poorly informed people in a hostile and incomprehensible environment was exacerbated by a network of thugs and Fascists with access to arms and CIA funding and a vested interest in keeping hysteria at a high pitch. These terrorized—and continue to terrorize—those information media they did not control.[8] Pressures to conform to the extreme right-wing consensus were so great that Cuban

Americans who disagreed either avoided Miami altogether or, when that was impossible—because almost all have relatives there—did their best to avoid political discussions.

Another group of young Cubans, mostly outside Miami, sought alliances with more "progressive" communities, especially Chicanos and Puerto Ricans. María de los Angeles Torres, who was sent out of Cuba by her parents as a little girl in the early 1960s, recalls how "as young Cubans became aware of the discrimination they faced in their adopted country and grew increasingly critical of the role of the United States in Vietnam, they came to question what really had happened in their home country."

These questioning young Cubans, however, were rejected by the Anglo-American leftists, who "relished having a connection to Cuba and authoritatively spewed the rhetoric claiming that we could not return for we were 'gusanos' who had abandoned the revolution. 'Yes, but I was six years old!' I'd say. They would respond, 'So what, you were obviously middle-class, and as such your class origins make you unworthy of return.'"[9]

Torres and others like her felt themselves drawn to the Chicano movement of the early 1970s, then heavily involved in the grape and lettuce boycotts in support of the farmworkers. But she did not feel fully at home among Chicanos, who "had a very exclusive definition of identity"—that is, exclusive of non-Chicanos. She felt more comfortable in CASA, a Chicago organization of Mexican political refugees from the repression of 1968, who "had a more inclusive definition of Latino identity."

When Harold Washington became Chicago's first black mayor and its most progressive one in many years, a number of Chicago Cubans, including Torres, were active in his campaign and his administration, presenting themselves as a bridge group between Chicago's two much larger Latino communities, the Mexican Americans on the near south and far-south sides and the Puerto Ricans in the northwest part of the city.[10]

Other Cuban-American liberals, like the Presbyterian minister Daniel Alvarez in Chicago, continued to oppose Castro but focused their political energies elsewhere, on problems nearer at hand. This is simply practical politics: An overly conspicuous opposition to Castro would tend to divide the liberals from potential allies.[11] Instead, they have simply agreed to disagree with other liberals on Cuba, so as to get on with the task of improving conditions for poor Cubans and other minority-group members, especially Hispanics, in this country. Alvarez, who left Cuba in 1960, built up and directed the settlement house Casa Central into the largest service complex for Hispanics in the United States. In 1990 he was appointed by Chicago's mayor Richard M. Daley as commissioner of human services.

Albor Ruiz found himself attracted to a more radical group of young Cubans who, beginning around 1969, began reexamining their whole attitude toward the Castro government. Lourdes Casal (1938–81), who had left Cuba at about the same time as Albor, in 1961, was a key figure—sometimes referred to as the "god-mother"—of this group. Given the open racism that was commonly expressed by the *exilio* in Miami, members of this dissident group seemed to take special pleasure in the fact that their intellectual leader was a brown-skinned, nappy-haired, unfashionably stout young woman with a ready smile who must have seemed like the personification of Mother Cuba.

This group would grow to include some two hundred activists and many more sympathizers who referred to themselves as *la tribu* (the tribe), united by their passion for Cuba and their extreme alienation from the majority of Cuban Americans.[12] The *tribu* first began to cohere around their magazine, *Areíto*, launched in Miami in 1974, but moved to New York after a series of bomb threats.[13] *Areíto* was then the only forum—and is still one of the few—where Cuban Americans who dissented from the Miami official line could discuss their intimate concerns in their own language. Since identity was as great a concern as politics, fiction, poetry, and graphic art figured prominently alongside political and sociological articles from the start.[14]

Casal had been permitted to return to Cuba in 1973, to satisfy her "almost obsessive interest" in the country.[15] Gradually, the Cuban government learned to trust the members of this little circle around her, and *Areíto* was soon publishing regular reports on other young Cubans who had returned to visit. In 1977, Cuba received the first contingent of the Antonio Maceo Brigade, a group of young Cuban-American volunteer workers organized by members of this group. The *tribu* was very active in bringing about "the Dialogue" between the Cuban government and members of "the

Cuban community abroad" (a new, neutral name for *el exilio*, hitherto known in Havana as *los gusanos*—the worms), which began in Havana in 1978.

*Dialogueros*—promoters of the Dialogue—knew that they risked death from Cuban-American terrorists who had a stake in maintaining the isolation of the Miami enclave. In 1979, Carlos Muñiz, a Cuban American who had started a travel agency booking trips to Cuba, was killed at his office in Puerto Rico, and in the same year another member of the tribe, Eulalio Negrín, who directed a Cuban-refugee services center, was shot down in Union City, New Jersey. Both attacks were claimed by the Cuban terrorist organization Omega 7.[16]

Besides poets there were also entrepreneurs in the ranks of the *tribu*. One of these was Francisco Aruca, who had barely escaped being executed in Cuba for his work in the anti-Castro Catholic underground. Aruca became the president of Marazul (Blue Sea), a full-service travel agency whose specialty was, and still is, chartering planes for trips to Cuba. Today he is the only Cuban-American radio-talk-show host in Miami openly calling for dialogue with Cuba, braving constant death threats and persisting even after his studios were physically attacked and an employee injured.

And the third and ultimately most important group pursued a radically different strategy. They avoided, or deemphasized, all such political distractions, whether of the Right or Left and instead devoted their energies to business careers. Perhaps the best known (and one of the best remunerated) is the president of Coca-Cola in Atlanta, Roberto Goizueta. Others are running food-processing industries or public relations agencies targeting the Hispanic market. One industry where Cubans began having an impact almost as soon as they arrived was communications, both print and broadcasting, where many of them already had experience from Cuba and where they turned their knowledge of Spanish from a handicap into a marketing asset in the new country. It was their good fortune that their massive arrival, beginning in the 1960s, coincided with the enormous growth of that part of the population of the United States that speaks their language and with the technical expansion of the communications media. Thus, Cuban Americans have been among the most prominent contributors to the image machine, especially as producers, executives, and on-screen hosts of Spanish-language television, and are also active in Spanish-language print media and radio, not just in Miami and Union City but across the country. It is thus that Cuban Americans have probably made their greatest contributions to constructing the Hispanic nation.

## Uniting the *Raza*

Meanwhile, Mexican Americans were experiencing an accelerated political development of their own. Growing militant nationalism by black Americans was both a threat and an example, stimulating Mexican Americans to reanimate and update their own nationalist aspirations. Their tradition of labor organizing and protest had never died out, and had recently been reanimated by César Chávez and the farmworkers. And while the Cuban revolution may have seemed culturally distant to the rural folk of the Río Grande Valley and the *vatos* of "East Los," another social uprising that was part of the same third-world tide had reached and stirred them—the peasant, worker, and student protests in Mexico that culminated in the bloody massacre in Tlatelolco in 1968. It was a time of proliferating social movements with revolutionary rhetoric and imagery borrowed from Mexican history—Benito Juárez and Emiliano Zapata being favorite icons—along with the berets and other paramilitary trappings borrowed from Cuba and the Black Panthers (who had borrowed much of their dress style and military terminology from the Cubans).

## César Chávez and the Farmworkers

By the beginning of the 1960s, if not earlier, the traditional strategies of Mexican-American labor agitation had just about reached the end of their useful life. Since before the Mexican Revolution, Mexican and Mexican-American workers had treated labor disputes as revolutionary war, to be won by meeting the brute force of employers and their armed goons with the brute force of the masses. It was at once a class war and a "race," or national, war between Mexicans, mostly workers, and "Anglos" (who might be Jewish, German, Irish, or Italian) who were owners or the owners' allies.

With boundless tenacity and courage, often facing machine guns and bomb throwers and sometimes, perhaps, hurling a bomb or a dynamite stick or two themselves, the workers had sometimes won a battle here, a skirmish there, securing pay hikes in the mines and other improvements in working conditions. But by the early sixties everything was changing. Industries were now less dependent on semiskilled labor and thus less vulnerable to strikes; more workers of Mexican descent now understood English and were familiar with American ways and were less inclined to messianic struggle; Taft-Hartley and other labor laws hounded radicals out of the unions and made it more difficult to strike; and, of paramount importance, there had been a revolution in communications, especially the spread of television to almost every middle-class household and to many poor ones as well.

One of the first to recognize the new opportunities and limits and to craft new strategies to seize them was a Mexican-American organizer from Arizona, César Chávez. In his farmworkers' movement Chávez would bring together several organizing traditions from all over America and as far away as India, packaging them so as to have the widest possible impact. While working within this movement, Mexican Americans, Puerto Ricans, Cubans, and other nonwhite working-class Americans discovered one another's heritages and learned to contribute to one another's struggles.

The story of César Chávez and the United Farmworkers Union (UFW) has been told many times and continues to be told by the organization he left behind at his death in 1993 and by some of the many people who were deeply affected by his movement, for better or for worse. He has been presented as a saint[17] or as a charlatan concerned primarily with self-glorification.[18] There is some plausibility to both portraits, and maybe they are not even contradictory: Like many saints, he was both an exceptionally persistent, self-abnegating man and a public relations genius.

A onetime farmworker himself, Chávez had been working for the Community Service Organization (CSO), which was organizing mostly middle-class communities on the principles of self-determination and self-interest elaborated by the self-styled radical organizer Saul Alinsky. In 1962 Chávez resigned because he wanted to work with the very poor, those the Alinskyites considered unorganizable, and began building a union initially known as the National Farmworkers Association.

There had been many efforts to organize farm laborers, going back at least to a 1903 strike of Mexican and Japanese sugar-beet-field workers in Ventura, California, by the outlawed Partido Liberal Mexicano. Agricultural labor militancy continued through the Great Depression, celebrated in John Steinbeck's novel *In Dubious Battle* and, with greater emphasis on Mexican participation, in José Antonio Villarreal's *Pocho*. In agriculture, however, strikes had proved ineffective, mainly because agricultural workers were so easily replaced. No great skill was required for most of the tasks, just a willingness to endure backbreaking labor in unhealthy conditions to earn a pittance. Another reason was that, thanks to pressure from the growers, agricultural labor had been exempted from the National Labor Relations Act (NLRA), so there were no guarantees of the right to organize or to strike.

Chávez nevertheless organized the poorest of Mexican-American workers into the first effective farmworkers union and by 1966 got several major growers to sign a contract and even succeeded in getting the state of California to pass the Agricultural Labor Relations Act in 1975, guaranteeing to farmworkers in that one state the types of rights industrial workers enjoy nationwide under the NLRA. Many of these accomplishments have since been undone, and at his death in 1993, Chávez's organization was a shell of its former self. But for a few years he was a player in national politics—a minor player, to be sure, but one who was taken into account. He accomplished this by gathering allies from far beyond the lettuce and beet fields.

Chávez's organization called its first strike (*la huelga*) when in September 1965 it decided to support an ongoing strike of Filipino field workers, members of the Agricultural Workers Organizing Committee in Delano, California. But *la huelga* under Chávez's leadership was not like other strikes. For one thing, it never ended, because it was not directed at a single employer for a limited set of demands which would be either clearly won or clearly lost in some finite period of time. *La huelga* was more of a prolonged social movement to change a whole series of conditions, and then to change some more. When a table-grapes contract with Schenley was signed in 1966, the strike continued, targeting other growers and other crops, and even after the passage of the California Agricultural Labor Relations Act, the "strike" continued, to enforce it and extend it, and so on. The slogan *La Huelga Continúa* (The Strike Continues) echoed a revolutionary slogan from the third world, originally from Mozambique, *A Lutta Continua* (The Struggle Continues), which had become an international symbol of tenacity.

Second, in a sharp break with Mexican-American labor tradition, Chávez insisted on nonviolence. This meant that even when a picketer or an organizer was physically attacked by a grower's agents or the growers themselves, as happened repeatedly, the picketer was not to fight back. And there were occasions when the provocation was severe. Mark Day, then a young priest working as a volunteer with Chávez's organization, recalled one case when women who were working on a ranch were deliberately sprayed with a highly toxic pesticide. When one of them asked the grower why he had done that, "he replied with a laugh, 'The spray makes grapes grow bigger, and it will make the women's breasts bigger, too!'"[19]

Third, Chávez found ways to touch the consciousnesses of people all across America, far from the California fields, and for them to feel part of the struggle called *la huelga,* even managing to bring the Kennedy family into the fray on his side. There were three main ways of involving so many people: the calls for consumer boycotts of the foods produced by growers who would not sign with his union; the welcoming of priests, ministers, students, and other volunteers from all over the country into the union's projects; and the staging of events for maximum publicity. In one famous scene, Robert Kennedy held up César Chávez's head and fed him his first solid food after a long fast. Another, even more memorable, was the union's long march from Delano to the California state capital, Sacramento.

All of these things worked together. Their nonviolence made the farmworkers appear more sympathetic, if not simply pathetic, and the aggressions of growers and local police especially grotesque. It also made the movement seem a close parallel to that section of the black civil rights movement led by Dr. Martin Luther

King Jr., which had already won support from liberal white Americans across the country.

Consumer boycotts were illegal under the NLRA, but Chávez and his lawyers cleverly argued that since farmworkers were not covered by the act, the prohibition did not apply. Thus, they turned a major disadvantage—their lack of NLRA protection—into an advantage. The boycotts may not have had a noticeable effect on the growers' bottom line (at least, according to the growers), but they gave people across the country a way to participate and made many of them more willing to send funds or contribute in other ways. And all of these actions were magnified by effective public relations and use of the media.

It has been argued that Chávez's organization did not always follow through in protecting farmworkers, that it used the clout it got from the early contracts to deny people work if they did not join and pay dues, that once it got a contract it did little to enforce its provisions and could not always provide the workers called for by the contract, and that its picket lines and spectacular long-distance marches were just for show, staged for television and the press with little regard as to whether the participants were bona fide farmworkers or not.[20] Such accusations, especially the last, miss the point. The movement was effective precisely because of the canny use of media. And if the UFW could not sustain itself as an organization over the long haul, it had already accomplished a great deal. It raised the self-esteem of farmworkers and made everyone else more aware of their existence and their problems, and that has to be good for future organizing in the fields.

From this point forward, in part because of César Chávez's strategic discoveries and in larger part because of the structural changes that had made his movement possible, the history of Mexican-American political consciousness ceases to be a separate story from that of other protesting groups in the United States. And it was at about this time, the late 1960s and afterward, that Mexican Americans began to get interested in the histories not only of their own ancestors but of the other Spanish-speaking groups as well, because in order to take maximum advantage of the new economic, political, and technological conditions in this country, they were going to have to work together. For those struggling on other fronts, far from the fields of Bakersfield and Delano, Chávez's movement demonstrated the effectiveness of coalitions with other sectors of society and of a public relations effort directed far beyond one's own industrial or ethnic group. And it had a powerful demonstration effect for others whose main work was in other sectors of the Mexican-American and other ethnic communities.

Arturo Vázquez remembers his first contact with the UFW as an event that changed his life. A Chicago-born son of Mexican immigrants, he was in 1966 a community organizer in a Puerto Rican neighborhood for a church-based association in Chicago, but with no clear political conception of the work he was doing and its possible meaning for people like him. Then the Anglo minister who was his boss, a man who was "really progressive," sent him, along with two other Chicago activists, to Delano, California, to join the farmworkers' march to Sacramento.

"And that's when the metamorphosis occurred. I couldn't relate to the [black] civil rights struggle because it didn't get under my skin, and that particular trip all of a sudden was like— everything began to fall in. And by the time I got to Sacramento I was like completely and totally vulnerable. I was just totally wide open to everything. And that's when I got to meet the guys who were organizing, hard-core farmworkers, people coming out of MECHA [Movimiento Estudiantil Chicano de Aztlán] and all that kind of stuff. And one guy that I really got close to was a guy named Flowers. He was with the Student Non-Violent Coordinating Committee. And he was organizing alongside the Mexican workers....So we got to talking, and by the time I got back to Chicago, it was like, all kinds of skin, just moulting, right? I was useless for about three months...."[21]

## La Raza Unida

One of the new movements that Vázquez and others like him were becoming aware of was what came to be called *chicanismo*, or what we might call the Chicano identity movement, which came to be associated with the myth of Aztlán and with *la raza*.

*Chicano* was an epithet that Mexican Americans had long used among themselves, at least since the 1920s. It may have started out as an abbreviation of *mexicano*, which some Mexicans pronounced as "meh-shi-ca-no." Or it may have started as a playful extension of *chico*, colloquial for "boy" or "buddy." (*Chica* means girl.)[22] Most likely it caught on and was repeated because it reminded speakers of both words at once. It was an insolent epithet that punctured class pretensions and thus could be a friendly declaration of solidarity or a wounding put-down, depending on tone of voice and context. For an outsider to call someone by this insiders' name was considered offensive, even to people who referred to themselves as *chicanos*. By taking this private word as their public name the young Chicanos were being deliberately provocative, alienating culturally conservative Mexicans and signaling to Anglos that they were impervious to insult and ready to fight.

In the spring of 1969, Rodolfo "Corky" Gonzales (a variant spelling of González), a forty-year old poet, ex-boxer, and head of an organization called Crusade for Justice in Denver, hosted the first annual National Chicano Youth Liberation Conference. A ceremonial highlight of the conference was the proclamation of "The Spiritual Plan of Aztlán" by Chicano poet Alurista. The people who settled in the Valley of Mexico, the Méxicas, or Aztecs, claimed that they had come from a land to the north that they called Aztlán. It is unlikely that they meant as far north as Denver or even as far north as Chihuahua, but the word "north" was enough for Alurista, and it is his Aztlán—an ancestral pre-Hispanic homeland embracing all of the U.S. Southwest—that has invaded Chicano imaginations, one more meme available to link up with others in the construction of the Hispanic nation. Although Chicanos sometimes like to frighten Anglos by talk of retaking this territory, what Alurista wrote of was a spiritual rather than political connection to the land.

The other major occurrence at the conference was the decision, promoted by Gonzales and a younger attendee, José Angel Gutiérrez of Texas, to create a national Chicano political party. The Mexican-American Youth Organization (MAYO), founded by Gutiérrez and other students at St. Mary's University in San Antonio (appropriately enough, in May, or *mayo*), decided to put the idea into practice in the Winter Garden area of South Texas, where there was a heavy Mexican concentration, with almost no Mexican or Mexican-American political representation. The students called their party La Raza Unida—(the United People).[23]

This was not the only organization to use the phrase. The Southwest (now the National) Council of La Raza, today an important Mexican-American lobbying organization based in Washington, had been founded the year before. The term *la raza* had long been used among Mexican Americans to refer to "our kind," appearing in José Antonio Villarreal's 1959 novel *Pocho* about Mexican Americans in California in the 1930s.[24] Some African Americans used the word "race" in the same way, to mean "those like us."

*Raza*, however, has less narrowly biological connotations than the English "race" (which, incidentally, derives from the Spanish word).[25] What the Chicanos imagined was an amalgam of Spanish, Aztec, and other cultural strains that have gone into the making of people like them, reflected more in their spirits or ways of thinking than in their genes. A person did not have to be brown-skinned to be part of the *raza* as long as his or her mentality was Chicano.

The party had a great success in its first, bitterly contested campaign, winning a majority of the school board and then of the city council of the little spinach-producing town of Crystal City, where the Anglo minority had always completely dominated these institutions. But efforts to build it into a significant political force outside the Río Grande Valley, especially in the more urban areas of California, made little headway. Although campaigning strenuously for its candidate for the California state assembly, the party got only 7 percent of the vote in its best year, 1971. Outside of South Texas it remained primarily a student movement, often tied to the newly created programs of Chicano studies, with students receiving credit for fieldwork courses for their participation in La Raza Unida.

In preparation for the 1972 presidential election, the Nixon White House set up "a secret operation...working as a task force labeled the 'Brown Mafia.'" The aim, according to researcher José de la Isla, was to reduce the Hispanic Democratic vote in any way they could, either by getting Hispanics to vote Republican, to vote for a third party, or not to vote at all.

"Idealism was dashed when many pumped-up activists realized that the White House was actively involved in getting funds for the South Texas Raza Unida party. The radical party was caught herding votes away from Democrats while taking money from the same Republican establishment that they criticized."[26] De la Isla sounds indignant about this, but given Raza Unida's past experience with the Democrats and the fact that they were the local hegemonic power, one wonders if taking money from the Republicans to destroy them could have seemed like such a bad idea.

The party ceased to exist by 1973, but not before having won inclusion of Mexican Americans in Democratic party politics in South Texas and having deeply affected the thinking of a whole generation of college students in Colorado, California, and other states with large Mexican-American populations. And, of course, many of the personal alliances made through party work live on to facilitate other political work.[27]

## Chicanos Against the War

For Mexican-American youth in Los Angeles and other great cities, both on and off campuses, more urgent even than the farmworkers movement or the Raza Unida party was the growing opposition to the war in Vietnam. In 1969 it was widely reported that Mexican American soldiers were dying at a higher rate than any other group in the armed forces, supposedly because they tended to choose high-risk duty.[28] Increasingly, their *hermanos* (brothers) were coming to think that was the wrong choice.

It's not hard to figure out why minority youth were drafted at higher rates than whites. Latinos, blacks, American Indians, and poor whites seldom had the skills or resources needed to avoid the draft legally, such as going to college and maintaining a grade-point average high enough for a student deferment or persuading a draft board of one's conscientious objection or pulling strings to get into the National Guard or to find some other soft billet. Tough kids who had been brought before a judge for a crime were often given the choice of the marines or prison; most chose the marines. And a lot of minority youth volunteered, for the obvious reason that their options in the barrio or migrant-labor camp looked grimmer than military life with its regular paycheck, food, housing, and uniforms. And for a few the very danger of war was more of an incentive than a deterrent, bringing the young soldier prestige back in the "nabe." Some Mexican American families in the Southwest (and also a number of families in Puerto Rico) had a tradition of military service going back to World Wars I and II and Korea or even further. (Young Cubans who had either missed or survived the Bay of Pigs invasion joined up for a more ideological reason: to get a second chance to fight communism.)

But this war was different. It was not clear to most Chicanos why the United States was there at all. The enemy looked too poor and weak to deserve all the punishment from B-52s, helicopter gunships, napalm, and reconnaissance, and despite the hopeful prognoses from the Pentagon it didn't really look as though we were even winning. Much of the drama and gore were televised and thus impossible to glamorize. And to a lot of the Mexican Americans and other people of color watching, the "gooks" looked more like kin than like fiends.

Thus, a growing number of draft-age Mexican Americans and other Latinos were becoming ambivalent about the war and ready to listen to antiwar agitators, who usually were students or came from other communities. A decisive event that radicalized great numbers of them was a huge rally called the Chicano National Moratorium Against the War in Vietnam, held in East Los Angeles's Laguna Park at the end of August 1970. It was to be a festive day, complete with a picnic, and according to most observers was proceeding noisily but peacefully when the police charged. By the time it was over, police had killed a highly regarded journalist, Rubén Salazar. One of the many participants politicized by that event was the writer Luis Rodríguez, then a young gangbanger looking for a cause.[29]

## Primitive Rebels

Then as now, there were lots of young gangbangers looking for a cause, young men caught up in a cycle of violence but smart enough to know there could be something better. In poor urban neighborhoods where drug trafficking and addiction, gunfire and police assaults, tuberculosis (and now AIDS), unemployment and stolen welfare checks, collapsing buildings, and culture war disguised as education are daily experiences, interethnic unity is not a marketing ploy or a politician's slogan. It is an outlaw's glorious dream. It means a union of the have-nots so that they can *take* and thus have. The real-life multigang federations of Latin Kings and Ñetas are the organized Lumpenproletariat, *la chusma movilizada* of the *barrios*.

In Moorish Spain, *"barrio,"* from the Arabic *barri* (exterior), referred to the undeveloped area beyond the walls of a city where Christians and other riffraff might be permitted to live. In contemporary Spanish, *barrio* may still be used to describe a community on the urban fringe, as in the shantytown *barrios* of Caracas, but as fringe areas have been engulfed by expanding cities, *barrio* has come to mean any "neighborhood," even a classy one such as Buenos Aires's Barrio Norte. For Latinos in the United States today, a *barrio* is an *inner*-city neighborhood, usually poor, where most people speak Spanish. In the 1960s each barrio typically had its own organization of youth so strongly identified with that neighborhood that, recalls a former Brown Beret who was active in recruiting them, "we didn't call them gangs, we called them barrios."[30]

The people in the barrios are like those British historian Eric Hobsbawm wrote about in his classic *Primitive Rebels* "in that they have not been born into the world of capitalism. . . . They come into it as first-generation immigrants, or what is even more catastrophic, it comes to them from outside, insidiously by the operation of economic forces which they do not understand and over which they have no control." Their response is to form what Hobsbawm called "archaic social movements."[31]

Hobsbawm was not thinking about gangs in East Los Angeles, Chicago, or New York, but he might have been. Their members may not be "first-generation immigrants", they may be second, third, or even later generations to enter modern, urban capitalist society, but for various reasons—racism among them—they have never really been assimilated. Thus, their organizations remain "archaic" in Hobsbawm's sense: they carry over values, such as attitudes toward honor and loyalty and the like, from a premodern, precapitalist social order, to defend themselves in the modern world. Perhaps "archaic" is an unfortunate word. It sounds like a put-down. It is not. It may be true that the old ways are best, it may even be that they sometimes work. They are archaic simply because they spring from an older social order.

The archaism of Mexican workers' struggles against mine

owners and growers in the 1920s and 1930s has already been described. A combination of *compadrazgo* (ritual kinship) and *machismo* (code of virility) developed in peasant and *charro* society gave those struggles a fierce intensity even when there was no rational hope of success—and that very fact sometimes won success against their terrified opponents. Something of those same traditions is preserved by those fighters' grandchildren and great-grandchildren in the barrios.

Like the classic mafioso of the nineteenth century, the Ñeta or Latin King of today or the Young Lord of the 1960s and 1970s "did not invoke State or law in his private quarrels, but made himself respected and safe by winning a reputation for toughness and courage and settled his differences by fighting. He recognized no obligation except those of the code of honour or *omertà* (manliness)"—a notion similar to *machismo*—"whose chief article forbade giving information to the public authorities." Gang colors, beads, ritual handshakes, "jumping in" of new members, scarring, and other bloodletting rituals all indicate carryovers from a culture very distant in time and space from the modern barrio.

Hobsbawm considered *mafia* to be "the sort of code of behavior which always tends to develop in societies without effective public order, or in societies in which citizens regard the authorities as wholly or partly hostile (for instance in jails or in the underworld outside them), or as unappreciative of the things which really matter (for instance in schools), or as a combination of both."[32] This describes pretty accurately the way people in the barrios see the police, the state, and the school system.

The reasons that Latino gangs are not just a footnote but an essential part of the story of the Hispanic nation is that for a period in the late sixties and early seventies they became something else—political movements—which suggests that that could happen again. That is, they became part of larger social movements that were devoted to changing the social order.

In some cases, as with the Young Lords, the initiative seemed to come from within, when a key gang member who had acquired a larger political vision (contacts with fellow prisoners in jail and reading were common ways) set about reorienting his homeboys to larger goals than gangbanging and drug dealing. In other cases, as with the Brown Berets, radical university students or other relatively sophisticated *activistas* began recruiting barrio youth to their organizations and found themselves and their organization as changed by the contact as were their recruits—pushed toward greater violence, for example.

It would be pointless to try to distinguish between these two etiologies in most cases, however. There was just too much going on. Young gangbangers and students were thrown together in jails after protest marches or met in college extension classes, learned from each other new techniques for dealing with the police (their mutual enemy), and sought each other out for drugs or sex or just plain curiosity. A denunciation of the "pigs" (police) as enemies of "the people" and of the Vietnam War as an example of the pigs writ large might start out as just one more pose for a street tough, just as an aggressive, fist-in-the-air stance might start out as no more than a pose for a radical student. But poses, when held long enough, develop their own momentum and generally require some appropriate action to sustain.

## Young Lords

Of all the movements that shook Puerto Rico and the stateside Puerto Rican neighborhoods in the 1960s and 1970s, one that still has resonance for today's youth is a street gang from a small Puerto Rican barrio in Chicago that became a multicity, multiethnic organization in which thugs imitated intellectuals and intellectuals sometimes learned to behave like thugs. The Young Lords even set up chapters in Puerto Rico itself. Their alumni today include prominent print and television journalists, such as Juan González of the *New York Daily News*, Felipe Luciano of *New York Newsday* and New York ABC newsman Pablo "Yoruba" Guzmán; university professors, such as Tony Báez of the University of Wisconsin-Milwaukee; and professionals with advanced degrees directing community-service agencies, including Iris Morales in New York, Omar López in Chicago, and many more. In New York, Geraldo Rivera, who has also gone on to a conspicuous television career, was their lawyer. Even those ex-Lords who are not in such visible positions are often active in volunteer organizations, like the ex-gangbanger who led the Young Lords into their first crude, violent but effective political actions, the longtime president of the organization, José "Chacha" Jiménez. What all this means is that the intense experiences the Lords shared in their revolutionary period—1969 to about 1973—are now being passed on to younger generations by experts in the talk of the streets.

These old Lords are well aware of the value of their experiences and are busy documenting them. Tony Báez and Iris Morales are both working on video documentaries, with separate but not necessarily conflicting perspectives. Although sprung from the same source, the Chicago-based group, in which Báez was "information minister" (because he was one of the few members who had been to college), and the New York–based organization, in which Iris Morales was one of those who introduced feminism as a concern into the *machista* atmosphere of Latino politics of the seventies, evolved quite differently. There are also memoirs in preparation by some of the veterans. In short, if these people fulfill their ambitious plans, we shall soon have available all the information we could possibly use on the Young Lords and their era. For the emergence of the Hispanic nation, the most important aspect of that history is how such a group of street youth acquired an empowering identity and a political mission.

The organization first appeared in the early 1960s among the preteens and youngest teenagers (hence, the name) in a Puerto Rican neighborhood of Chicago on the near North Side, around North Avenue and Clark. The families there had come mainly from two working-class barrios, La Plaza and Borinquen, of the Puerto Rican town of Caguas, so they knew one another's families and backgrounds well and had the same reference points. "Just like immigrants, they would just bring the whole town," recalls Chacha. They were thus able to reproduce a little bit of what was familiar in the very alien environment of Chicago, and the kids who became Young Lords were tied together in multiple ways.

Unlike some of the older gangs, the Young Lords made no pretense at being an athletic club. "From the beginning, the Young Lords, we were there for protection," said Chacha. He and other Puerto Rican kids were getting chased and sometimes beaten up by the Romas (an Italian gang), the A&A's, and the Oasis (a "hillbilly" group—that is, Appalachian whites), and black gangs from the projects. "So we kind of just followed suit. We started our little gang in the Puerto Rican area 'cause we were being chased." Chacha was one of the seven cofounders.

"Black and purple were the colors. In fact, we got the colors from *West Side Story*," the film of the Leonard Bernstein–Jerome Robbins musical which was released in late 1961, when Chacha was 13. "In fact when that movie came out, that was the only thing that we had to look up to, in terms of Puerto Ricans, you know, was a movie about gangs. And we were going to that Biograph theater, where Dillinger got shot, so when that came out, I remember there was like a miniriot at the theater. There was one usher that was Puerto Rican, and he was with us and was trying to stop the fight, but we're still jumping on the Italians and— We fought Italians and Irish at that time, I guess, like New York. After that everybody started dyeing their shirts purple."

In contrast to Polish Chicagoans, well represented on the city council and with Dan Rostenkowski already in the U.S. House of Representatives, the Puerto Ricans did not yet have any important cogs in the local political machine, and their sections of the neighborhood were grossly neglected in terms of such things as street repair and fire protection. Puerto Ricans were also subject to police abuse. In the summer of 1966, in the wake of an especially brutal police beating of two young men, neighborhood youth went on a rampage against police and local merchants that lasted days. The image of a pair of squad cars, overturned and blackened by smoldering flames on Division Street, was a vivid memory, representing for Puerto Rican youths one of their few triumphs in the class war. That had caught the city's attention, and now some of the resources of the War on Poverty—federal funds, but administered by the city—were being channeled into an "urban development center," where Art Vázquez worked.

The Young Lords acquired a reputation for their near-maniacal aggressiveness in assaults and robberies with "fists, or bats and chains, and knives, and then once in a while some firearms,"[11] according to Chacha. The gang expanded to other neighborhoods until, at its gangster (i.e., prepolitical) peak, in about 1966 or 1967, it had four branches across the city, some with Cuban as well as Puerto Rican members, and a girls' section called the Young Lordettes. Each of these branches, according to Chacha, had forty or fifty members. The core, however, remained the little group of relatives who traced their roots to Caguas.[33]

Then Chacha did another stint in jail (assaulting an officer, stealing cars and so on), but this time it politicized him. He was impressed by the large number of angry blacks hauled in to jail after the riots following the death of Martin Luther King Jr. in April 1968 and then by the presence of so many undocumented Mexican workers, for whom he translated. And he began to read. Up to then he had been "apolitical, never watched any news, never read any books or anything, but I was in the hole and nothing else to do so I began reading the books."

He started with the Catholic monk Thomas Merton and "even went to confession in my cell.... It was a change in my life came over me, and I didn't care who laughed or whatever.... I'd never read a book through before. It took me about a month. I was like in a monastery." Next he read about Martin Luther King and then Malcolm X, "and when I came out I said, 'This is what I want to do.'"

While in jail he had joined a program to get his GED; the professor took the class to the 1968 Democratic Convention, where he saw the Black Panther leader Bobby Seale and then watched the hippies getting beaten up by the police. This "didn't faze me too much. I didn't really care except I just really wanted to get out of there. They're not going to beat me up! That was my thing. I was dressed up like a gangbanger, you know. And they knew me, the police knew me. So they'd let me walk right through the line, 'Hey, Chacha, how ya doin'?' I didn't look like a hippy"—with his hat tilted back—"and those big gowster pants, you know with the pleats and cuffs and your little handkerchief in the back and like an Italian knit, and you had your little walk. Every neighborhood had their little walk and whatever."

After jail and a month lying low with his girlfriend in the suburbs, Chacha got back to the street in 1969 and found the barrio changed. Urban renewal was in full swing, and in the course of the few months of his absence, familiar buildings had disappeared and others, obviously not intended for the likes of him and his family, were under construction, transforming his barrio into the upper-middle-class neighborhood Old Town. One day, jiving with a gang brother in army green who was just back from Vietnam,

Chacha turned to say something smart to a "white chick who was rapping with some neighborhood guys who just wanted to get into her pants."

The "chick" suddenly turned to him and his buddy and berated them for "killing babies for LBJ." She referred to herself as a "Communist," and like many middle-class students of the day had moved into the barrio to organize the revolution. Chacha was dumbfounded. She told him that if he was so tough, he ought to be doing something to save his neighborhood, and persuaded him to try to bring neighborhood people to a meeting of the Lincoln Park Conservation Community Council, an all-white middle-class group that was politely discussing the fate of the community.

"I didn't know anything about organizing. I just went in [to the bars] there and shouted at the guys, and they shouted back and then I'd say, 'Let's settle this outside,' and we'd go outside and fight."

He managed to gather fifty or so of the younger gang members and associates to go over to the meeting. When they walked in, they saw about a dozen well-dressed white people up on the stage and another dozen in the audience and a model of the proposed new neighborhood, with unfamiliar little wooden buildings on the familiar pattern of streets.

"Hey, look at this!" Chacha remembers shouting. "You see your house there, Alfredo? How about you, Louie? You don't see yours either? Let's smash this m——." And smash it they did.

Chacha announced to the group that there would be no more meetings. "And then I tried to get fancy. I said, 'Until you get Latinos, blacks and poor white representation.' I made it up right on the spot. I figured we had to tell 'em something....And they agreed later to do that." Besides smashing the urban-renewal display, they flooded the bathroom and broke all the chairs and windows. "The whole place was demolished. And then we split up and nobody was caught, nobody got arrested, so the next day we're giving each other fives, you know, we did a good job."

And this was how the Young Lords, former delinquent terrors of the northside of Chicago, discovered their revolutionary vocation. Chacha brought as many of them as he could into his new, still-vague political project, with only partial success—he admits, with a mix of pride and regret, "We have Young Lords now that are big leaders in, say, like the Latin Kings or Disciples," gangs not known for progressive politics. "Yeah. That have been in jail most of their lives, so that's all that they could relate to. So they go to jail, and that's where they go to, they stay with the gang."

A major boost to the Lords political project occurred later that same year, in 1969, when a group of radical Puerto Ricans from New York saw a televised news report of a Young Lords takeover of a church to demand local community services. In August a few of the New Yorkers, including Pablo Guzmán (now the ABC newsman), traveled to Chicago to meet with Chacha and his lieutenants and returned with a charter to found a New York branch of the Young Lords. The New York organization was not a gang transformed by politics but rather a group of already politicized young men and women—some of them with gang backgrounds, to be sure—who admired the bravado of Chacha's group and were ready to don the purple beret.

Chacha never exercised effective control over the New York group. Though a man of considerable personal magnetism, Chacha could never completely control the unruly elements in his own Chicago organization. While trying to coordinate with Chicago, the New Yorkers developed their own extensive programs. They, too, took over a Protestant church, turning it temporarily into a day-care and community-service center until expelled by force of police batons, organized a self-help community cleanup project in defiance of the city's sanitation department, founded and distributed a famous newspaper, ¡Palante! (slang for Forward!), and set up branches in Philadelphia and even in Puerto Rico, where their big Afros and insistence on having women in the leadership met a chilly reception.

In Chicago, Chacha Jiménez pursued his contacts with Bobby Seale as well as with Fred Hampton, the charismatic young leader of the local branch of the Black Panther party. The relationship between the two organizations continued even after Hampton and Mark Clark, a Panther leader from Cairo, Illinois, were slain in their beds by police in December 1969. The Panthers and the Young Lords entered into an alliance with another crowd of tough street youth, the Young Patriots, made up mainly of kids whose families had come from the Appalachian Mountains of West Virginia, and had settled in Chicago's uptown neighborhood. Black, brown, and white, they called their alliance the Rainbow Coalition—a name later appropriated by other organizations. Sometimes together, sometimes separately, they pursued programs of direct action to bring to their neighborhoods services, such as day care, free breakfasts, and vocational training. If that required seizing a church or other building, they would do it. Later, when Chacha went into hiding because there was a warrant out for his arrest—he had been involved in much more serious stuff before, but this time it was because he had taken some lumber to complete construction of a day-care center—he traveled to cities across the country (and beyond) and in Los Angeles started a Young Lords branch made up mainly of young Chicano students.

The New York Young Lords tried to carry their revolutionary message and style to Puerto Rico, competing for political space with the Puerto Rican Socialist party (PSP) and other radical groups demanding independence. It seemed to them an obvious step to take. After all, Puerto Rico was a classic case of the kind of colonialism Fanon and Guevara and others wrote about, despite the United States' claim that the island was not really a "colony" but a "commonwealth."

The PSP, a Marxist-Leninist party that emulated the Communist party of Cuba, was based in the island of Puerto Rico but in 1971 formally set up a *Seccional*, or U.S. "section" with branches in New York, Chicago, and other U.S. cities. Thus, radicalized young stateside Puerto Ricans were sometimes torn between joining the Young Lords or the *Seccional*, and a few actually joined both— though not at the same time. Both organizations advocated Puerto Rican independence, both supported revolutionary movements in the third world, and of course both strongly opposed the U.S. war in Vietnam. But there was a great cultural difference: The PSP was run by island Puerto Ricans with island values, the Young Lords was run by stateside sons and grandsons of Puerto Ricans.

Thus, even in the U.S. *Seccional*, PSP activists felt inhibited if they were not fluent in Spanish, which was the language of all party activities and of the party newspaper, *Claridad*. In the Young Lords, English slang, laced with Spanish, was the favored dialect. Since, as in all radical movements, verbal ability was as important as revolutionary deeds for achieving power, this was an important consideration for would-be members whose Spanish was shaky.

Also, the Young Lords was more permeable by other stateside trends of the time, particularly black power and feminist consciousness. In the Chicago organization race never seems to have been an issue, but the Young Lords in New York and Philadelphia spent many hours of intense, soul-searching debate over their own and their communities' attitudes toward race. Darker-skinned members like Felipe Luciano let their hair grow into the big Afros that identified them with the Black Power movement. In the PSP this was viewed as ridiculous and petty bourgeois; racial differences were not to be accentuated because they distracted from the common class struggle. And although feminists like Iris Morales in the Young Lords report that they had a hard time getting respect from the brothers in the movement, for feminists in the PSP—and there were some, mainly New Yorkers—it was virtually impossible.

The Young Lords' attempt to build a base in the slums of Puerto Rico was as big a flop as the PSP's strenuous efforts to build a mass base in the United States. Each was just too culturally odd in the other's setting. It was not clear that the sons and daughters and grandsons and granddaughters of Puerto Ricans in the United States shared the same aspirations as those who had lived their lives mainly on the island. They certainly did not have the same customs or language; few of those brought up in the States were fully fluent in Spanish. Were they, then, really all parts of the same "nation," as the PSP insisted?

There just did not seem to be any mass constituency on the island demanding independence, whether as a socialist republic or any other kind. Was it then any business of the stateside Puerto Ricans which status—commonwealth, statehood, or independence—that island Puerto Ricans chose? Or should the statesiders instead focus on improving conditions for Puerto Ricans in American cities? These would be among the most divisive issues for Puerto Rican intellectuals and activists throughout the 1970s, and their arguments continue to reverberate to this day.

## Brown Berets

Somehow Chacha and his energetic Young Lords also found time in 1969 to travel to Denver to meet with Corky Gonzales and others in the Chicano movement. Pan-Hispanic coalitions were being forged from the ground up. One of the Chicano organizations with which the Lords felt the greatest kinship was the Los Angeles–based Brown Berets. They had come into existence in a very different way but by 1969 had a social composition similar to that of the Lords.

The organization had sprung from a youth group in the East L.A. Episcopal Church of the Epiphany. The original name was Young Citizens for Community Action (YCCA).

"And then they went through the cultural awareness," says Carlos Montes, an early member who was then a student at East Los Angeles College. Keeping the initials, they renamed themselves Young Chicanos for Community Action and, with a small grant from the Episcopalian parish, opened a coffeehouse in East L.A. to work with youth.

"And then one day they became the Brown Berets.... It was a symbol of our brown skin and being proud of being brown, cultural pride, and the beret meaning we're more militant." Berets of whatever color were by now associated with the Black Panthers, Cuba, and other revolutionary movements around the globe.

. The new name was also a symbol of a change in strategy, from focusing on the concerns of college-bound youth in the schools and churches to reaching out to young Mexican Americans who weren't even thinking of college but instead were organized in the neighborhood car clubs and gangs. The focus now was on stopping police brutality and pushing for reforms in the public school system.

Thus, rather than a gang that became politicized and sought to educate itself, like the Young Lords, the Brown Berets were a politicized group of students who recruited gang youth.

"We worked for peace among the gangs," says Montes. "Let's stop the shooting, let's work together, the enemy is the police. So we would actually go out and meet with the different barrios.... We didn't call them gangs; we called them barrios."

The Brown Berets soon had chapters in El Paso, Santa Barbara, San Francisco, and Oakland, but their major force continued to be in Los Angeles. There they organized a campaign for bilingual education and Chicano studies, helping to organize a two-week student strike of all the high schools in East Los Angeles, the so-called Chicano Student Blow-Out of March 1968.

But they were heavily harassed, mainly by the LAPD. As "Information Minister"—in effect, the press officer—Montes "was responsible for speaking at the rallies and publishing a newspaper, and since I was organizing in the neighborhoods as well as in the campus, the leadership of the Berets was pretty visible. So they"—the police—"came after us."

"They infiltrated the group and started fomenting violence and dissent," says Montes, who, along with twelve others, the "East L.A. 13," was indicted by a federal grand jury for "conspiracy to disrupt the peace, conspiracy to disrupt the school system. We ended up beating that one as unconstitutional."

In 1969 they were again indicted, this time on state charges. A young undercover cop, posing as an ex–barrio (gang) member, had infiltrated the organization and "was basically trying to get people involved in violent actions to get them busted," says Montes. The agent instigated an attempt to firebomb a Safeway store, a target because the Berets were picketing it in support of César Chávez and the UFW's boycott of grapes. More provocatively, the infiltrator set up the group for a charge of conspiracy to commit arson against the then governor of the state, Ronald Reagan.

"Reagan was speaking at a conference on education having to do with education for Chicanos. And he was the one that was against bilingual education and other social programs for Chicanos, and there was a major demonstration against him inside the banquet room and outside the hotel and inside the hotel. And this cop set a fire in a rest room and blamed it on the Brown Berets and the other students that were there. So ten of us were indicted on that."

Montes, who (unlike most of the U.S.-bred Brown Berets) is not actually Chicano but born and raised in Mexico and fully bilingual, went "underground" by fleeing to Mexico, where he remained until the cases were finally thrown out. Now back in Monterey Park, near Los Angeles, where he works for Xerox, he stays in touch with his old comrades, especially those who "are still active in the movement one way or another," some of whom became attorneys, union activists, or teachers. Others "just didn't do anything" after the glory days of the 1960s and 1970s. But in the last couple of years, he says, "I've run into a whole new group of people that I work with that are my age and younger that work on the issue of police abuse." Like Chacha Jiménez, who is now a drug counselor and youth organizer in Grand Rapids, Michigan, Montes devotes his evenings to barrio youth, in his case working with the volunteer organization PODER, organizing the young people and teaching them their rights and how to file a complaint against the police.

"And how to organize! Empowerment....When we have a family that's been a victim of police abuse, the father or a son has been beaten up or killed...we try to get the extended family in the neighborhood to organize, to form a committee, have a petition, workshops, and organize to educate themselves and fight against the sheriff abuse."

This current of protest from twenty-five years ago remains an important component of the Hispanic nation.

## "National Liberation"

The events of the late sixties and early seventies changed the ways Mexican Americans, Puerto Ricans, and Cubans thought about themselves and their people. Concepts of identity and ethnicity underwent a "paradigm shift," in the term that T. S. Kuhn, a historian of science, introduced in this period.[34]

The underlying causes of the shift were demographic and technological: The post–World War II baby boom had produced a huge number of young adults, ready for action and looking for guidance, and the phenomenally rapid growth of television during their adolescence had given them new sources of guidance and new models of action. Television spread from 9 percent of U.S. homes in 1950 to 96 percent in 1970, magnifying the impact of the events of the civil rights movement that was developing precisely in that same period.[35] This generation of 1969 had seen the loosing of fire hoses and police dogs on peaceful black demonstrators in the South; the aftermath of the assassinations of the Kennedys, King, Malcolm; black protests and riots in Los Angeles, Newark, Detroit, Chicago, Boston, and other cities; and much else. Television not only informed, it inspired new forms of protest designed in part for the cameras; the raucous hippy-yippy-radical spectacle of protest at the 1968 Democratic National Convention, the brutal finale of which Chacha Jiménez witnessed, was probably the largest of these. The dramatic actions orchestrated by César Chávez in the organization of farmworkers, especially significant to young Latinos in California and the Southwest, were also communicated by television. The war in Vietnam—likewise televised—brought issues of domestic civil rights together with international struggle: American's own colonized people, blacks and Latinos especially, being heavily overrepresented as cannon fodder to crush a people's liberation movement.

It was an era of experimentation in music, clothing styles, personal relationships, and consciousness-altering drugs. But within the festival were other, darker dramas in which dark, poor people were seen to be assaulted by and resisting police in American cities or repressive authorities in the third world. To Latinos, the protagonists of these poor people's struggles in Asia, Africa, and Latin America seemed not so different from themselves.

The old order would not hold; some new principle was needed to put the world back together again. For young Latinos anxious to define an identity that would connect them to historical events, the principle that offered the most exciting possibilities was "national liberation."

Some first heard the phrase in connection with the Algerian *Front de Libération Nationale*, which led the fight for independence from France (1954–62). The movie *The Battle of Algiers*, celebrating an early episode of that war, was a popular attraction at political gatherings. *Front de Libération Nationale* was also the formal name of the Communist guerrillas of Vietnam, the so-called Vietcong, and of peasant-based revolutions around the globe, continuing in more recent times down through the Sandinista National Liberation Front and the *Frente Farabundo Martí de Liberación Nacional* of El Salvador.

Besides the powerful images of armed, youthful defiance, which would have attracted attention regardless of the cause, the concept of "national liberation" offered a wealth of attractive role models, from Algeria's Ben Bela through Lumumba and Ho Chi Minh to Che Guevara. Its combination of Marxism and nationalism allowed it to draw on several rich intellectual traditions, from Marx and Freud to the Tunisian Jewish writer Albert Memmi, the radical *Martiniquais* psychiatrist Frantz Fanon, and such Latin American revolutionaries as Hugo Blanco (the Peruvian anthropologist who organized *guerrillas* of Indian peasants in his homeland) Fidel Castro, and, once again, Che Guevara. And for young people angered by injustice and looking for direction, the slogan "national liberation" gave the order. In Fidel Castro's words, *"El deber de todo revolucionario es hacer la revolución."* (The duty of every revolutionary is to make the revolution.) Another popular saying of the day put the same idea in an American idiom, "If you're not part of the solution, you're part of the problem."

The clincher was that national liberation legitimized one's own Latino experience. The phrase stood for a line of thought that reinterpreted the humble jobs of one's parents and every other humiliation one had experienced growing up, transforming them from episodes of shame to battles in a struggle akin to liberation struggles everywhere. For young Mexicans in Texas or California, Puerto Ricans in New York and Boston and Connecticut, and all the others who had at some time been made to feel ashamed of speaking Spanish, of being dark-hued, or of having relatives whose music and other customs seemed too foreign, the concept of national liberation was also a personal liberation. It not only made it all right to be a Latino, it turned Latino-ness into a privilege, a vanguard position in the world revolution.

A key concept associated with national liberation was "solidarity," which meant alliances among various struggling peoples. The rationale was that all were fighting the same enemy: U.S. and Western European imperialism. Thus, by aiding my brother, I was also aiding myself to defeat the foe. This concept was celebrated in numerous "solidarity" organizations in the United States and abroad and a constant theme in the radical press of the 1960s and 1970s, giving a romantic allure to the very practical and sensible politics of coalition. It was in the name of solidarity that various Chicano, Puerto Rican, and other Latino groups began exploring the alliances that would become key to building a wider Hispanic identity.

Not every concerned young Latino bought this whole collection of ideas, but nobody could escape being aware of them. If one disagreed, it was not enough to laugh at the military posturing or condemn the intellectual eclecticism of the young radicals; one was challenged to come up with a convincing alternative, to show

how different ideas—whether derived from the usual alternatives of Christian faith or secular American populism—could better answer the questions posed by worldwide and domestic movements in the name of national liberation.[36]

For Art Vázquez, as for a lot people of his generation, Latinos and non-Latinos, a lot of seemingly different struggles were beginning to come together and to make a new kind of sense.

In June 1966, as Vázquez was trying to figure out his own politics after returning from marching with César Chávez, a police beating of two young Puerto Rican men on Chicago's Division Street, then the heart of the Puerto Rican community, sparked an explosion of anger against the accumulated abuses by police in the neighborhood. It raged for days, and when it was over, two police cars had been burned, scores of people were injured, and damage to non–Puerto Rican stores in the neighborhood was extensive.

"I was trying to figure out what was going on and trying to get it all together," recalls Vázquez, "trying to analyze stuff, and then the Puerto Rican riots broke out, and all of a sudden I was galvanized into action and started organizing stuff around the Puerto Rican riots. And so I began helping community organizations get off the ground in Chicago—Latin American community organizations. At that time there weren't any, any at all. The Spanish Action Committee was first founded, it emerged out of the Puerto Rican riots in the Puerto Rican area. LADO emerged at that time, in Pilsen"—the Mexican-American neighborhood—"there was a thing called ALAS that started, and I was involved in that."

One of the people working with him in ALAS was a Cuban, Luis Cuza, who was one of the first Cuban Americans Art had ever met who was "progressive." Cuza was working for an older Cuban, a Presbyterian minister named Daniel Alvarez, who directed a settlement house named Casa Central, and Cuza and Vázquez "began to work on getting together a Latino civil rights group in the Lincoln Park area, and later he started organizing the Young Lords."

Another person Art ran into about this time at one of the demonstrations for the Farm Workers was Clark Kissinger, an SDS (Students for a Democratic Society) organizer (working in a Chicago community) "and doing antiwar stuff." They started talking, with a few other comrades of Kissinger's, and "we decided to do a little study group around the Vietnam War." Then, with the backing of this little group, Art got selected (by drawing straws) to run for the state senate, against Esther Saperstein, who was the darling of the liberals of the Democratic party, on an anti–Vietnam War platform. Art got thrown off the ballot, with no explanation, but he learned something about hardball politics, and his group actually got the county to liberalize its rules for admitting unendorsed candidates onto the ballot.[37]

Like Art Vázquez, every Latino concerned about his or her community, from the young Marxists in paramilitary gear to trade-union officers to Catholic and Protestant theologians, was obliged to confront "the national question": Who are we as a people? What rights do we have *vis-à-vis* other peoples? And what is our national destiny?

Outrage demanded action, and often it was only after taking action—in the moments of calm following a building takeover, a confrontation with police on a march, or an exhausting fortnight of organizing a huge conference or a demo—that the activists would stop to ask themselves, not in reproach but in wonder, "Who am I to be doing these things?"

Who indeed? It had dawned on almost everybody that their identities were at least partly up to them. They certainly did not need to accept the labels that had been imposed on them because of their ancestry or what other people called them. Afros or long, straight hair, ostentatious jewelry, and colorful, new-styled clothes were among the ways of signaling the rejection of the old self. That part came pretty easily. What was tougher was settling into a relatively stable new self, and on this there were endless discussions, especially in radical groups like the Young Lords or the Brown Berets, where people strove to settle even the most intimate questions collectively. In these groups, the whole question of who one was, the internalization and projection of a "self," had to be recast and radicalized.

The radicalized concept of "identity" set it in a wider context and linked it explicitly to current events. To know who one was was to discover one's true place in the flow of world history, including the history that was being made at that very moment. Thus, you had to know history to know who you were, and only by knowing who you were—where you fit in the flow—could you know what you had to do.

This was hardly a new idea: After all, from the most ancient times and in all societies, elders have recounted the stories of the tribe to teach younger members their roles and duties. What was new was that in the late 1960s young people were inventing their tribes and *choosing* their elders. Patrice Lumumba, Fidel Castro, and César Chávez were just a few of the popular choices. And Latinos, Chicanos, Boricuas, Nuyoricans, persons of color, and La Raza were among the eclectic new tribes that would go into forming the new supertribe of the Hispanic nation.

In their extremely disorderly way, with persistence, ingenuity, and sometimes sheer recklessness, the generation of 1969 conquered much territory for their new supertribe and its many constituencies. The incorporation of Mexican Americans into Democratic party politics in South Texas, the creation of Latino-oriented institutions like the Eugenio María de Hostos College of the City University of New York in 1969, and of Puerto Rican, Chicano and Latino Studies programs at other universities were just a few of those gains. In the same period, the movement laid the groundwork for the extension of the Voting Rights Act to protect language minorities in the Southwest in 1975,[38] the passage that same year of the Agricultural Labor Relations Act in California, and the general realization by politicians that Latinos were a constituency that had to be taken into account. None of this would have happened if the Latinos, both with and without their purple, black, or brown berets, had not made it absolutely clear that they could be more of a nuisance outside the system than inside.

# 6

# Forging the National Agenda

IN THE 1980s the evolution of self-awareness and self-assertion of the Spanish-speaking peoples of the United States entered a new stage, what we might call its postrevolutionary, or to anticipate the argument of the next chapter, its prepostmodern stage. Its most obvious feature was the shift from outlaw to routine politics, from attempts to storm the citadel of power to networking in its outer corridors.

This shift in strategy is not what we might expect from the rapid growth of the Hispanic population in that same period—a growth of 61 percent between 1970 and 1980 and another 53 percent from 1980 to 1990, by the Census Bureau's count.[1] Ever larger urban concentrations of poor, mostly young people who are culturally separated from those who hold wealth and power, would seem to be just the sort of sea for urban guerrillas to swim in. But while there continued to be plenty of outlaw behavior in those barrios, especially by gangs involved in drugs and theft; outlaw politics of the sort practiced by the Young Lords, Brown Berets, and countless other self-styled revolutionary groups in the previous decade virtually disappeared.

In part this was due to the heavy blows the revolutionaries had suffered. But it was also because of their gains in that struggle. In a variety of ways, Latinos had forced their way into the system. Not as far as they wanted, certainly, and not in numbers in any way proportional to their populations, but there were now enough of them inside to engage in and begin to change routine politics.

Routine politics is simply the politics that everybody expects,

143

the routine ways of maintaining, exercising, and transferring power. This does not always mean lawful politics; in many places, bribery and vote fraud may be quite routine, so expected and accepted that they are not deviations but parts of the system. And in the southwestern United States, Mexican-American U.S. citizens had routinely been denied the opportunity to vote through poll taxes, literacy tests, and other ruses, even though such discrimination was on the face of it contrary to the U.S. Constitution—and was finally made explicitly illegal by an extension to the Voting Rights Act in 1975.

Whenever there has been an opening, the Spanish speaking have tried to work within the system. This has meant using the courts to challenge abuses (which is why many Hispanics become lawyers), educating those they consider *nuestra gente* (our people) to know and use their rights (which is why so many become community-service professionals or clergy), and lobbying for change. But lobbying, when it takes the form of street demonstrations—about the only form of lobbying available to the poor—can easily be perceived as, treated as, and finally turned into an outlaw act by the police. Every good street demonstration has an air of defiance mixed with festival, which can be very disturbing to the forces of order. Thus it was that the 1970 Chicano National Moratorium Against the War in Vietnam, a people's lobby in the form of a picnic and rally in Los Angeles's Laguna Park, ended up with two Brown Berets and a journalist slain by police.

For Hispanics to make themselves heard, they have repeatedly had to resort to outlaw acts, like the bloody Plan de San Diego uprisings in South Texas in 1915, the wildcat strikes and battles with National Guards in the western mines between 1917 and 1924, the raids of Reies López Tijerina's Alianza Federal de las Mercedes to recover ancient land grants in New Mexico in the mid-1960s, the occupations of public buildings by Young Lords and Brown Berets in 1969 and 1970, or, more colorfully, the draping of a huge Puerto Rican flag over the Statue of Liberty in 1977 to protest the imprisonment of Puerto Rican Nationalists. Violence or the threat of violence has always been the engine that forced change in routine politics.

Outlaw politics turn into meaningless acts of vandalism unless rebel energies can be guided by some charismatic, that is, nonroutine, authority.[2] Today the word charisma is often used to to mean little more than charm or personal magnetism, so that a routinely elected politician, such as John F. Kennedy, is described as "charismatic," and the word is almost always meant as a compliment. Its original meaning is quite different and more disturbing: Charisma is the force field holding together a movement that is hurtling itself against the established order. It is the force of Attila the Hun, the Ayatollah Khomeini, and Adolf Hitler, as well as of more universally admired figures like Boadicea and Joan of Arc, leaders who destroy in order to create.

The charismatic force increases as the movement succeeds; it dissipates when the movement falters. Thus, to maintain maximum authority, the leader must take the movement from victory to victory; if he suffers a setback, he must find some other point to attack and win in order to recover his and his movement's strength. Fidel Castro is the clearest living exemplar of the type; Mohandas Gandhi, Benito Mussolini, Emiliano Zapata, and Juan Domingo Perón are a few of the others who have appeared in this violent and overly charisma filled century.[3]

However, focusing exclusively on the personal qualities of the leader obscures the social dynamic of leadership. Ample anecdotal evidence testifies that the personal force field attributed to some individuals is a real phenomenon. One Cuban defector described an awesome force that seemed to push hard against his upper body when, to receive an award for something, he first physically approached Fidel Castro. People who worked closely with César Chávez have spoken of the powerful and inexplicable feelings he aroused of love and desire to do his bidding. Holy men and women have a similar effect. But not on everybody and not all the time.

And that's the point. The charisma of the leader evolves and is strengthened in the process of leadership, for it is a joint product of the followers and the person they look to to lead them.[4] In the United States in the sixties and seventies, there were plenty of talented and magnetic rebel leaders with potential charisma, but none who attained the full charismatic glory of "Smasher of the System," for reasons having little to do with the relative strengths of their personal magnetism. The leader who triumphs has to pick the right social vehicle at the right moment. César Chávez picked the wrong vehicle; farmworkers were a declining force in American labor, hardly the most strategic base for revolution. For Carlos Montes, Felipe Luciano, Chacha Jiménez, and others, it was not the right moment; the urban Latino masses they sought to mobilize were not yet large enough or self-confident enough to fulfill the task. When that time comes, we may look back to these figures as the precursors.

To focus on the collective dynamic of these movements rather than the power of an individual leader, I prefer to speak of their "outlaw politics" rather than their "charismatic authority." They were "outlaw" in that they defied the routine, even when their behavior was technically within the law. The Brown Berets, for example, took pains to stay within the letter of California law but were still considered outlaws because they violated the unwritten norm of Mexican docility in the face of authority. The Young Lords, of course, were outlaws from the start.

As Pablo "Yoruba" Guzmán, who was the New York–based Young Lords' information minister, recalls, "By our sixth year, it was over. Partly because of destabilization by arrest and government infiltration, but mainly because we were young, and prone to mistakes."[5]

The price for the outlawry of the sixties and seventies had been horrific: leaders killed, imprisoned, or driven underground, careers and families disrupted, comrades turned against one another, organizations paralyzed by court actions. COINTELPRO (Counter-Intelligence Program), the FBI's notorious campaign of infiltration, provocation, and sabotage of leftist organizations, deliberately stimulated paranoia and exacerbated authoritarian tendencies within the liberation movements, causing splits and defections.[6]

Not only were Latinos in the Marxist national liberation movements up against a ferocious and unscrupulous opponent, by 1973 they were finding themselves with fewer allies. The end of the draft and of U.S. direct involvement in the war in Vietnam had eliminated the strongest cause of radicalism among young whites, whose support had often been critical. And when they were no longer able to offer free breakfasts, vocational training, and other services or even maintain an open presence in the barrios, the radicals also found themselves cut off from the Latino masses. A few die-hards formed underground paramilitary organizations like the Puerto Rican *Fuerzas Armadas de Liberación Nacional*, or FALN (founded in 1975), to continue the struggle by armed assaults and bombs, but by this time most Latino radicals realized that the game was up. Unlike what they imagined had happened in China and Cuba, in the United States it was not—at least at that moment—possible to combine mass action with armed struggle. To reach the masses, they were going to have to lay down their arms.

Consequently, some veterans of the Marxist Left—those who did not give up the struggle altogether or isolate themselves in terrorist cells such as the FALN—sought to reconnect with the masses. They entered into dialogue with non-Marxists and even anti-Marxists in the labor and barrio movements, including clergy and lay-people who combined social and religious commitments. What these non-Marxist reformers were doing—what they had been doing all along, in some cases since the 1940s—was trying to defend the Latino masses through the ordinary, routine politics of educating their constituents and organizing them into trade unions and neighborhood councils to petition for services. The Marxists threw their energies into the ongoing campaign of the Hispanic masses to break into the routine politics of lobbying and elections.

Actually, the relations between the non-Marxist and especially the religious-community workers, on the one side, and the Marxists on the other had always been more fluid than the labels suggest; for many of the revolutionaries, joining forces with lay and religious leaders in the barrios was like coming home. Long before Art Vázquez experienced his "road to Delano" political conversion—on the march on which a Chicago preacher had sent him—he had been a seminarian; after he rejected all church doctrine and became a committed, even doctrinaire, Marxist, he applied his new views to his community organizing work, side by side with church folks. The Brown Berets, we recall, had started out as an Episcopal youth group. Chacha Jiménez had at one time aspired to become a priest and was reading Thomas Merton along with Malcolm X in prison shortly before leading the Young Lords into political action. And Pablo Gúzman, information minister of the New York–based Young Lords, describes himself as a "former altar boy of Our Lady of Pity."

Not only were the Marxists deeply touched by religion, many of the Spanish-speaking clergy, Catholic and Protestant, had come to a deep appreciation or at least a tolerance of Marxism, especially after a decade of "liberation theology" and "Christian base communities"—neighborhood-based community-action groups that were a little like revolutionary party cells except that they spent a lot of time praying and discussing theology. To fudge the doctrinal differences between them (which continue to be deep and important), Marxists and Christian-inspired organizers alike adopted the new occupational title of the eighties: "activist."

What the combination of these forces produced was a kind of routine politics with an outlaw edge. Legal actions, such as demonstrations, were pushed with greater aggressiveness, and illegal or semilegal actions, such as squatting in unoccupied apartment buildings, grew to become so common and so ritualized as to be routine, for the police as well as the activists, and were resolved through routine legal processes, usually without violence.

The activists' incursions into routine electoral politics were almost invisible at first; they worked so close to the grass roots that they escaped serious attention or resistance—contesting local school board elections, for example. But they were getting ready to challenge candidates for more powerful statewide positions and to lobby for national legislation, efforts which would require larger coalitions among organizations with diverse ethnic compositions, subcultures, and histories. To succeed, they would also have to exploit divisions within the national Democratic and Republican parties and their local manifestations. It would be a subtle and complex game, with many players all keeping score in different ways.

To achieve an effective coalition, the "activists" and their no-less-active (but less in-your-face) allies knew they would have to work out a list of demands and goals—the elusive "Hispanic agenda"—that could satisfy broad sectors of their various constituencies.

## One Agenda or Many?

Over and over the question comes up in Hispanic publications: With a population so large and with so many media at their disposal, why have Hispanics not had more success—as compared, for example, to Jewish or Irish Americans or other interest groups—in promoting their political agenda?

"Think about it," West Coast journalist Guillermo Torres recently demanded of readers of *Hispanic Link Weekly Report.* "When was the last time a Hispanic rights group overloaded the fax machines and telephone and telegraph lines to Congress, the White House, or the national news media on behalf of an issue important to Hispanics?"

He complained that "the largest or most well known Hispanic advocacy groups—the League of United Latin American Citizens, Mexican-American Legal Defense and Educational Fund, and National Council of *La Raza,* as examples—are in the business of quiet lobbying," in contrast to "the network of fanatics" of the National Rifle Association, which "has terrorized Washington for years," and "the Religious Right," which "still can stand Congress on its head overnight."

To initiate "a Hispanic advocacy group with fire in its belly," Torres proposed "a conference of the major Hispanic groups representing people of Mexican, Puerto Rican, Cuban, Spanish, Filipino, and Central and South American descent." The conference would create "an umbrella organization" that might call itself the "National Hispanic Council...American Hispanics United...National Association of Hispanics...or something similar with the word 'American' or 'National' would suffice."[7]

Some elements of corporate America are also interested in bringing Hispanics together. At a January 31, 1994, meeting at the headquarters of the Coca-Cola Company in Atlanta, company executives presented a proposal for a Unity Convention in 1996 of national Hispanic organizations to leaders of seven of those organizations: National Image, the Cuban American National Council, the U.S. Hispanic Chamber of Commerce, the American G.I. Forum, SER-Jobs for Progress, the National Puerto Rican Forum, and LULAC (League of United Latin American Citizens).

Rudy Beserra, an assistant vice president of Coca-Cola, sought to assure everybody that this was not a case of "corporate America trying to tell [them] how to do [their] job. That's not it at all. It's getting the biggest bang for your buck."[8]

Whether the metaphor is "bang for your buck" or "fire in the belly," such a grand coalition has been an aspiration at least since the *Congreso Nacional de los Pueblos de Habla Española* (National Congress of the Spanish-Speaking People of the United States) was first convened in Los Angeles in 1938.[9]

So why hasn't it happened?

There are at least three reasons, beginning with the very multiplicity of organizations claiming to represent Hispanics or some segment of them. Each organization has its own bureaucratic inertia and its turf to defend, two facts which interfere with collaboration. Thus, in response to the Coca-Cola proposal for a "Unity '96" convention, LULAC and the U.S. Hispanic Chamber of Commerce, two of the biggest bureaucratic machines in the Hispanic universe, said they had "already locked in dates and sites for their 1996 conventions and would be reluctant to change plans." And even if they and other groups should agree to hold a joint convention, they can expect stubborn disputes over who is to run it and how and whose pet issues will be most prominently addressed. Unsurprisingly, the greatest enthusiasm for such an event comes from smaller outfits such as the National Latino/a Lesbian and Gay Organization, unable to hold an ambitious convention or attract much press on their own.[10]

A second reason is disagreement over whom to include, the old question of ethnic "identity" and who has the right to claim it. Guillermo Torres's list leaves out Dominicans (who are neither Central nor South American), but this is surely only an oversight owing to his living in California. (Dominicans are fast becoming a power in New York City, but few of them have moved out west.) More controversial are his inclusions of Filipinos and Spaniards. True, Filipinos were colonized by Spain for almost as long as Puerto Rico, and most have Spanish names, even though very few still speak Spanish. They thus would have as much right as anybody to consider themselves Hispanics, but it is not clear that many of them want to. Many Filipinos are active in forming a very different and even more diverse panethnic community, that of Asian Americans.[11] Finally, Torres's inclusion of Spaniards will not please those who still despise the *gachupines*. And if we include Spaniards, what about Portuguese, who don't speak Spanish but a language that's pretty close to it? In August 1994 the California state legislature declared both populations, Spaniards and Portuguese,

"Hispanics" for purposes of affirmative action in minority con-tracting. Mexican-American state legislators and contractors were infuriated by this inclusion of Europeans in their protected market, saying such things as "How can a Spaniard possibly be Hispanic?!"

Even if a consensus could be reached on who is and who is not in the imagined community, the third and most serious obstacle to Torres's proposed advocacy group is lack of agreement on what he describes vaguely as "an issue important to His-panics." Is there an issue important to all Hispanics, rural and urban Mexican Americans, inner-city Puerto Ricans, Dade County Cubans, and all the many other Hispanic populations equally? And more important to them than to non-Hispanics? How many such issues are there where they all have a common interest?

"There is no such thing as a Latino issue!" insists Art Vázquez. And it is certainly true that immigration law is of as much concern to Asians, Haitians, and Irish as to Latinos. Bilingual education, another frequently mentioned item on the supposed "Hispanic agenda," is an issue for dozens of linguistic minorities in the United States, although the Spanish-speaking are by far the largest. The problems affecting Hispanics, Vázquez argues, are "systemic issues," parts of the total U.S. social and political system, so it is that system that must be addressed.[12]

Something like Torres's proposed Hispanic advocacy group may sooner or later be formed—in fact, a number of organizations like it have been formed in the past—but it probably won't matter much. The real Hispanic agenda is a more diffuse thing, and it is taking diffuse political actions to carry it out.

### Power Tools: The Organizational Matrix

The Hispanics' political machine, if we can call it that, is even more diverse and contradictory than their image machine, but in an apparently chaotic and anarchic fashion, it, too, is fashioning a product. It is increasing Hispanic power.

At the base of the operation are the innumerable Latino voluntary associations, chartered for a variety of purposes that ostensibly have nothing to do with lobbying or elections; if they did, of course, they would lose their not-for-profit status. Most have the very broad aim of promoting and defending the group's cultural heritage, which may mean sponsoring parades and festivals and publishing glossy folders on Hispanics' contributions to America, holding conferences, and especially in recent years, conducting research on social and economic conditions of their supposed constituents. Other associations have more narrowly defined purposes, such as preventing school dropouts or teen pregnancy, while others define their purpose in the broadest terms possible: to shape public policy.

Until recently, the only way to keep up with the more notable of the activities of these organizations—other than subscribing to their mailing lists—was to read *Hispanic Link Weekly Report*, a newsletter founded in 1982 by the American-Mexican husband-and-wife journalist team, Charles Ericksen and Sebastiana Mendoza, and published in English from Washington, D.C. The *Link*, still indispensable, is now supplemented by Internet sites, including the popular and elaborate Chicano/LatinoNet (http://latino.sscnet.ucla.edu).

No Hispanic politician can afford to ignore this web of associations or to alienate any significant part of it. It is here, in the conferences and newsletters and public statements of these groups, that contacts are made, funding sources are identified, potential campaign issues are floated and tested. It is also where many budding politicians get their start, as high school students in some after-school activity or later as a volunteer or staff member, learning the ropes, shaking hands, and exchanging business cards. The mass of Latino voters may be only dimly aware of these groups' existence and rarely have any idea of the scope of their activities, but the politically ambitious learn about them very quickly.

The largest and very nearly the oldest of the broad-purposed voluntary associations is LULAC, long identified with Mexican Americans of the Southwest but now trying to reposition itself as the body that speaks for all Hispanic groups. The effort has not been without conflict and comedy.

LULAC was founded in Corpus Christi in 1923, two years after its precursor, the Order of the Sons of America, was established by Mexican-American veterans of the Great War in San Antonio. The bloody suppression of the rising of the Plan de San Diego in 1915 was still fresh in memory, the Mexican Revolution had still not subsided, and the participation in the war had made especially acute the question of what it meant to be both a Mexican—a person exposed to discrimination—and an American, as the name "Sons of America" underlined.

The league was a response by middle class Mexican Americans in San Antonio, Corpus Christi, and the Río Grande Valley to Anglo Texans' formulation of what they called "the Mexican Problem," which for Anglos meant how to keep the increasing number of Mexicans under control. Although its early publications were in Spanish, over the years LULAC became much more of an English-speaking Mexican-American than a Mexican organization, focusing mainly on civil rights. Women were actively involved from very early on.[13]

Whereas Hispanic organizations in the nineteenth and early twentieth centuries were interested mainly in holding their communities together as cultural entities, interest groups such as LULAC that developed in the 1920s–1950s had a more outward focus, seeking social equality with the dominant Anglo population.[14] In the radical seventies, the young hotheads saw such organizations and their goals as insufferably stodgy—liberation was not about gaining the privileges of the oppressor but about eliminating the system of privilege. But then, in the eighties, with the utopian project now in abeyance, LULAC and its brethren were again appreciated for their size and stability—necessary bulwarks against the rollback of civil rights that threatened during the Reagan years. After the still sharper rightward turn of U.S. politics in the congressional elections of 1994, stodgy old LULAC looks positively progressive.

A more narrowly targeted strategy, seeking to lift the group by raising its most talented members, was tried in the East. Aspira was founded in New York in 1961 to keep Puerto Rican kids in high school and college-bound and to "develop leadership." In 1980, Aspira built on its local success to go national, with centers in Puerto Rico, Pennsylvania, Illinois, Florida, and New Jersey. It proved to be effective, and its distinguished alumni now include Bronx borough president Fernando Ferrer, officers in foundations and service organizations, university professors, numerous judges, and other elected officials—people who in most cases would not have made it through high school without the encouragement and intensive counseling, instruction, and group activities of the Aspira clubs. New ethnic-studies programs worked to similar ends at the university level.

Organizations like the Mexican-American Legal Defense and Education Fund (MALDEF), founded in San Francisco in 1968, and the Puerto Rican Legal Defense and Education Fund (PRDLF), founded in New York four years later, were at first poised between the outlaws and the establishment, defending the former against the latter. But their real, longer-range purpose is to shape public policy on issues of concern to their respective constituencies. A particularly interesting organizational form that emerged in the eighties is the policy institute, which, while it, too, must refrain from lobbying, conducts research and takes positions on public issues affecting Latinos. Operating as small-scale think-tanks, such institutes put together social-research data, organize conferences, and issue position papers to orient Latino politicians. Three that are particularly active are the Tomás Rivera Center, in Claremont, California, the Latino policy Institute in Chicago, and the Institute for Puerto Rican Policy in New York. The last named publishes *Crítica,* a lively journal edited by Howard Jordán and full of political gossip, penetrating cultural critique, and irreverent commentary—it's simultaneously funny and informative, a welcome relief from the many more solemn organizational documents.

There are also special-interest-group consortia, such as the Inter-University Program for Latino Research, the National Association of Chicano Studies, the recently formed Puerto Rican Studies Association, and the National Puerto Rican Policy Network, and professional associations, such as the Association of Hispanic Mental Health Professionals. A professional association especially relevant to our subject is the National Association of Latino Elected Officials.

Two mainly Latino organizations initiated by Saul Alinsky's Industrial Areas Foundation (IAF) in Chicago have served as important power bases in their respective areas. The Community Service Organization (CSO), founded in Los Angeles in 1947, has worked in Latino and other nonwhite neighborhoods to promote community control, with support from organized labor and local churches. The CSO, incidentally, is the organization that César

Chávez was working for when he quit to found what became the United Farm Workers Union.

In 1973, Ernie Cortés, a Chicano trained in community organizing by the IAF in Chicago, returned home to San Antonio and founded Communities Organized for Public Service (COPS), with support from the local churches. Like all Alinsky organizations, its emphasis, too, has been on community control, in this case in the mainly Mexican-American barrios of the city. Despite its unappealing acronym, COPS would grow to be the most important parapolitical organization in San Antonio, the tenth-largest city in the United States. In 1977, COPS won a major victory against the Anglo establishment, the adoption of a district-based city council system instead of the at-large system, in which Mexican-American candidates had always been swamped by better-financed candidates from outside their neighborhoods. Since Mexican Americans were a majority in five of the ten districts, they were able to dominate local politics for the first time since San Antonio was lost to the Anglos in 1836.

An organization that signals the transition from the turbulent seventies to the cautious eighties is the National Congress for Puerto Rican Rights (NCPRR), which held its first convention in the South Bronx in 1981. Its founders had come mainly out of the Young Lords and the Puerto Rican Socialist party (PSP), which would have been an impossible combination just a few years earlier—in the days when each group had more candidates for membership than slots, the Young Lords and the PSP had gone to some pains to exaggerate their differences, but now they could hardly afford such doctrinal niceties. The NCPRR is a small organization, rather like the vanguard parties from which it descended, which claims a membership of five hundred to one thousand and a core of some fifty to seventy-five activists, with chapters in New York, New Jersey, Pennsylvania, and Washington, D.C. Despite its radical heritage, the NCPRR's agenda and even its rhetoric have generally been noninflammatory. Besides support for bilingual education, it claims to fight against discrimination against Puerto Ricans and try to achieve a 'better life for the community.'" It also urges Puerto Ricans and other Hispanics to register to vote.[15] The most distinctive elements from its radical past were its opposition to U.S. intervention in Latin America and the high priority it put on women's issues, especially involuntary sterilization in Puerto Rico and the United States. Neither of these was a major theme for the old-line Latino voluntary associations. While not destined to become one of the major players, the NCPRR gave the old radicals a place to hang their berets in the era of routine politics.

## Following the Money

When some of the earliest organizations like LULAC were getting their start in the 1920s and 1930s, they depended entirely on members and a few well-off sympathizers for funds. In more recent years, since the early sixties, all the voluntary associations have depended very heavily on grants from foundations and government agencies. Donors inevitably influence the priorities of recipient agencies and even their continued existence and so have to be considered as part of the Hispanic organizational matrix.

The biggest financial impact on the life of the barrios came in the 1960s as part of President Lyndon Johnson's War on Poverty. The federal government pumped money into "minority" (non-white) and poor white neighborhoods by funding local initiatives in education, health care, and housing programs, with the aim of "maximum feasible participation" by the people of the communities being served. Many people who had seemed destined for lives of poverty got the training and encouragement to start careers, and the salaries paid by the new community-service agencies, which were staffed by people from those communities, and purchases of supplies by those agencies had a multiplier effect, boosting the economies of the neighborhoods. Many organizations, including Latino organizations, got their starts with such funding.

But, of course, there were problems. "Maximum feasible participation," as interpreted by local administrators, often seemed to mean that whatever neighborhood group could participate the loudest got the funding, a process memorably satirized in Tom Wolfe's book *Mau-Mauing the Flak Catcher*. Daniel Patrick Moynihan, one of the architects of the program, also criticized its execution in a less amusing book, *Maximum Feasible Misunderstanding*.[16] Much of the antipoverty money went to paying staff salaries that were quite generous relative to licit barrio incomes generally, creating resentment among those who hadn't got the job or didn't think the money was deserved. The figure of the grassroots opportunist living well on the government's largesse was captured in the sarcastic phrase "poverty pimp." Besides problems of barrio-based inefficiency and abuse, which undoubtedly occurred, there was often gross interference by the municipal political powers. In Chicago, where Art Vázquez got his career start as an organizer and Chacha Jiménez got the beginnings of a college education through federally funded programs, Mayor Richard J. Daley was able to block funding for organizations and individuals who opposed him, thus turning the local War on Poverty programs into parts of his patronage machine—which was why Vázquez left for a less remunerative but also less limiting job with a church group.

Federal funding for community organizing of the type that was promoted in the War on Poverty is much more restricted these days, so the voluntary associations either don't do such organizing or they turn to the private foundations for help. The NCPRR, true to its radical heritage, is one of the very few that refuses to seek government money for any of its programs so as not to become an accomplice of the state. However, concern about programmatic control by a donor agency comes up in other, quite middle-of-the-road organizations as well.

The issue surfaced at the beginning of 1994 when the San Antonio office of MALDEF hired a critic of Southwestern Bell, one of its usual donors, as its regional counsel. In his previous position as Texas public utilities counsel, Luis Wilmot had accused the company of abusing its telephone monopoly by overcharging customers. Southwestern Bell then turned down two grant requests from MALDEF. Although the company later said it would continue to fund future MALDEF projects, the point had been made.

For Hispanics, the main private funding source has been the Ford Foundation, which has helped fund almost all the organizations named here. The foundation itself established MALDEF and the Southwest Council of La Raza (forerunner of the National Council of La Raza [NCLR]) in 1968, after commissioning a study which concluded "that Mexican Americans were disorganized and fragmented and in need of a national organization to serve their social, economic and political needs," writes the best-known critic of these programs, the Republican politician and scholar Linda Chávez, who was executive director of the U.S. commission on Civil Rights under President Reagan. MALDEF and the NCLR now receive funding from a variety of places, but their chief source over the years has continued to be the Ford Foundation, which, Chávez reports, gave $9.6 million to the NCLR and $14.2 million to MALDEF between 1968 and 1991. "Indeed," she writes, "the Ford Foundation virtually created the infrastructure of the contemporary Hispanic movement."[17]

Since Chávez is a declared enemy of the contemporary Hispanic movement, this judgment is not meant as a compliment. When she quotes a onetime head of the Southwest Council of La Raza, Henry Santiestevan, that "without the Ford Foundation's commitment to a strategy of national and local institution-building, the Chicano movement would have withered away in many areas," it is with regret that it did not wither away. Her complaint is that the organizations funded by Ford and other grants sources, such as Carnegie, Rockefeller, and the philanthropic arms of Coors and other corporations, encourage a separate ethnic identity and thereby slow down Hispanics' "assimilation" into the American "mainstream." We shall return to this argument in a later chapter.

Some of the ways in which the foundations, and Ford in particular, do indeed contribute to the production of Hispanic identity are illustrated in the career of Bill Díaz, a former program officer at Ford. Born in New York City and reared in its suburbs by parents who had immigrated from Puerto Rico many years earlier, Díaz was always aware that he was Puerto Rican, because his family was "very Puerto Rican" in the food they ate, the music they listened to, and their pride in being Puerto Rican. But since the family was white and middle-class, he "grew up more or less as a sort of regular American kid," his Puerto Rican background not impinging on his life in any way he was aware of.

At Fordham University, he studied political science, with no thought of ever working with Puerto Ricans. But then, in 1980, a few years out of college and bored with his job with the Manpower Demonstration Research Corporation, he learned of an opening at the Ford Foundation for a Hispanic program officer to create a think tank called the Hispanic Policy Development Project. He applied and was hired. "I didn't set out to become a professional

Latino," he says, "though in some ways that's the way I turned out, at least while at Ford."[18]

The foundations have filled a vacuum that was left when other types of organizations ceased being major sources of social intervention in the barrios of America. Churches and church associations, such as the National Council of Churches, and individual denominations, such as the United Methodists, used to be far more visible in poor communities, with programs in the churches themselves and settlement houses offering a variety of counseling, training, educational, and even health-care services. Today the revenues of the traditional churches have declined drastically, according to Daniel Alvarez.

Alvarez, a Presbyterian minister recently arrived from Cuba, was invited in 1964 to take charge of a modest settlement house called Casa Central, which had been founded ten years earlier by a group of Protestant pastors in a North Side Latino neighborhood in Chicago.

"It was supported mainly by the churches," he recalls. "There were no government funds and a small contribution from the Chicago Missionary Society. But it was a small agency, with a small budget."

In 1974 he took a leave from the agency to work for Governor Walker of Illinois as his head of the Spanish-Speaking Affairs Office, and when he returned to Casa Central two years later, he says, "I came back with a lot more knowledge that there was government money for private agencies—something I hadn't been aware of before." And with government grants he led the agency into new programs of child care, prevention of child abuse, and on to create the country's first and, as far as he knows, still the only nursing home for the Hispanic elderly.

In his view there has been "a tremendous decline" in the importance of the churches and their commitment to social work. "For example, in Chicago there were institutions that brought together the churches, such as the Religious and Race Council, several other councils—they closed down, ceased. The Chicago Federation of Churches closed down. At this moment there is no institution that groups together the churches the way there was twenty-five years ago."[19]

He attributes this to *"una decadencia de la espiritualidad"* ("a decline of spirituality") in the society generally. In any case, he believes it would be impossible for hospitals today to set up a social agency like Casa Central, even on the modest scale it had at its beginnings, much less to found hospitals like Chicago's Presbyterian Hospital or Wesley Memorial or universities like Northwestern, Loyola, De Paul—to mention only a few of the major church-created institutions in Chicago. "The church can hardly maintain itself."

Despite Alvarez's pessimism, churches are still important bases for community organizing in Latino neighborhoods all over the country, even if they are not as well bankrolled as in the past. San Antonio's COPS (discussed above) is a famously effective organization that still relies mainly on church support. But increasingly the churches have had to leave the more ambitious projects to the foundation-funded groups.

## The Declining Role of Organized Labor

There was another type of organization that was once far more active in poor urban communities, including the barrios. This was organized labor.

Whereas the churches sponsored support services to the needy as an expression of their commitment to Christian charity, unions more typically initiated projects to meet direct practical needs of housing, credit, and training, benefiting Hispanics as members of the larger working class. Early in the century the Amalgamated Clothing Workers (which later became the Amalgamated Clothing and Textile Workers Union [ACTWU]) created "America's labor bank"—the Amalgamated Bank—to give workers and small entrepreneurs access to credit. Its customers today in Chicago and New York are mostly struggling immigrant workers, but far more of them speak Spanish or Chinese than Yiddish or Italian. ACTWU, with the International Ladies Garment Workers Union (with which it has recently merged to form the Union of Needletrade, Industrial and Textile Employees), the International Brotherhood of Electrical Workers, and other unions made impressive investments in low-income housing after World War II. Unions also set up college programs and clinics to serve workers and their families. Most important, they served working-class communities, including Hispanic ones, by funding organizing drives of their workers.

From the Hispanic's point of view, union power was not without problems—bigger, Anglo-dominated unions at times helped bust up, instead of build, smaller unions of Spanish-speaking workers, and within the bigger unions Hispanics were often frustrated by obstacles to their advancement to positions of authority.[20] Still, unions were a major factor in their lives, a terrain for struggle, to be sure, but also more often than not a valued ally.

Back in 1938 it had been the Congress of Industrial Organizations, the CIO, that sponsored the first *Congreso Nacional de los Pueblos de Habla Española* (National Congress of the Spanish-Speaking People of the United States). Organized by Luisa Moreno, the first woman vice president of the California State Industrial Union Council (C.I.O.), the event was originally planned to be held in Albuquerque, New Mexico. Invitations went out to people from all sectors and all the Spanish-speaking national groups (Mexicans, Puerto Ricans, Spaniards, Cubans, Central and South Americans). But then "the House Un-American Activities Committee [HUAC] descended upon Albuquerque, and using its congressional powers and immunities, proceeded to vilify and accuse the congress's sponsors as Communists, Radicals, and unpatriotic elements." HUAC succeeded in scaring off local sponsors, which was why the congress was moved to Los Angeles, "where it took place very successfully and enjoyed almost twenty years of active political life."[21]

As another of many possible examples of initiatives for Hispanics, in 1968 it was the United Auto Workers (UAW) that provided the start-up money—$60,000—for what would become one of the country's largest antipoverty agencies. UAW President Walter Reuther asked Esteban Torres, an active Los Angeles unionist and former gang member, to set up the East Los Angeles Community Union (TELACU). Neither the UAW nor Torres, who has been serving in the U.S. Congress since 1982, is now associated with TELACU, which is now the largest federally-chartered Community Development Corporation (CDC) run by and for Hispanics.[22]

Union membership, revenues, and power have declined precipitously in the past few years, and unions are no longer able to do as much in the communities as they once did. In fact, union power has declined so much that the United Farmworkers Union is itself partly dependent on foundation support.[23] In its beginnings, as we have seen, that union drew heavily on an amalgam of church and union support.

The decline of church-based interventions and the virtual disappearance of union-based interventions in working-class communities have left the field open to the social experimentation of foundations and the cautious bureacratic measures of federal agencies. The government agencies are in turn largely influenced in their policies by foundations and the organizations they support, such as MALDEF and the NCLR, that have made it their business to analyze, define, and—within the limits of their not-for-profit status—lobby for public policy. This shift has placed greater emphasis on the imagined community of Hispanics.

The progressive churches saw and continue to see their mission as Christian charity toward all mankind, without ethnic distinction. When they created or create projects targeted especially at Hispanic communities, it is simply because that is where they see a greater need, not because of any special spiritual quality attributed to people who pray in Spanish. Traditionally, American churches have been agencies that facilitated the integration of immigrants into the new society, in part by introducing them to coreligionists of other ethnic backgrounds. The Roman Catholic church fulfilled this function for the Irish and then later for the Germans, even when the latter attended mass in German.[24] Both Catholic and Protestant churches are fulfilling that function today for the Spanish speaking, who join with other parishioners in activities defined by their common beliefs rather than their ethnic differences.

The unions have always organized on the basis of class; although common ethnicity has been a vitally important bond, class rather than ethnicity has defined the boundaries of the solidarity group. Mexican-American workers in the California fields learned—sometimes with great difficulty—to build unions and organize strikes together with Filipinos and "Okies," and Spanish-speaking workers from Mexico, Central and South America, and the Caribbean are learning to organize not just with each other but also with the Chinese, Korean, Vietnamese, and other Asian, European, and African immigrants in their industries.

But the logic of the foundation-sponsored organizations has

to be different. They are not likely to get corporate funds if their declared aim is to organize the working class, nor can they openly direct their work at a particular confessional group. Instead, they have defined their clientele as "minorities," one of which is the Hispanic, or Latino. Thus, they are contributing in a major way—though not in as decisive a way as Linda Chávez, among others, believes, because they are as much following as creating a trend—to the construction of that imagined community and are helping to create a class of "professional Latinos."

## Getting Elected

The entire matrix of Hispanic-oriented organizations supports the advancement of political power, but some organizations are more directly involved in achieving that clout than others. None has played a more important role than the Southwest Voter Registration and Education Project (SVREP).

The SVREP was founded in San Antonio in 1974. Under its founder and president, Willy Velázquez, it increased the ranks of Mexican-American voters and educated them, making available materials in their own language, helping them understand the issues, and encouraging them not to be intimidated by what may have looked like a mysterious electoral process. The project developed operations throughout the Southwest and also established a research institute to provide itself and anybody else who was interested carefully analyzed polling data on Mexican-American citizens. The mere fact of reporting these data drew attention to a group whose opinions had never seemed to matter much to politicians. Ed Pastor, now a Democratic U.S. congressman from Arizona and since 1994 the head of the Congressional Hispanic Caucus, credits the organization for making possible the elections of numerous Hispanic candidates in the region, including himself.[25] Another who was clearly benefited by both the SVREP's and COPS's political education and registration of Hispanic voters was Henry Cisneros, a Harvard-educated native of San Antonio who returned and in 1981 became the city's first Hispanic mayor since Spanish colonial days. He rapidly emerged as the Democrats' most articulate and telegenic spokesman on behalf of Hispanics.

Of course, the SVREP had to be nonpartisan, registering

Republicans and independents as well as Democrats, but it happened that most of the people they registered voted Democratic. The affinity of Democrats to the organization became especially apparent when Andy Hernández, president of the SVREP since Velázquez's death in 1988, resigned to become the Hispanic outreach director for the Democratic National Committee (DNC) in 1994. Actually, the very fact that the DNC thought it needed a Hispanic outreach was largely due to the effectiveness of the SVREP in increasing the Hispanic vote.

Other Latino groups in other parts of the country studied and emulated the SVREP's approach, though seldom with as dramatic effects. In 1977 the National Puerto Rican Coalition was founded with the aim of increasing voter participation in areas of Puerto Rican concentration in the Northeast and Midwest. There was also a Midwest Voter Registration and Education Project. In these regions the Latino populations were more diverse, and the quarrels between their organizations were more acrimonious, making it impossible to coordinate voter education efforts as smoothly as the SVREP had done in its home territory. Still, these efforts surely did increase voter awareness and probably voter turnout (though the effect of the MVREP and the NPRC on this is impossible to measure). Partly due to the work of these groups, enough Latinos had been elected by 1979 for the founding of the National Association of Latino Elected and Appointed Officials (NALEO).[26]

In the 1984 presidential campaign Hispanic politicians worked very hard to convince strategists in both major parties that there was a sizable Hispanic vote and that they could deliver it. They seem to have imagined that Hispanics were going to vote as a bloc, to the extent that they voted at all, for whichever party could find the magic formula. Hispanic politicians in each party were happy to encourage this delusion, which made them much sought after in their respective parties.

Toney Anaya of New Mexico, at the time the nation's sole Hispanic governor, headed up the Democrats' Hispanic Force 84, which sought to link organizations across the country that were trying to register and mobilize Hispanic voters and to bring Hispanic concerns to the attention of all the presidential candidates, Democrats and Republicans.[27] In response, the GOP formed the Republican National Hispanic Assembly, chaired by Cuban-

American physician Tirso del Junco, who described its aims: "to bring to the Hispanic community the Republican philosophy, with the hope that eventually we will develop an organized Republican political structure within the Hispanic communities like California, Texas, New York, Miami, Colorado, Denver, Arizona, and New Mexico."[28] Del Junco sought to persuade his fellow Republicans that the Hispanic vote was inherently conservative on family values and economic issues and thus could be delivered to the Republicans—if not in 1984, then sometime soon.

In fact, the only reliably Republican stronghold in Hispanic America is Southeast Florida, which is Republican with a Cuban accent. There, especially in Dade County (Miami, Hialeah, Coral Gables, and their environs), the Republicanism of Cubans is almost entirely a product of their obsession with punishing Fidel Castro. But in other respects the Cubans are not typical Republicans; they often support Democrats and tend to be especially liberal on labor issues.[29]

In 1993, the NALEO and the National League of Cities identified 196 Hispanic mayors of the United States' 19,300 cities. The greatest number were in Texas, sixty-eight; California, forty-two; New Mexico, forty; Arizona, nineteen; and Colorado, twelve. There were others in Florida, Michigan, Illinois, New Jersey, Idaho, Utah, Washington, Wyoming, and Kansas. Their role models, mentioned by several of these ambitious mayors, are Henry Cisneros (ex-mayor of San Antonio) and Federico Peña (of Denver), who not only managed major cities but have continued to play important political roles. Only twenty-two of the Hispanic mayors were women, including six in Texas and two in California. As Matilde Aguirre, mayor of Sweetwater, Florida, observed, "Hispanic males—all males—have a hard time responding to a woman in a higher position than themselves."[30]

Including the 196 mayors, the NALEO found 1,476 Hispanic municipal officials in the United States in 1993, up 45 percent since 1983. A few of these were in what some have called the lower tier of American politics, including those in "minority" slots—state and local commissions created specifically to deal with Latinos.[31] But even such relatively powerless jobs may be springboards to higher office.

## Hispanic Caucus (Congress)

There has not been a Hispanic in the United States Senate since José M. Montoya of New Mexico was defeated in 1976, after serving two terms (first elected in 1964). Nor is there currently any Hispanic in a governor's mansion (except, of course, the governor of Puerto Rico). Thus, the highest elected position held by a Hispanic is a seat in the U.S. House of Representatives.

Redistricting is mandated by the U.S. Constitution to maintain representative equality after a shift in population. In preparation for the 1992 congressional elections, the commissions charged with drawing the new boundaries were under court constraints to draw them so as to give maximum opportunities for minority populations to elect a candidate of their own, by creating what were called "majority minority districts"—that is, congressional districts where African Americans, Hispanics, Asians, or another minority group were a majority of the voters.

This created some bizarrely shaped districts, especially where the targeted minority was widely dispersed. In New York City, for example, a new Hispanic-majority district, the Twelfth, takes in a cluster of blocks in Puerto Rican and other Latino neighborhoods in southeastern Brooklyn, extends north and then sharply east before forking north and east to take in narrow bands of the borough of Queens, while to the west it leaps across the East River into a fairly compact part of the Lower East Side. This district is not a community in any sense; the people at the ends of its various forks could not even get to each other easily by New York's extensive public transportation system. But together these tenuously connected fragments of the city have a population that is 58 percent Hispanic, which met the chief redistricting criterion. In a six-way race for Congress, the winner was Nydia Velázquez, who had never before held elective office. Born and raised in Puerto Rico, she was far more fluent in Spanish and culturally closer to her many new immigrant constituents than were her New York Latino opponents. Her most serious rival in the primary was Stephen Solarz, a congressman whose old district, which had evaporated with the new boundaries, had overlapped partially with the new Twelfth.

Illinois's new Fourth Congressional District in Chicago is even stranger. On a map, it consists mainly of a large blob in the area just southwest of the Loop and another sizable blob in the near northwest, from which juts a northward-thrusting peninsula, the two blobs connected by a very narrow band that goes *around* a different congressional district (the Seventh) that cuts across the city from Lake Michigan almost to its western boundary. As the *Congressional Quarterly's Politics in America 1994* explains, "Drawing the 4th required a creative touch. Most Chicago Hispanics live in two blocs, one northwest of downtown and the other nearby to the southwest. However, a direct linkup would have cut through the black majority 7th District. To avoid this, the 4th takes in a mostly Hispanic section of the North Side, follows a narrow, 10-mile band along the northern border of the 7th to the Cook County line, then moves south and east along the 7th to hook up with the other Hispanic concentration."[32]

The resulting district has a population that is 65 percent Hispanic, but hardly homogeneous. The two Hispanic concentrations were geographically separated for a reason: The people to the southwest are overwhelmingly of Mexican origin, including many new arrivals who do not vote, whereas the northwest area is where Chicago's Puerto Ricans have traditionally lived, although they, too, have been joined by Mexicans in recent years. Mainly because so many of the Mexicans are recent immigrants, Hispanics are only 38 percent of the voters, and voters of Puerto Rican origin are probably nearly equal to those of Mexican origin. The winner in 1992 was Luis Gutiérrez, a Puerto Rican on the Chicago Board of Aldermen who was backed by Mayor Richard M. Daley. These two cases, the New York Twelfth and the Illinois Fourth Congressional Districts, show the exaggerated contortions people are willing to go through to create a real physical, national territory for the imagined Hispanic nation.

After redistricting and the 1992 elections, there were seven more Hispanic members of Congress than there had been, making a total of seventeen (not counting the nonvoting members representing Puerto Rico and the Virgin Islands). Hispanic politicians had hoped to have eight new members, but in the new Texas Twenty-ninth District in East Houston, drawn so as to have a 61 percent Hispanic majority, the local Hispanic politicians were so divided that an Anglo, Gene Green, won the Democratic primary in a runoff after a five-way race and then handily beat his black Republican opponent.

In addition to the winners of the seven new seats, there was an eighth new Hispanic congressman. Henry Bonilla of San Antonio defeated the Democratic Mexican-American incumbent, Albert Bustamante, to become the only Mexican-American Republican in the House. Bustamante had alienated voters by being one of the more flagrant abusers in the House banking scandal—with thirty *cheques calientes* (hot checks), as the Republican candidate reminded voters—and other problems.

Besides Bonilla, the only other Hispanic Republicans in Congress are both Cuban-born representatives and both from Miami, Ileana Ros-Lehtinen (first elected in 1989) and Lincoln Díaz-Balart (a freshman in 1992). The other Cuban American, Robert Menéndez of Union City, New Jersey (where he was formerly mayor), is a Democrat. A son of Cuban immigrants, Menéndez has made his career as a liberal Democrat, liberal on every issue but Cuba. In Union City this position makes sense, since his constituency is not just Cuban but is very largely working-class Puerto Rican, with many Hispanics from all the other countries, and their concerns are mainly jobs and housing.

The longest-serving Hispanic congressman is Henry B. González, Democrat from San Antonio, a member of Congress since 1961 and chairman of the Banking, Finance and Urban Affairs Committee when the Democrats were in the majority. Another who has been in the news is Bill Richardson (D-N.M.), a self-defined Hispanic despite his Anglo name: Born of a Mexican mother and American father, he was raised in Mexico City and speaks Spanish more fluently than most of his colleagues in the Hispanic Congressional Caucus. His Hispanic and specifically Mexican ties became relevant when he had the task of shepherding NAFTA through Congress and could listen to, and present persuasively, the arguments of both the Mexican and U.S. sides. In the ideologically split California delegation, the Hispanic Democrats Esteban Torres (the former union man), Xavier Becerra, and Lucille Roybal-Allard (daughter of now-retired longtime congressman Edward Roybal) make up a liberal contingent.

All seventeen won reelection in 1994, with no new Hispanic members. But, of course, their relative positions changed, since the Republicans are now in the majority, and one of the first things that Speaker Newt Gingrich did was abolish the funding for special committees, including the Hispanic Congressional Caucus.

There may be more Hispanic Republicans coming up in South Texas, encouraged by Bonilla's victory. *Hispanic Link* reported that some Mexican-American Democrats were switching parties, including "Pete Nieto, who switched during his first term in the Texas legislature to become the first Mexican-American Republican in that body." Speaking of the Democratic leadership in impoverished South Texas, Nieto said, "The guys that run the social programs are the new patrones. The ranchers used to tell everybody how to vote. Now the poverty pimps tell everybody how to vote."[33]

## Tiers of Power

Many economists have argued that Hispanics and other minority groups operate in the bottom half of a "dual labor market." That is, they compete against one another and sometimes exploit one another in an economic sector of low-paid, mostly nonunion, off-the-books jobs in an economic subsystem that is in effect walled off from the better-paying jobs that can lead to the middle class. In other words, you can't get here from there.

Similarly, University of Colorado political scientist Rodney Hero argues that there is a dual political market, which he calls "two-tiered pluralism." The top tier is mainly closed to blacks and Latinos. It is the dominant political system, often called the "establishment" or the power elite, where people compete for real power as U.S. congresspersons, governors, and the like. Beneath it is a subordinate, parallel tier of lesser offices—minor judgeships, county clerkships, commissioners on unimportant commissions—that is walled in by such strict racial and ethnic segregation that few of its prisoners ever break out. This restricted subordinate system operates on the same pluralistic (or market) principles as the larger one, but for much smaller stakes.

Hero's glass-ceiling argument is perhaps an overly static portrayal of what is really a very fluid situation, where the relative power of all political positions is in flux and opportunities for advancement can come in surprising ways. It also underestimates the ingenuity and agility of office seekers. Latino politicians have long since learned to move back and forth from voluntary associations to government positions as the political winds change, and may even exert greater influence on public policy when they are out of government employ. One example of this circulation of elites from government to nonprofit leadership is Luis Miranda, who lost his job as New York City Democratic mayor Edward Koch's adviser on Latino Affairs when Koch was defeated in 1989, kept himself well connected by founding and presiding over a coordinating agency for dozens of Latino nonprofit agencies, helping tem get funding for their programs, and four years later was appointed by Republican mayor Rudolph Giuliani as head of the New York City Health and Hospitals Corporation. Some Latinos have become important political players without ever seeking political office; Angelo Falcón of the Puerto Rican Policy Institute seeks to influence policy makers by his scrupulously nonpartisan reports on Latino political opinion research, and Dennis Rivera, president of the Health and Hospital Workers Union "1199," has become a key figure in the Democratic party's efforts to attract Hispanics nationally. Among those who do make a career in politics, it is certainly true that there are Latinos who never got beyond the least influential jobs. But lower-level political work can also be a valuable training ground for those aspiring to higher office.

One example of such success is the two successive elections of a Mexican American, Federico Peña, as mayor of Denver, thought by many to be the state's most powerful elective office. Peña went on to become President Clinton's secretary of transportation. In Denver, Hispanics were only 18 percent of the total population and about 10 percent of the voting-age population. Hero attributes Peña's 1983 election to his "strong ties with labor, neighborhood organizations, environmentalists, the handicapped, young professionals, and the elderly." He had worked for MALDEF and the Chicano Education Project and had been a highly visible member of the state House of Representatives. He got help from the American Federation of State, County and Municipal Employees (AFSCME), the Denver Area Labor Federation, the local chapter of IBEW, and the SVREP, to increase registration of Mexican-American voters, getting a record voter turnout of 63.5

percent in the general election and 71.7 percent in the runoff (against another Democrat)—up from 53.3 percent in the previous (1979) election. However, as mayor he was unable to fulfill the high expectations for more jobs and prosperity in their neighborhoods, and next time around his victory was much narrower.

"There is ample evidence that the election of Hispanics stimulates political interest and participation by Hispanics," writes Lawrence Fuchs, "which was also true for the Irish, Germans, Italians, and others."[34] Success builds on success. The careers of Peña, Cisneros, and the humble political beginnings of some of the Hispanic members of Congress—one of whom, Solomon Ortiz of Corpus Christi, started his political career as the Nueces County Constable; several others had no prior political experience— suggests that more and more Hispanics will be breaking into the upper tier of power.

### How "Mexican" Are You?

One problem facing Hispanic politicians in any major area is the great diversity of interests and prejudices among their Latino constituencies. This is true even within groups that outsiders' tend to think of as homogeneous, such as Mexican Americans. One historian has maintained that despite the deep divisions of class and history, there is "a social-psychological continuum" based on language and kinship ties that "connects Mexican immigrant workers to all Mexicans who are U.S. citizens."[35] In some sense this is probably true; certainly many Mexicans believe in such a connectedness, which explains the attempts to create all-embracing Mexican-American organizations under the rubric *la raza*. But not everybody in this supposed community feels equally "Mexican." Some are much more attached to Mexican cultural traditions—the Virgin of Guadalupe, enchiladas poblanas, and other culinary specialties, Mexican patriotic holidays, Mexican music and films and so on—than are others. University of Texas political scientist Rodolfo de la Garza, who has studied this issue extensively, concludes that "there are not likely to be many issues around which the Mexican origin population will rally en masse." The only one he can think of would be discrimination against all people of Mexican origin, without regard to whether they are *tejanos* or *hispanos* or recent immigrants, workers or managers, white or brown, and this is an unlikely scenario.[36]

Also, the same kinds of bonds that exist among Mexicans also exist between Mexicans and other Spanish speakers in the United States, to whom they are often joined not only by language but by friendship, common work experiences, and even marriage. The creation of a common Mexican-American identity may be a way station in the formation of the larger Hispanic nation.

Richard Rodriguez, a California writer of Mexican parentage who looks upon the whole Hispanic-agenda notion with some irony, has written of the rise of Henry Cisneros that he was suddenly "unveiled" by Democratic party officials "to the constituency he was supposed already to represent. He must henceforward use the plural voice on committees and boards and at conferences. We want. We need. The problem, in this case, is not with the candidate; it is with the constituency. Who are we: We who have been to Harvard? Or we who could not read English? Or we who could not read? Or we who have yet to take our last regard of the lemon tree in our mother's Mexican garden?"[37]

Toward the end of the 1980s, Cisneros tried to bring Hispanic leaders together to formulate a national Hispanic political agenda, no doubt expecting this to be a much simpler task than it has turned out to be. Even though Mexican Americans are a large majority of the nation's Hispanic population, what Rodriguez calls "the tumult of pigments and altars and memories" among the different groups is too great for any one of them to define what it means to be "Hispanic."[38]

## "Boricua First!"

Mexican Americans are such a huge majority of the Hispanic population, nearly two-thirds of the total, that many members of our country's second-largest Hispanic group, the Puerto Ricans, are worried. They fear that any Hispanic agenda that gets worked out will necessarily be a Mexican-American agenda in which the Puerto Ricans' particular concerns will be lost. At the same time, the more assertive style of some of the Puerto Rican activists— they are, after all, mostly New Yorkers—has the more laid-back Chicanos of the Southwest fearful that they may be taken over.

By the end of the decade leaders of most of the Latino organizations began trying to adjust their strategies to the new demographic realities, especially the growth and diversification of the Hispanic population and its greater dispersal. In most cases this meant simply paying closer attention to the doings of other Latino communities, reporting on them in their newsletters, and occasionally sponsoring joint events. For example, Puerto Rican organizations in the Northeast cosponsored events for Dominicans, Colombians, and other Latinos and in New York helped the New York Dominican Guillermo Linares win a seat on the city council.

But LULAC and the NCLR made a different sort of adjustment. Both decided rather abruptly that they should no longer limit their scope and appeal to Mexican Americans but should also represent not just the newcomers but Puerto Ricans, who were already represented by dozens of organizations.

By 1990, LULAC had decided it was going to live up to its name and represent all "Latin American citizens," not just those of Mexican origin. The organization broke with precedent to elect as president José Vélez, described by *Hispanic Link* as "a multi-millionaire born in Nicaragua of a Puerto Rican father, [who] was...an anomaly in this most venerable of Mexican-American groups."

Vélez "Puerto Ricanized" the organization at a pace that seems to have left the Texans bewildered. At their 1994 convention in El Paso, 120 out of 604 voting delegates were from Puerto Rico (they outnumbered the entire Texas delegation), and they controlled the election of the new president, Belén Robles, an El Paso native. In the words of *Houston Chronicle* columnist Lori Rodríguez, who covered the convention, "Puerto Ricans are a very different breed of Hispanic. Beyond style, their focus on pet issues like international politics, statehood for the commonwealth, and minority procurement contracts for their businessmen raise fears among the more traditional LULAC members that the group will stray too far from its original civil rights mission." She quotes longtime Texas LULAC leader Johnny Mata: "The Puerto Ricans are good for LULAC in a way, they bring in so much energy and enthusiasm and we need that. But we have to watch them. We wouldn't want them to take over our group."[39]

Vélez, incidentally, was indicted for fraud shortly after, suggesting that the Texans hadn't been watching closely enough.[40]

While Mexican Americans were fearful of a Puerto Rican takeover of their most venerable organization, Puerto Ricans were startled by a move by Mexican Americans to step on their turf. One of the best-connected organizations in Washington is the NCLR, founded as the Southwest Council of La Raza in 1968 and "National" (with headquarters in Washington) since 1970. In July 1994, the NCLR's longtime president, Raúl Yzaguirre, already a member of the White House Advisory Commission on Educational Excellence for Hispanic Americans, was named chairman by President Clinton. (He later resigned claiming his opinions had not been taken sufficiently into account.) The NCLR had always been considered a Mexican-American organization, but in 1992 it hired a Puerto Rican researcher and won a grant to carry out research on joblessness among Puerto Ricans. Instead of rejoicing, Puerto Ricans complained that their organizations were being out-maneuvered in grantsmanship by the larger organization.[41]

Inter-Hispanic ethnic rivalry also surged when President Clinton had an opportunity to appoint a Supreme Court justice to replace retiring Justice Harry Blackmun. Puerto Ricans mustered the support of most of the major Latino organizations, including the Hispanic National Bar Association, LULAC, and, of course, PRLDEF to endorse a Puerto Rican federal judge in Connecticut, José Cabranes, for the slot. Even the Congressional Hispanic Caucus—most of whose members are Mexican Americans—broke with its tradition of not endorsing specific candidates and voted to endorse Cabranes.

But MALDEF and the NCLR refused to climb onto this bandwagon, saying merely that they wanted "a Latino"—with no stated preference as to which Latino—to be the nominee. The Cabranes boosters did not consider this helpful. Worse, from their point of view, the Latino Issues Forum in San Francisco endorsed a different candidate, former California Supreme Court justice and current member of the U.S. Commission on Civil Rights, Cruz Reynoso.[42]

In the end, President Clinton selected Ruth Bader Ginsburg for the job, and it seems unlikely that Cabranes or any other Latino was ever under serious consideration. Nevertheless, this interethnic dust-up, little noticed on the outside, provoked considerable ire within Latino circles. The controversy reflected a real anxiety on the part of many Puerto Ricans that their unique identity might be swallowed up by the much larger Mexican-American presence.

Puerto Ricans, when they want to emphasize the special character of their local traditions, often refer to themselves as *borincanos* or *boricuas*, derived from the Taino Indians' name for the island of Puerto Rico, "Borinquén." In the wake of the Supreme Court nomination dispute several Puerto Rican organizations banded together in a campaign under the slogan "Boricua First!" As they put it in a campaign brochure in August 1994, although there were "more than 2.7 million Puerto Ricans in the United States and 3.6 million residing in Puerto Rico, they "remain invisible at the tables of power....Our issues continually get lost when the discussion is put in simplistic Black-White or 'minority' terms, and get diluted within a larger Hispanic or Latino agenda."

But, with one exception, just what those uniquely Puerto Rican issues are is something no five Puerto Ricans are likely to agree on. The exception is the political status of the island of Puerto Rico. Whether it should remain in its peculiar condition as more than a territory but less than a state, or become a state, an independent nation, or something else is a complicated debate that obviously affects Puerto Ricans more than anyone else. The undefined status is a terrible distraction for social activists, whether left or right, especially on the island. It should be resolved so they can get on to other things. But it is not an issue of great moment to most of the 2.7 million Puerto Ricans, or children or grandchildren of Puerto Ricans, living in the United States.

In the period around 1972–74, the militants of the Young Lords and the Puerto Rican Socialist party tried to make this the dominant issue for Puerto Ricans in the States as well as on the island. But it is unlikely ever to assume such centrality in the thinking of stateside Puerto Ricans. Among those for whom the status issue is important, there is no one position that is clearly more popular, or deemed more patriotic, than another, and the arguments for one status or the other get very technical and confusing, especially when they focus on the economic implications for the island. Most stateside Puerto Ricans are not entirely sure what their position is or if it matters—past history suggests that Congress will dispose of Puerto Rico as it sees fit, with little regard to the opinions of Puerto Ricans either there or here. These expectations may change, however, if the growth of the still small Hispanic caucus in Congress makes that body more responsive.

## The Continuing Issue of Cuba

One of the most divisive issues for Hispanics continues to be U.S. policy toward Cuba. In Congress, José Serrano of the Bronx, who chaired the Hispanic Congressional Caucus in the 103rd Congress (1992–94), has been a strong voice for lifting the economic embargo, along with Charlie Rangel of Manhattan. Rangel, incidentally, despite his Hispanic surname (his father was Puerto Rican), participates in the Black rather than the Hispanic Congressional Caucus, but given the increasing Hispanicization of his district, he has had to take an interest in Hispanic questions. Both Rangel and Serrano received what they regarded as credible death threats from Cuban organizations in 1994 when they proposed lifting the embargo.

The most effective single-issue lobbying organization dealing with Cuba has been the Cuban American National Foundation (CANF), now headed by the wealthy businessman and 1961 Bay of Pigs invasion veteran Jorge Mas Canosa. The CANF lobbied for and got U.S. government funding for the anti-Castro station Radio Martí, which began broadcasting to Cuba in 1984, and later for TV Martí. These have probably had little effect on people in Cuba (reception has been easily jammed, and there was little information on these stations that was not available to Cubans by ordinary radio picked up from Miami and elsewhere). However, this government-funded operation has enormously increased the prestige of Mas Canosa in the enclave and enabled him to reward supporters with jobs. The CANF also persuaded the Clinton administration to set up camps in Guantánamo for the thousands of Cubans who embarked from the island in makeshift rafts in 1994, once it became apparent that they would not be accepted directly into the United States.

A rival group headed by Carlos Alberto Montaner has tried to align itself with slightly more liberal forces in the United States, advocating negotiation with, rather than the unconditional surrender of, the Cuban regime. Both Montaner's and Mas Canosa's operations show the desire to break out of the old Miami enclave politics, where Ortodoxos are still fighting Auténticos (two pre-Castro political parties) and none of it matters beyond Hialeah. These younger—mostly generation of '69—Cuban Americans use their connections in the enclave as a fund-raising base and to rally enough visible support to make their lobbying plausible in Washington.

The alliance with the traditional Right in the United States, or even with the moderate Right, as Montaner has attempted, has been complicated for most Cuban Americans because of the class and racial prejudices of these sectors. That is, Cuban Americans, if they were not both rich and white, have not always felt welcome among either the GOP or southern Democrats. And rich white Cubans like Mas Canosa who do have good GOP connections have offered little to the mass of poorer Cuban Americans except patriotism.

One of the oddities of Miami politics is that foreign policy has long been an issue in campaigns for even the lowliest local office as candidates try to top one another's calls for U.S.-government action against Cuba in order to pull in the Cuban-American vote—even though the local official has no authority over such policy and would bear no responsibility for its consequences. But the Cuban obsession is losing its effectiveness even in Miami, where non-Cuban voters especially are tired of hearing about Cuba and want to know what the candidate will do for the city. In the 1993 mayoral election, Miriam Alonso, a Cuban who focused her campaign on opposition to Castro and communism, got 64 percent of Cuban votes but only 36 percent of those of other Hispanics and lost the three-way election to Steve Clark, who won 45 percent of the total vote, against Alonso's 39 percent.[43]

## People of Color or People of Language?

Benjamin Chavis, during his brief tenure as executive director of the National Association for the Advancement of Colored People (NAACP), invited Latinos to join. The historically English speaking, African-American association should, he argued, embrace all "people of color" and under his direction organizing committees were set up in the heavily Latino Crotona section of the Bronx and even in San Juan, Puerto Rico.

"I think there are mutual interests here," Chavis told reporters in July 1994. "Our cultures are similar. Our histories of oppression are similar. Don't forget that a large segment of Latinos also are of African descent."[44]

As Chavis says, "If Latinos and blacks want to fight each other then both are going to lose because America in the twenty-first century is going to be a colored nation, in all hues of color."[45]

The recruitment of Latinos by the NAACP posed a challenge to leaders of established Latino organizations. On the one hand, they were pleased that the best-known and longest-established African-American organization was taking an interest in their issues. In this vein, U.S. congressman José Serrano of New York said of the Latino recruitment, "Why not?" As chair of the Congressional Hispanic Caucus he had been working to bring his group together with the Congressional Black Caucus for joint lobbying and thought Chavis's initiative could only help to highlight common interests.

But there is the problem of turf: Raúl Yzaguirre, president of the NCLR, praised Chavis for reaching out but warned, "If he wants to position the NAACP as a spokesman for all minorities, that's unacceptable."

And Luis Núñez, president of the NPRC, sounded downright huffy when he heard about it. "Everybody thinks we all should get together," he said, "but I don't think the NAACP has approached this in a coherent way. They haven't talked to us and we aren't exactly an unknown quantity."[46]

Maybe the proper criterion for unity is not color, or in any case not only color. Latinos are still Latinos even when they are white, and insisting—as some very fair skinned Puerto Rican and Mexican activists do—that they are "people of color" seems perverse, even to others in their own communities. Maybe social class is more relevant. Or perhaps what is needed is some concept that combines both color and class and still manages to tap into all the tumultuous emotional energy of one's own particular *pueblo*. Perhaps it is some kind of nation.

The people lumped together as Hispanics start out with just

two things in common: their Spanish-language heritage and the fact that they are lumped together as Hispanics. Anyone trying to establish a common agenda must build on these two facts.

As we have seen, Spanish-language mass media exploit the heritage for commercial reasons—to sell an audience to advertisers who are selling other things—and in so doing inevitably promote group consciousness among that audience. The virtual Hispanic nation of Univisión and Telemundo is thus a kind of by-product of the selling of Hondas, Miller beer, and Sazón Goya.

The politician starts from the other end, from the group consciousness to linguistic concerns. He or she must identify the shared concerns of potential constituents and get them to act on them as a group, and speaking the language is an incidental but usually necessary part of what it takes to do that. Politicians who represent or seek to represent Hispanics generally make an effort to speak Spanish even if they have to take lessons to do so. Even though almost all Hispanics who vote understand English (except for Puerto Ricans, they have to to become citizens), in scores of communities Spanish is still the insiders' language, the one that must be used to touch intimate emotions. Whether in Miami's Calle Ocho, New York's Washington Heights or Jamaica, Queens, and other barrios, South Central Los Angeles, or Magnolia in Houston, one doesn't need to speak English to work, shop or be a power broker.[47] And if you are running for office, you definitely want to be able to speak to the local power brokers.

On occasion, the correct and eloquent speaking of Spanish becomes an overt issue in electoral campaigns. Thus, in a 1990 contest for a seat on the Dade County Commission (Miami), one candidate had to defend himself in Spanish against the accusation that he was not "really" Cuban. Unlike his opponent, he had been born in the United States. Fortunately for him, he came up with an effective response, that "the hope of our homeland Cuba is in our generation."[48]

But as this example shows, in politics, unlike mass communications, language is more likely to be used to *divide* than to unite communities. Not only whether or not one speaks Spanish but the particular accent with which one speaks will define whether a candidate is one of "us" or one of "them."

The political process, jockeying for power, discrediting your opponents, coming to terms with financial backers and others who can help, bargaining my support on your bill for yours on mine, does not necessarily lead to Hispanic unity. When Hispanic candidates run against one another, as will be happening more frequently both because of the increase in Hispanic-majority districts and the increasing numbers of Hispanics becoming eligible to vote, they themselves may resort to crude ethnic slurs. It may seem electorally advantageous for a Puerto Rican to disparage Mexicans, or vice versa, or to play up minor differences even within one's own ethnic subgroup. Mexican candidates in California or Texas, Puerto Rican candidates in New York, and Cuban candidates in Miami have attacked one another vigorously on grounds that exaggerate divisions rather than bring people together. Thus, in 1992 conflicts among Mexican-American politicians in Houston allowed an Anglo, Gene Green, to win a congressional seat in a district that had been designed (by redistricting) to have a Hispanic majority. In New York City, New York Puerto Rican candidate Elizabeth Colón attacked Nydia Velázquez as being less in touch with her constituents because she was an Island Puerto Rican. Kika de la Garza, a Democratic congressman from Texas's Fifteenth District since 1964, is attacked by Mexican-American rivals for being an old Hispano, descended from Spanish land grantees and thus unresponsive to the masses of Hispanic poor in the district.

Latinos of diverse backgrounds have at times joined together in sustained and effective political struggle. For example, Puerto Ricans and Mexicans have joined in electoral and other coalitions in Chicago and Milwaukee, a Dominican won a New York City Council seat with crucial Puerto Rican support, Mexican-American candidates in California draw votes of Central Americans, and so on. But inter-Latino coalitions to support Latino candidates or promote Latino issues are containers of so many conflicting forces—class and narrow ethnic rivalries, conflicting personal ambitions, conflicts of values or vision—that they soon explode into fragments unless they find a satisfying answer to the second question: Why coalesce at all?

Those who do find an answer, identifying the larger aims of their group, are sure to discover that ethnicity is an imperfect guide to alliances. Not all Latinos are potential allies, even for an ostensibly pro-Latino project, nor are all non-Latinos likely enemies.

Stereotyping does not necessarily lead to a feeling of solidarity or to common action, but it may—especially if the individual discovers that the stereotype, no matter how absurd, is inescapable. A Spanish-surnamed person's initial reaction to such stereotyping is often to say, "No, that's not me, you're thinking of those other guys, the ones from country X." That is, the victim seeks to distance himself or herself as much as possible from Spanish-surnamed persons with other accents, other colors, or other income levels. But repeated encounters of this type tend to build up a rage that can be directed against the presumed authors of the stereotypes.

Besides the labeling, the most we can say is that there are a few widely shared problems, common to many Puerto Ricans, Mexicans, Cubans, Dominicans, Central Americans, and others. Among them: lack of a voice in political decisions, ignorance of the majority language, and limited access to good jobs and housing. For many individuals, these problems are exacerbated by undocumented immigrant status, racial discrimination, or both. And finally, especially among immigrants or children of immigrants, there are often behavioral and psychological problems due to cultural displacement.

But none of these problems is universal. There are plenty of people with Spanish surnames who are well off, culturally assimilated, English dominant, socially white, politically vocal, and clinically sane. There are others with darker skin who have also adjusted to this society and are also prospering, at least by their own definitions. Such people are found not only among the wealthier Cubans in Dade County but among all the Hispanic groups—Mexicans, Puerto Ricans, or South Americans—in all parts of the country. These are sometimes the ones most interested in "delumping," or distancing themselves from the problems of other people who just happen to have similar surnames.

Also, if we consider only the poorer, more discriminated against, and lesser assimilated Hispanics, none of their problems are exclusive to Hispanics, but are shared by poor blacks and all other cultural minorities.

## The Real Agenda

Yes, as Luis Núñez grouses, everybody thinks everybody should get together, but when appeals for Hispanic unity—or, even more problematic, unity between Hispanics and other "people of color"—are heeded at all, the forces summoned are so disparate that they check one another's efforts. This is why umbrella organizations are reduced to the feeble, token gestures Torres calls "the business of quiet lobbying."[49]

Much of the political activity by Hispanics is nonelectoral, not quite outlaw politics—that is, not in open defiance of the established system—but outside it, premised on different values and goals.

Of course, there is a lot of collective behavior which may not lead to sustained efforts to redistribute power. Street gangs, like those Luis Rodríguez writes about, for example, may get politicized, but only under exceptional conditions. Trade-union agitation may be politicized at the top—Dennis Rivera, the dynamic president of the Health and Hospitals Workers Union "1199," is a savvy participant on the left edge of the Democratic party—whether or not politics are on the minds of the militants.

This means political analysis should also focus on these other agitators in local issues; there may be key, gifted political leaders who don't bother to vote.

We also need to look at the students. Agitations such as that at Cornell in November 1993, supposedly over defacing of a Latino artwork, the 1993 hunger strike for a Chicano Studies Program at UCLA, or the large and rowdy demonstrations against tuition increases at state schools in New York over the years and again in 1995 are rehearsals or practice confrontations for later, adult politics.

By the 1990s, the rough contours of the Hispanic agenda have begun to become apparent. Cuban Republicans and Mexican-American Democrats from California and Puerto Rican Democrats (and the occasional Mexican-American or Puerto Rican Republican) and the various political tendencies among smaller groups, such as the scattered Central Americans, Dominicans, and Colombians, have found areas in which they can agree. Theirs is a compromise agenda, to be sure, not fully satisfying the desires of any of its constituent groups, who continue to pursue their own more narrowly defined agendas. And ethnic rivalries between Chicanos and Puerto Ricans, Puerto Ricans and Dominicans, Central Americans and Cubans, and so on, can still be fierce. But there is a broad consensus which draws Hispanics together and distinguishes them from other forces in American politics.

But whether there are any especially Latino or Hispanic issues has by now become beside the point. There is a Hispanic agenda, although it is usually an unspoken one. It has two main points. First, it is clear that in order to have any credibility at all with their supposed constituents, Hispanic leaders have to be seen to be defending the interests of the working poor. This is because much of their constituency is the working poor, and because even a Hispanic who is a well-off professional is likely to be insulted and stereotyped by assumptions about the working, and nonworking, poor. These must be uplifted as part of the defense of one's own dignity, so that one does not need to feel embarrassed about being Hispanic. This priority means that politicians must defend social services and job and housing creation—or risk very serious challenges from other Hispanic politicians who do. It also means it will be very unlikely for a Hispanic politician of either party to support measures like one proposed by the Republican majority of the 104th Congress to cut off Medicare, unemployment, and welfare benefits to legal aliens. It will be hard to get many of them to agree to harsh measures like California's Proposition 187 against *illegal* aliens, partly because many of their constituents have relatives who are illegal aliens, partly because even their other constituents are worried that they will suffer discrimination because they are suspected of being illegal, and partly because most of their constituents believe it is just plain unfair to deprive children of education and their parents of health benefits no matter what their status.

The second and more important point on the Hispanic agenda is both broader and deeper. It is to make the Hispanics' presence felt and respected. That is the broadest Hispanic agenda: respect for themselves, their language, and their culture. It is the one point that Democrats and Republicans, Cubans, and Mexicans (and everybody else), middle-class and poor Hispanics, can all agree on.

# 7

# Image Makers

TO A COMMUNITY STRUGGLING TO BE BORN, the sights and sounds and phrases by which it represents itself matter. When a Hispanic arts official declares that public funding for the arts "is a matter of life or death," she is scarcely exaggerating.[1] The imagined community is literally inconceivable without its images.

The blatant display of private passions in murals on expressway walls, the retelling or invention of communal histories in movies and books, and the making of a distinctive noise are all urgent efforts to shout: "We are!" (*"¡Somos!"*). And in that shout the culture makers define a "we," a *nosotros* (implicit in *somos*) that can then be conjugated with even more politically charged verbs like *recordamos*, *queremos*, *exigimos* (we remember, we desire, we demand).

It is different for people whose images of themselves are confirmed every day by their experiences in the dominant culture. Middle-class Frenchmen in France, say, or Japanese in Japan, or English-speaking white Americans in the United States see faces and hear accents like their own whenever they deal with people in authority and see these and other aspects of their culture reflected back to them on television and billboards. They do not need artists to do this and so look to art, if at all, for more private, personal purposes reflecting individual talents and tastes. In a settled, established society producing, viewing, or collecting art are activities that set one and one's circle apart rather than bringing the entire culture together.

In contrast, in a community that is just imagining itself into being, like the Hispanic nation, artists perform their more ancient function of summoning the entire people not on the basis of the shared tastes of a few but claiming to represent the shared peoplehood of all. Or rather, others read such claims into their art, even if the artists themselves are trying to do something entirely different. No matter how idiosyncratic, how intensely personal their vision, their work will be regarded as a totem of their tribe.

The idea that there *is* a Hispanic community is now so thoroughly accepted by critics, dealers, and funding agencies that they presume any artist who has a Spanish surname is somehow representative of it—even if the artist objects. Thus, to get support or to be included in an exhibit, an artist may have to accept the "Latino-Hispanic" label.

But it is not the Anglo art establishment alone, or even primarily, that creates this presumption. The Hispanic mass media boost any *artista* (the word covers performers as well as composers, writers, and visual artists) they can conceivably claim as one of their own, even one with such shallow U.S. Latino roots as the Spanish crooner Julio Iglesias, who qualifies because he has a following in the United States and a home in Florida. Other artists from Latin America who have no special links to Latino communities in the United States, such as the Venezuelan sculptor Marisol, the Colombian painter and sculptor Fernando Botero, or the Cuban painter Wifredo Lam (whose influences were mainly French and African) are likewise extolled as "ours" ("*los nuestros*"). Closet Latinos who started their careers under non-Latino names—like Rita Hayworth and Gilbert Roland—are sometimes "outed" posthumously. It is as though the publicists believed that Hispanics truly were a single biological race whose virtues could be demonstrated by a few outstanding specimens.

Latino intellectuals, especially those in ethnic studies departments in universities, also demand totemic readings. In their courses and writings and by the very act of participating in programs or departments called Chicano, Cuban, Puerto Rican, or Latino Studies, they require us to look at the work of writers and other artists of Hispanic background for what they say about *nosotros*, the collective self. And they may severely scold those who, like West Coast writer Richard Rodriguez, renounce their Latino fealties.

Apart from such institutional pressures, many Hispanic artists feel compelled to confront the issue of identity for their own reasons. Just as James Baldwin found he had to write "about being a Negro" in order to "unlock the gate" to write about other things, José Antonio Villarreal had to write about growing up "pocho"; Piri Thomas, about being a black New York Puerto Rican; and Richard Rodriguez, about unbecoming Mexican.[2] Visual artists like Ana Mendieta, Andrés Serrano, the members of the Royal Chicano Air Force, Judith Baca, and Pepón Osorio have created powerful images that are both intensely personal and emblematic of their social condition. Even in music, no matter how eclectic their influences—American jazz being especially powerful—Latino musicians from Willie Colón to Linda Ronstadt have wanted to go back to their "roots" in the rhythms of their ancestors.

## The Hispanic National Anthem

Music has been the vanguard of the Latino cultural invasion. Long before the physical presence of *hispanos* in the United States had become a political issue, Xavier Cugat, Desi Arnaz, Carlos Gardel (the *zorzal criollo*, or "Argentine songbird") Tito Puente, and Machito had found North American fans. Ernesto Lecuona's songs became so popular—"The Evening Breeze" is one of them—that few Americans even thought of them as foreign.

"Latin music is excited," comments Cuban-American culture critic Enrique Fernández in the *New York Times*. "While the English-language love song drips with honey or violates your ears, Latin ballads are full of something foreign to American culture: passion."[3]

Not exactly. "Passion" is hardly foreign to American culture. Americans feel so deeply about some things that we fought a civil war that was even bloodier than the Mexican Revolution, and all those people marching or acting for or against abortion, budget cuts, or gun control are *intense*. What I think Fernández really means is: Latin music, and Latino culture generally, is much less embarrassed about openly expressing sexual desire. Perhaps Anglos like Latin music because it says what they feel but cannot easily say.

As the Spanish-speaking population has grown, so has the

number of its musical *artistas*. Recording and performing in Spanish in the United States, they draw huge audiences from other Spanish speakers in this country and throughout the Spanish-speaking world plus a sizable minority of English-speaking Americans. The Cuban Americans Gloria Estefan and Jon Secada and the late Mexican-American *artista* Selena Quintillana have been among the recent Grammy winners who have drawn enormous audiences. The Panamanian Rubén Blades and the U.S. Puerto Rican Willie Colón, sometimes together and sometimes separately, also draw enormous multicultural audiences. And there have always been *artistas* who, while little known to Anglos, had a large enough following in their own communities in the United States to make a modest living from their work.

For the deracinated children and grandchildren of Puerto Ricans and other Hispanics on the U.S. mainland, the surge in popularity of Latin music has often been the main stimulus to their re-identifying themselves with things Hispanic. Sometimes this works in very specific and measurable ways. New York sociologist Clara Rodríguez (herself of Puerto Rican descent) was struck by the great popularity among high school students in New York of the all-boy pop singing group from Puerto Rico, Menudo, in the early 1980s.

One surprising development, she notes, "was the development of Spanish-language readership" among high school girls. "Young girls who had never read or studied Spanish were buying *Las Noticias del Mundo* so that they could read the Menudo articles that appeared every day. Working their way through those articles, they learned more Spanish than they could in a year's schoolwork."[4]

Every national movement needs to make its national noise.[5] The national anthem of the Hispanic nation is written *en clave* (in code) on key and in many cases to the rhythm of the *claves*, the short, thick dowels that are clacked together to keep time in much popular Caribbean music. It is not a single melody or set of lyrics; it would be hopeless to try to get everybody concerned to agree on one choice out of such a wealth of possibilities. The anthem is a whole family of sounds, it is the idea of making certain kinds of music, very diverse in rhythm and intent, yet all recognizable as somehow *nuestro*, unmistakably "Latin."[6]

### "Sailing Out" of Despair

Not only is it evident that the imagined community could not exist without its artists; more poignantly, it is also true that some of its artists could not exist without imagining that community. In the grimmest neighborhoods and prisons of the United States, there are some who claim to find the strength to survive only in poetry, painting, or other art that connects them to something beyond themselves. What these barrio and prison artists find, or think they find, when they dive deep inside themselves to that place where art comes from is not the weakness of one wretched individual with a drug or liquor habit, a lengthy police record, or too many hungry babies, but the strength of a whole imaginary nation. Sometimes, as in the case of the New York Puerto Rican playwright and screenwriter Miguel Piñero, whose drug habit finally killed him, the connection is not enough to save them from self-destruction. Sometimes it is.

One of those who is still alive and producing, despite many episodes of degradation and close calls with death, is the Chicano poet Jimmy Santiago Baca, who remembers, "I was born a poet one noon, gazing at weeds and creosoted grass at the base of a telephone pole outside my grilled cell window. The words I wrote then sailed me out of myself, and I was transported and meta-morphosed into the images they made.... I wrote to sublimate my rage, from a place where all hope is gone, from a madness of having been damaged too much, from a silence of killing rage."[7]

Certainly there are image makers of Hispanic origin in the United States whose ethnicity seems irrelevant or is at most a minor theme in their work.[8] But for most, institutional and com-munity pressures, combined with their own personal artistic and psychological needs, make a preoccupation with ethnic identity inescapable.

### Doubly Plural

The cry of ¡*Somos*! (We are!) is heard often in Hispanic gatherings. Some organizations even make the word part of their name, as does the annual meeting of Hispanic community and political leaders in New York *Somos el Futuro* (We are the future) or as an acronym for the entire name, like the West Coast organization SOMOS. But these reiterated declarations of unity beg the main question: Who are this "we" they're talking about?

The Hispanic "we" is doubly plural, a *nosotros* of *nosotroses*: we Chicanos, we Boricuas, we Cubans, and so on, and it is not always clear whether the speaker is referring to just his or her own group, to all Hispanics, or to some subset. These groupings are further divided by class, length of time in the United States, and more parochial prejudices like creed and color. To the politicians, these divisions have so far proved insuperable obstacles to creating a viable Hispanic lobby—mostly because they themselves exploit the divisions to get elected, each claiming to be a more authentic representative of the tribe than any of his or her rivals.

But the diversity that is an obstacle course for politicians can be a playground for image makers. Artists are far better positioned than politicians to induce people to see what they have in common, for what they seek is not the biggest slice of a finite vote but a place in our imaginations, which are infinitely capacious. Chicano imagery is not pitted against images of Puerto Rican, Anglo, African, or any other origin. Instead, all meet and combine into new imaginative possibilities.

## The Past as a Working Hypothesis

The assertion of identity begins with the reinterpretation of the past, which is a never-ending project. The promoters of a new identity want to be able to declare definitively, "We are what we are because we got this way, and these are the events that made us." Nothing about the past, however, is definitive. The past is multiple and various, so filled with events real and fictitious that they can be combined to tell many different stories, and all interpretations are subject to shifts as people begin asking new questions about the present.[9]

Nobody has understood this better than the Chicano, Puerto Rican, and other Latino artists, who link all manner of memories to create a new past. Public memories of documented political history mingle with myth and more private memories and, further, with the ambiguous signals that emanate from religious icons, movies, and consumer products. And because they are artists, which means they have given themselves license to create, and because they work in a postmodern age, where images from everywhere are instantly accessible, they often draw on several of these memory categories simultaneously.

The main goal for all of them is to develop a set of images that draw strength from their history to empower them in the present. In this pursuit, Chicanos, Puerto Ricans, Cubans, and the more recent immigrant groups discover their convergences as they undertake a *reconquista* of the imagination.

Like Spain's fifteenth-century "reconquest" of its territory from the Moors, the Hispanic *Reconquista* of the imagination is a counteroffensive against political and cultural colonization. The artists have been among the first to understand that Hispanics in the United States and even in Latin America needed to recover the power to define who they were and the events that had made them.

The loss of control by a Hispanic group over its own narrative occurred most clearly in the former northern provinces of New Spain. There marginalization was not just a metaphor but a literal historic event. Within a few years of Mexico's cession of these lands to the United States, their Mexican *plazas* had been turned into Mexican-American *barrios*.

The *Plaza de Armas* (so-called because military revues were sometimes held there) was the geographic and ceremonial center of towns like San Antonio, Albuquerque, San Diego, Los Angeles, and indeed every city laid out according to the Law of the Indies. This open rectangle, extending between the cathedral and the town hall, was where edicts were proclaimed, bulls fought, religious processions initiated, markets and all manner of public events held. The streets demarcating its four sides were the beginning of the street grid for the entire town.

*Barrio*, which as mentioned earlier derives from the Arabic for "outside," still usually means a marginal settlement on the outskirts of a city.[10] One of the most striking examples of the plaza-to-barrio transformation occurred in Albuquerque after New Mexico became a U.S. territory. Because the Spanish-speaking town, built around its plaza, was surrounded by valuable agricultural land that the *hispanos* would sell only dearly, the new railroad, when it came, simply bypassed the old town completely and thus avoided paying for an expensive right-of-way. The new Anglo town grew up around the new depot, and Albuquerque's Old Town became the Hispanic barrio and it remained so until its recent redevelopment.[11] A similar process occurred in Los Angeles (Olvera Street) and other cities, where new urban growth occurred away from the old urban centers, leaving Spanish "old towns" on the margins—decaying, ramshackle, and from the outsiders' viewpoint, picturesque barrios. Eventually this picturesqueness would itself come to have commercial value for the Anglo society. The revived interest in our national roots around the time of the U.S. Bicentennial in 1976 and the growing influence of the preservationist movement during the 1980s spurred developers to transform the areas once again. In both Albuquerque and Los Angeles, what had started as ceremonial *plazas* and then become decaying *barrios*, have now been turned into Hispanic theme malls.

Besides being physically displaced from the center, the Mexican Americans were also subjected to expropriation and displacement of their symbols. The displacement came as a new and alien version of Hispanicness was introduced. A few wealthy Anglo settlers in the 1880s and 1890s, looking for a historic past to call their own and finding the actual ruins unimpressive, copied the much-admired (and much-romanticized) feudal antiquity of Europe, and in the former Spanish possessions from Florida to California, imitation Spanish castles and cathedrals were especially popular. Such designs, remote from the cultural memories of the actual Spanish-speaking people in those areas, imported a standard of supposedly high or authentic Spanish culture, of which the architecture, customs, and accents of the local Hispanics were considered mere degraded versions.

In parallel with the fad of medieval and aristocratic Spain, some Anglos of a more populist, democratic bent, particularly in California, turned their sentimentality to the much simpler old missions, whose old ruins had been romanticized in Helen Hunt Jackson's popular novel *Ramona* (1884). There they sought and found antecedents to Americanize the "arts and crafts" movement they had imported from England toward the end of the century, since almost everything the early missions used had been handcrafted locally. The simplicity of the old missions, whose proportions had been determined less by an aesthetic code than by the availability of materials—for example, whether there were large enough trees around for long roof beams—was codified as a "style." Over the next years architects in Anglo California and the Southwest would design mission-style railroad depots, hotels, and even gas stations, often decorated with paintings by Anglo artists of their versions of colonial times. Places were given Spanish or pseudo-Spanish names—there is an Anglo-created town in Arizona, for example, called El Mirage, whose current inhabitants, almost all Mexicans, pronounce it "El mih-RAH-hay," which means nothing in their language. (The Spanish word for mirage is *espejismo.*) In a more blatant gesture that showed what the cultural appropriation was all about, Anglo ranchers got themselves up in costume to celebrate "Old Spanish Days" festivals— *they* were the "grandees" now; the Spanish speakers, their peons. This cultural history explains why Mexican-American artists in the late sixties and early seventies, in the cultural renascence that was the expressive side of *Chicanismo*, would be mainly concerned with reappropriating the imagery and with celebrating aspects of Chicano culture that the Anglos had not refashioned.

The nature of cultural marginalization and colonization has been different and perhaps more complex for the other Hispanic groups, descendants of more recent immigrants, because they were trying to maintain a culture far from their ancestral grounds. Of course, any immigrants, no matter where they are from, are culturally decentered upon arrival. And most, unless they are wealthy, are at least temporarily marginalized in a low-rent district where other people understand their language. In the case of those from Latin America, however, the cultural decentering and marginalization had begun long before migration.

Some aspects of this process in Cuba and Puerto Rico following the 1898 U.S. invasion have already been described, including the restructuring of schools and government institutions on U.S. models and, in the case of Puerto Rico, with English as the medium of instruction. But U.S. culture also penetrated the imaginations of people in those and other Latin American countries in other ways and, much more deeply, through the distribution of phonograph records and movies, particularly in the years just after World War II. The countries of Latin America were a major target for Hollywood exports; although together these countries had less than 10 percent of the world's population, they accounted in 1949 for nearly 20 percent of America's foreign film market.[12]

Such a deep colonization of their fantasy life necessarily affected the attitudes and even actions of many Latin Americans. Here, for example, is the explanation by a working-class woman from Havana, given twenty years after the fact, of how she decided to take the drastic step of emigration to the United States in the mid-1960s:

> I was born in Cuba and didn't leave the island until I was twenty-eight years old, married, and the mother of three children. But I grew up in Hollywood. All throughout my childhood my mother, my brother and I would go to the movies at least two or three times a week....
>
> Ever since I was a little girl I had these grand visions of wearing long satin gowns and fancy hairstyles and living in great fancy mansions with marble staircases. Or else I would imagine myself having my own apartment in New York City and living alone and independently like many of the heroines in the American movies of the 1940's....
>
> When I decided to leave the country I thought it was because the revolution had betrayed me, had betrayed my ideals of a free and just society. But years later I began to realize that the main reason why I'd come to the United States was that I thought I could make those old Hollywood dreams come true, that I could turn the fantasies of my youth into reality.[13]

Alongside the gowns and marble staircases of an imaginary United States, what Latin Americans saw of their own cultures on the silver screen was Paul Muni in the title role of *Juárez* (1939), Tyrone Power in *The Mark of Zorro* (1940), *Blood and Sand* (1941), and the *Captain from Castile* (1947), Marlon Brando in the title role of *Viva Zapata* (1952), and Donald Duck as one of *The Three Caballeros* (1945). As singer-composer, actor, and recent Panamanian presidential candidate Rubén Blades has put it, "Since the silent era of films, Latin culture and its character have been grotesquely distorted and misrepresented."[14]

What the dominant society has fashioned from Latin American culture has often been caricature, adapted to the needs of the dominants for their entertainment. Thus, high on the agenda of all Hispanic artists, not only the Mexican-American ones, would be to take back their imagery.

## Telling the Stories

The heavy borrowing of imagery by outsiders did not necessarily remove it or destroy it in the communities that had generated it. People continued to worship in the old churches, for example. Nor had everything been borrowed. Much of the culture remained hidden from the makers of cowboy movies, novels, festivals, and other works with Hispanic themes. Or, if not precisely hidden, was considered unusable by the Hollywood image factory. Among the things that were hidden from all but the most astute observers were the intimacies of childhood, the conflicts and satisfactions of growing up in a culture whose values were sharply different from those of the dominant society.

The ethnic memoir, whether fictionalized or presented as fact, has long been a favorite genre in American literature, and is well represented by African-American, Jewish-American, and other minority writers, and now by Hispanics.[15] In their autobiographical fiction and memoirs they can strive to come to terms with their own lingering cultural conflicts while permitting outsiders to glimpse the experiences that have shaped their distinctive world-views. In the case of Hispanic writers, we see how vastly different are those experiences and worldviews that must be melded to make a united Hispanic nation. Growing up Mexican American has not been at all the same as growing up Puerto Rican American or Cuban American, and even within each of these national-origin groups the range of childhood experiences has been very great. Hispanics themselves are very curious about these differences and read one another's memoirs avidly, seeking and often finding common threads—the often comical mix of reverence and blasphemy, the strong sense of obligation to kin, the alternating waves of pride and embarrassment at speaking an alien tongue in an Anglo world, the initial bewilderment when one first encounters color prejudice.

For someone brought up in one culture to participate effectively in another one that is radically different requires a tearing away from the values, language, and relationships of one's earliest experiences. Remembering and coming to terms with those early years can be therapeutic, a way to put the pieces back together again and get on with one's life. The personal memoir is also a way of affirming the validity of all those things, not just skin color but also psychological and behavioral traits—gestures, attitudes toward relationships, music and food preferences—that continue to make one recognizably different from those who have grown up in the dominant culture. The little incidents of childhood are especially cherished because they were uniquely one's own—the least accessible to outsiders and thus the least corrupted by ethnic caricatures they encountered later.

## Up From Mexico

The earliest English-language Hispanic memoir, thinly disguised as fiction, was José Antonio Villarreal's novel *Pocho* (1959). This Mexican word—from the Uto-Aztecan (Mexican Indian) *potzi*, describing an animal that is short or tailless—here refers to a U.S.-reared person of Mexican origin who is comically inept and thus "tailless" in two cultures. As Villarreal's protagonist Richard Rubio explains to a girl who has just arrived from Mexico, "I am a Pocho, and we speak like this because here in California we make Castilian words out of English words."[16]

Richard (born Ricardo) is the only male child of a proud but barely literate veteran of the Mexican Revolution and his ignorant and docile peasant wife. Growing up in the multiethnic farming community of Santa Clara, California, in the 1930s, the boy watches his family's old Mexican traditions crumble as he and his sisters grow up as English speakers and his father, no longer a man on horseback but a pedestrian storekeeper in a foreign land, finds little support for his pretensions of Mexican dignity. Even Richard's long-suffering mother finally rebels against her husband's authority and his adulteries.

More reflective than embittered, the old man eventually explains to Richard what he has learned in what is probably a version of the author's own take on life in the United States.

> That is the wonder of this country of yours, my son. All the
> people who are pushed around in the rest of the world come

here, because here they can maybe push someone else around. There is something in people, put there only to make them forget what was done to them in other times, so that they can turn around and do the same thing to other people. That is why they teach their children to call you a cholo and a dirty Mexican....It is not in retribution because they remember they were once mistreated, my son; it is because they forget.[17]

Of the *pachucos* of the 1940s with their zoot-suit costumes and bizarre slang, Villarreal writes,

They had a burning contempt for people of different ancestry, whom they called Americans, and a marked hauteur toward México and toward their parents for their old-country ways....They needed to feel superior to something, which is a natural thing. The result was that they attempted to segregate themselves from both their cultures, and became truly a lost race.[18]

The boy resolves to determine his own values and to become a writer. The novel ends in 1942 when, at seventeen, he joins the navy to see the world and fulfill his destiny.

The book has been labeled as "somewhat of an embarrassment" by one Chicano critic.[19] Mainly, this is because while the book contains valuable testimony of its period and thus cannot be ignored, it is hardly upbeat about Chicano identity. The three identity options suggested are old-style Mexican, like Richard Rubio's father, which is obviously unsuited to modern U.S. life; "pachuco," which Villarreal considers pathetic; and "pocho," an in-between state where, the author seems to imply, the Mexican American is bound to remain. Second, it is not very sophisticated literature, its episodic structure generating little dramatic tension.

A more mystical fictional memoir that Chicano critics generally treat with more respect is Rudolfo Anaya's *Bless Me, Ultima* (1972). It is told in the voice of a child who was protected by the magic of the old *curandera* (spiritual healer) Ultima as he became a man in rural New Mexico. It occupies a unique place in our literature as testimony to a little-known peasant way of life here in the United States. The dreamy narrative idealizes this existence but does illustrate an authentic variant in Mexican-American life.[20]

One of the most controversial works of Mexican-American

biography has been Richard Rodriguez's meditations on his culture-rending California childhood, *Hunger of Memory*.²¹ This elegantly written memoir challenges the validity and usefulness of Chicano consciousness and for this reason has provoked strong condemnation by self-defined Chicanos, similar to the charges of "self-hate" leveled at members of other ethnic groups who question the group's assumptions.

Rodriguez was the youngest son of parents who had immigrated from Mexico shortly before his birth. In their Sacramento home, everything familial and intimate occurred in Spanish, while everything public and authoritative in the boy's life occurred in English. The nuns in his Catholic school urged the parents to stop speaking to him in Spanish, which they dutifully did—and because their English was halting, this language shift suddenly cut him off from the easy and intimate discourse he cherished in family life. But then, not only because of the nun's urging but because of everything he saw around him, Ricardo became Richard and dropped the accent over his surname. He deliberately chose English, the "public" language, and in *Hunger of Memory* he urges other Hispanics to do the same. He is critical of bilingual education, which he sees as perpetuating the Hispanics' linguistic inferiority in this society.

Rodriguez's mastery of English has been a resounding success: Along with the Cuban-American journalist Enrique Fernández and a few others, he has been one of our most eloquent and prolific "insider" commentators writing in English on the evolving culture of the Hispanic nation. He remains an insider because, even though he has decided not to be a Chicano, Richard Rodriguez cannot escape, and has given up trying to escape, the "Hispanic" identity thrust on him by others. He cannot escape because of his Mexican-Indian looks, his surname (even without its accent) and because of his own preoccupations; after all, he brought up the topic of his identity in his first book. Although he has written on many other topics, including his life as a gay man in San Francisco, his most recent collection of essays goes back to questions of identity, with the title *Days of Obligation: An Argument With My Mexican Father*.²²

Some of his critics have been disappointed by Rodriguez's refusal to be a spokesman for Chicanismo. One has complained that his "undialectical opposition between self and society...is a perfect example of our tendency to disguise the force of ideology behind the mask of aesthetics."[23]

But Rodriguez is not disguising ideology so much as artfully expressing his ambivalence. When dealing with such a subtle and complex notion as "identity," we should be skeptical of voices that are not ambivalent. There really are two sides to the issue, gains and losses associated with emphasizing one's cultural peculiarity as a Chicano or Hispanic or stressing instead what one has in common with the outside Anglo culture, and it is important to be reminded of these gains and losses.

The interpenetration of these two cultures was made evident in a startling way by an apparently authentic Chicano memoir that turned out to have been the work of an Anglo. Following by two years the publication of *Hunger of Memory*, the next big *escándalo*, or *cause célèbre*, in Chicano and Latino literary circles generally was *Famous All Over Town* (1984), by the mysterious but obviously talented Danny Santiago.

Told in the first person in a vigorous mix of English street slang and the Chicano dialect called *caló*, the novel tells the story of Chato Medina, a Chicano adolescent in East Los Angeles in trouble in his school, in a neighborhood being torn apart by new construction, and with a family where the father is boastful and arrogant in Spanish but turns meek and ashamed when he has to switch into English to deal with the *gabachos*—the quaint old Mexican term for Anglos. The boy is getting to feel like an absolute nobody until finally, in an exuberant gesture of self-affirmation, he goes on a wild spree, painting his *placa* (the stylized signature of a graffiti artist) on everything in sight, which is the only way he can imagine to become "famous all over town."

Danny Santiago had already won praise for his earlier short stories, and *Famous* won an important literary prize, the Richard and Hinda Rosenthal Foundation Award from the American Academy of Arts and Letters. Naturally, the Hispanic media wanted to interview this young Chicano author who showed so much promise, but only his agent knew how to find him. It turned out, after the author was flushed from hiding by the press, that he was in reality a seventy-something ex-playwright named Daniel L. James, who had been a radical in the 1940s and had given up writing after being blacklisted. In recent years he had been a social worker in East Los Angeles.

Latino writers cried foul. They considered that the old *gabacho*—who has since died—had posed as something he was not in order to steal recognition that was due their own works. James appeared to be deeply embarrassed by having his cover blown and said that after his painful experiences during the McCarthy years the only way he could write at all was as his alter ego Danny Santiago. This is not so hard to understand; Argentine writer Jorge Luis Borges confessed that he himself did not write his works but that they were instead composed by *el otro yo* (another self), also (as it happened) named Borges. James, too, had another self to do the writing; he called his "Santiago" (the Spanish name for St. James).[24]

One aspect of the book that infuriated some Chicanos was its ironic tone—but only after they learned that the author was himself not Chicano. Chicanos mock each other and themselves all the time but, like most people, cannot tolerate mockery by an outsider. As long as James was able to maintain his persona as "Danny Santiago," they were able to laugh with him. When his *otro yo* was redefined publicly as an imposter, Chicano nationalists were outraged. But they should have looked at the book more closely. In comparison to Rodriquez's *Hunger of Memory* and certain other books by authentic Mexican Americans, such as Adalberto Joel Acosta's *Chicanos Can Make It* (1971), the protagonist of *Famous* is much more affirmative about his ethnic identity and far more defiant of the dominant society.[25] Surely there is room in the Chicano and Latino consciousness for both these provocative works, *Hunger* and *Famous*.

A younger writer, Dagoberto Gilb, has recently brought us insights into a far different kind of Mexican-American life, that of the working class in our Southwest border region. The short stories in his collection *The Magic of Blood* (1993) deal with construction workers and drifters, and construction workers who unwillingly become drifters, men who are fully integrated into a common ethos of the whole Southwest proletariat, of whatever race.[26] This, Gilb seems to suggest, may be a glimpse of the future not only of the border but of all those places where the Hispanic and Anglo nations collide. It is a society still riven by conflicts, but the

important ones are based more on differences of class than on
color or accent.

## Jumping the Puddle

The first important Puerto Rican memoir written in English was
Piri Thomas's story of growing up among violence, decay, and
drugs in Spanish Harlem in the late forties and fifties, *Down These
Mean Streets* (1967). This was the precursor of the literary move-
ment that in the mid-1970s would take the name "Nuyorican" (for
New York Puerto Rican).[27]

Earlier generations of Puerto Rican writers in New York, such
as the radical journalists Bernardo Vega and Jesús Colón or the
poet Julia de Burgos, remembered life on the island (Puerto Rico,
not Manhattan) and were most comfortable writing in Spanish.[28]
They had a clear idea of who they were and no reason to question
their membership in one of the great cultural and intellectual
traditions of the world, the one that had begun in Spain and been
enriched by its mingling with other cultures in the Spanish-
speaking New World. And this may be why they felt no urgent need
to write exhaustively about their own childhoods. Childhood had
been the least problematic period of their lives.

But the New York–born children of the poor and mostly poorly
educated Puerto Ricans who "jumped the puddle"—*brincaron el
charco*—in DC-7s to La Guardia Airport in the 1940s or who had
arrived earlier packed onto steamers, like the famous *Marine Tiger*,
lost their connection to that proud Spanish tradition. In a climate
and concrete canyons that were nothing like the place their parents
remembered, surrounded by people who had no comprehension
of and little sympathy for their culture, these children knew Puerto
Rico only as a chimera glimpsed in photographs and the stories of
their elders.

Piri Thomas's was the first of this generation to write of being
made to feel ashamed of speaking Spanish and of looking neither
quite white nor quite black. That he could not only survive the
mean streets but write a book about it—and in proper English,
which must have astonished his early teachers—was a major
triumph. He wrote of his confusion about whether he was "black"
or "white" because he "came out" dark like his father and his

siblings were lighter, like his mother—a confusion that was entirely the product of encounters with the racial values outside his household, because within his Puerto Rican family such distinctions had not carried any special privileges. His meditations on such experiences, a process of discovery and healing for himself, helped other New York Latinos find a vocabulary to talk about their own experiences and thus heal themselves.

There have been many New York Puerto Rican memoirs since Thomas's, adding detail and variation to the basic urban narrative. But more recently a memoir has appeared that recounts a Puerto Rican childhood dramatically different, closer to the experience of many of the immigrants who arrive here from other, poorer countries of Latin America. Esmeralda Santiago's book *When I Was Puerto Rican* tells of a girlhood in tropical rural poverty and wretched slums from which she only later arrived, in early adolescence, at a tenement in Brooklyn.[29]

The title has disturbed some American-reared descendants of migrants from the island, for it seems to imply that one can cease being Puerto Rican. Santiago has claimed that she was not trying to be provocative, but merely to describe what was for her an obvious transformation. Until early adolescence, her only language was Spanish, her wisdom a mix of barnyard observation and the cryptic, resigned complaints of women about the infidelities of men, and her knowledge of the United States limited to her father's muted anti-imperialism and occasional glimpses of pink-skinned people who did not know how to behave. One scene lampoons the stiff, overdressed American experts who lecture the women in the rural hamlet on nutrition, recommending completely inappropriate and inaccessible foods, like apples, while confessing ignorance of the nutritional value of the local breadfruit. And no reader will soon forget the little girl's terror in the Santurce slum, when she has to pee over a hole in the floorboards above the horridly putrid sewage of the *barrio*.

When such experiences are what "being Puerto Rican" calls to mind, then clearly attending the High School of the Performing Arts in New York, graduating from Harvard, and becoming an English-language journalist in Massachusetts, as Esmeralda Santiago did later, is something different.[30]

## Revolutionary Repercussions

Oscar Hijuelos, who grew up in New York as the son of Cuban immigrants, represents still another kind of Hispanic experience. He is one of those artists who have had an ethnic identity thrust upon them from outside. "Until relatively recently," he told a Cuban-American interviewer, "when the category of Latino writer was created, I always considered myself a working-class writer." But *Mambo Kings Play Songs of Love*, his second novel, won him a Pulitzer Prize, a movie contract, and a lot of attention from reporters who needed a way to peg him. "Working-class writer" is apparently no longer an active journalistic category, but ethnicity is in, so he found himself labeled a "Latino."

"How would you describe a twelve-year-old kid who goes down to the Village to listen to jazz on a Sunday afternoon?" he asked, describing himself. "Or who went to the Apollo Theater in Harlem to watch James Brown or played softball in Harlem, alongside a Dutch-Italian friend? Those experiences were not specifically Cuban at all, but simply part of being raised in New York."

His most famous creations are the brothers Néstor and César Castillo, onstage and on-page stars of *Mambo Kings Play Songs of Love* (1989).[31] Although told as a memory of Néstor's young son, that is merely a narrative device. The main stories are of the two men and, secondly, of Néstor's long-suffering wife, Delores (for *dolores*, sufferings). Néstor, morose and self-absorbed, and César, a boisterous and generous hedonist, migrate from Cuba to New York in the forties—as did Hijuelos's own parents. The two enjoy a brief moment of fame as the Mambo Kings in their otherwise hard and unglamorous working-class lives. Enveloped in his longing for a past that never was, Néstor ignores the love and real possibilities around him and kills himself in a car crash about halfway through the book, leaving his brother free to take over the rest of the novel. César is Néstor's temperamental opposite, a man who leaves no opportunity for a good time, whether music, booze, or an attractive woman, unseized. We follow the slide of César's musical career but never of his spirits until, bloated from drinking and overeating, he literally explodes from inability to resist pleasure. A reader may feel sorry for the old fool for not taking better care of himself, but envious, too, because he has had a hell of a good time.

Pressed to define his relationship to "Cubanness," Hijuelos has said, "I would say I am a New York working-class writer whose first books have been meditations on certain emotional responses to having been brought up with Cuban parentage."

Distancing himself further from any social or political obligations that might be imputed to him because of his Cuban heritage, he added, "I don't presume to write a novel about the Miami exile community. Many of my relatives came up from Cuba after Castro, but I don't know what it really feels like growing up as an exile in Miami. There's a whole world of literature there that is waiting, and will come, and is being written now. There's room for many different points of view."[32]

One of the people producing that literature about the Cuban exile community is Cristina García, whose fictionalized memoir of Cuban-American childhood is evocatively titled *Dreaming in Cuban*.[33] Told from the point of view of eleven-year-old Pilar Puente, who, like the author, was born in 1959—the year of the triumph of the Cuban revolution—and is raised in Brooklyn, the novel is taken up mostly by the girl's dreams about the members of her family who have been separated by the revolution. What she dreams is the story of three generations of women; their male partners appear only vaguely and incidentally. There is a grandmother who remains in Cuba and is a fervent *fidelista*, a mother who has good reason to hate the revolution (she was raped by a *miliciano*) and is an absolutist on the subject, and young Pilar, who longs for reconnections with relatives and a place she knows less from memory than from dreams.

What was extraordinary about the novel, and gave it such a strong impact on other Cubans who have grown up in this country, was that it treated sympathetically the people—or at any rate the women—of "both Cubas," the real island of Cuba and the imaginary Cuba re-created by the exiles. The exile characters are emotionally complex, filled with recrimination and bitterness against the revolution but also with their warmth and close family loyalties.

## Other Realities

Among the Hispanics who have come from other parts of Latin America—Dominicans, Colombians, Hondurans, Peruvians, Salvadorans, et al.—there are many who are writing about the experience, almost all of them in Spanish.[34] Some of this work is very provocative and deserves a wider audience. The market for books in Spanish in this country is rapidly growing, but of course those writers who want the widest possible audience, and especially those who have been here long enough to feel comfortable in the language, will be writing more and more in English.

Julia Alvarez's comic fictionalized memoir *How the García Girls Lost Their Accent* is the first such work in English by a Dominican American. It is a series of episodes in the lives of four sisters and their parents after they flee to the United States from the Dominican Republic to escape the dictatorship of Rafael Leonidas Trujillo (in power from 1930 until his assassination in 1961). The running joke is that Papi, there a distinguished physician who here cannot learn English, find a decent job, or abide American "libertinism," strives futilely to maintain old-country patriarchal discipline over his rapidly Americanizing and sexually inquisitive daughters. Mami (Mommy), much more adaptable, supports the family, negotiates internal peace, and doodles inventions of gadgets that she never tries to produce. It has funny, charming moments that are probably recognizable to immigrant daughters from many ethnic backgrounds.

Jaime Manrique has produced the first English-language fictional memoir by a New York Colombian. About a young adult's difficulties in being allowed to act like an adult, Manrique's funny picaresque, *Latin Moon in Manhattan* (1992),[35] deals with a common cultural dichotomy. The hero and narrator is a grown man who is happily and nuttily gay, hip, and American in his English-language life in Manhattan, but when he returns to his mother's neighborhood and her Colombian friends, he cannot escape being put into the closet by an immigrant community that cannot imagine that its ways are not the best ways and its doings are not the center of the civilized world. The comic high point is the narrator's wedding to a flamboyant lesbian—who is dealing in her own way with the same dilemma—in a spectacularly formal affair in a Queens restaurant that is only momentarily disturbed by a narcotics gang that drops in uninvited, guns blazing.

## Writing in the Central Plaza

Hispanic writers like José Antonio Villarreal and Rudolfo Anaya, even if they wrote in English, were long isolated in a barrio of the American imagination, regarded by the few who had heard of their work as interesting but marginal phenomena. This is no longer true. Writers like Gilb, Hijuelos, Judith Ortiz Cofer, Sandra Cisneros, and many others are mingling with everybody else in its central plaza. They are absorbing and responding to other American writers, from Faulkner to Raymond Carver. And today's American writers and readers, of all ethnic backgrounds, are responding to them. What we learn from them is not just the folklore of an eccentric minority but something important about what it means to be an American. And as more and more Americans speak and think with a Spanish accent, what they have to tell us will be increasingly important to hear.

## Creating an Intelligentsia

Parallel with their struggles for political representation and community control, Puerto Ricans, Chicanos, and other Americans of Spanish-speaking background fought in the 1960s for a beachhead in the universities. Universities were, of course, gateways to middle-class prosperity and respectability: a way out of the barrio. This was why the Puerto Rican organization Aspira (founded in New York in 1961) established dropout prevention programs in public high schools through after-school clubs where Puerto Rican students could take pride in their history and culture and where they were constantly encouraged and guided to prepare for college. Better college preparation was also one of the main demands of Chicano students in the Los Angeles high school "blowouts" of 1968. Latinos on both coasts experienced their high schools as colonizing institutions where their language, style, and talents were constantly disparaged. The high schools had to be changed before there could be a significant increase in the Hispanic college population.

There had always been Hispanic scholars and philosophers, both clerical and lay, from the earliest days of the Spanish colonies. Few were academics in the modern sense, and none of them had tenure. Among those intellectuals who had the greatest influence on U.S. Hispanics in the nineteenth century, José Martí was a freelance writer and lecturer, Ramón Emeterio Betances had his medical practice to fall back on, and the Mexican and occasional San Antonio resident Francisco I. Madero was another journalist. Bernardo Vega, perhaps not one of the most original thinkers but a man who spent much of his time writing and thinking, rolled cigars for a living.

However, the milieu that could support an independent Spanish-speaking intellectual in the United States virtually disappeared after World War I. In fact, in the next decades freelance opportunities diminished for everybody, whether they worked in English or Spanish. Television, radio, and movies took over more of the media market but in the United States offered few opportunities for Spanish speakers, whether as writers or performers. Cuban band leader Desi Arnaz was the first and for a long time the only Latino visible on television. Television also sucked up most of the advertising dollars, so that magazines that paid fees to writers became scarcer and paid less. Those who could afford to devote themselves fully to the independent development of ideas in the United States were reduced to small clusters of journalists at the few surviving high-brow journals and university professors. Hardly any of them were people with Spanish background, and the few that were, like the Venezuelan-American journalist Tom Ybarra and the philosopher and Harvard professor George Santayana (whose father was a Spaniard), rarely concerned themselves with Hispanic communities in this country.[36] Not for lack of brainpower but because of the lack of education and employment opportunities for their thinkers, the barrios were nearly bereft of serious and well-informed intellectual leadership. This was what the student activists and their faculty allies in the late sixties intended to provide.

Around 1965 university enrollments had begun swelling because of the baby boom and because so many young men were seeking student deferments from the draft for the war in Vietnam. Thanks to programs like Aspira and a few enlightened high school teachers and counselors, a small but growing number of those students were Hispanics, although hardly any of their professors were.

If escape from the barrio was the initial reason for going to college, after young people got there, something else happened to them. They encountered students of different backgrounds. The diligent ones found their way to the library and often to a few sensitive and patient teachers, and they learned to pose more articulate and more probing questions. Like the Jewish, Italian, and other working-class youth who had preceded them in the 1920s and 1930s and the African-American youth whose college enrollments were also increasing in the 1960s, the first-generation Hispanic college students became tremendously impressed by the power of ideas and of the university as an incubator for ideas.

This student population growth created a demand for more college professors and for increases in their salaries. Having so few alternative opportunities, Latinos of scholarly bent naturally saw these jobs, as well as increased student enrollments from their communities, as worth fighting for. Beginning in 1969, as part of that broader protest movement of the day, Hispanic students, scholars, and their community allies argued, demonstrated, and lobbied for academic programs modeled on the still-new field of black studies. And because it was the sixties, the era of "power to the people," many of these students came to believe it was their historical obligation to "seize" the institutions—as the white radicals had already proclaimed—to make their power accessible to their communities. In the wake of takeovers by mostly white student radicals at Berkeley and Columbia, in 1969 a group of mostly Latino students seized central buildings of New York's City College. In that same year, responding to loud demands, the City University of New York (separate from City College) created a new bilingual campus in the Bronx, named for the Puerto Rican patriot Eugenio María de Hostos, who had first arrived in New York just a hundred years earlier.

Following up on the creation of the *Raza Unida* party, which had been started by students in Texas, the National Association of Chicano Studies was founded in 1972 to give faculty and students a platform for reading papers and to coordinate a push for more Chicano studies on campuses. Its Puerto Rican counterpart would not come into existence for another twenty years. Meanwhile, Puerto Rican studies programs and departments were being established, the most important being the Centro de Estudios Puertorriqueños at Hunter College of the City University of New

York, which, under the direction of political economist Frank Bonilla, grew to be the principal depository of documents on the Puerto Rican diaspora and a major research institution. By the end of the 1980s this movement had created departments or research institutes on dozens of campuses, variously called Chicano, Puerto Rican, Cuban, Hispanic, or Latino studies, or some combination.

In Chicago at the beginning of the 1970s, pressure from Mexican-American and Puerto Rican community and student groups, up against the counterpressure of an academic establishment that distrusted ethnic studies, produced a hybrid, the Center for Latino and Latin American Studies at the University of Illinois, Chicago, in which the "Latino" scholars—focusing on local community folk—shared little beyond a budget and occasional faculty meetings with most of the "Latin Americanists," those specializing in the countries of Latin America.

These ethnically defined university programs have always had to defend themselves from two different kinds of attacks. One comes from those representing themselves as speaking for that imprecise thing called "the community," a code word used by different groups to refer to very different sectors and interest groups outside the university. Typical charges are that the studies program is not doing enough to widen access to the university or is not conducting the kind of research that is "relevant" to the community's problems. Some of these programs have gone to great lengths to avoid or answer such objections. For example, the Centro de Estudios Puertorriqueños at Hunter College has insisted, over the strenuous objections of its host institution, on keeping its section of the Hunter College library accessible to community people so that anyone who is going to that section is admitted without having to show an ID. Others, such as the Latino and Latin American Studies Program at the University of Illinois, Chicago, have had more of a reputation of being inaccessible to the community.

The other kind of criticism is almost the opposite, that the program is too concerned about pleasing the "community" and is simply not serious as a scholarly enterprise. Critics ask what such a department offers that could not be better studied in other departments with established academic credentials? Why, for example, could not Hispanic-American literature—if there is any worth teaching—be taught in the English department, along with Faulkner and Oates and all the other significant American authors? Or if it is in Spanish, why not teach it in the Spanish department? And why not teach Puerto Rican or Chicano or Dominican or Cuban history in the history department, their community life in the anthropology and sociology departments, and so on? Shelby Steele says that the answer is that these separate ethnic groups want to be "nations unto themselves"[37] and decries the tendency.

Steele complains about what he calls "the New Sovereignty...bestowed upon any group that is able to construct itself around a perceived grievance," his main example being "America's university campuses, where, in the name of their grievances, blacks, women, Hispanics, Asians, Native Americans, gays, and lesbians had hardened into sovereign constituencies that vied for the entitlements of sovereignty—separate 'studies' departments for each group, 'ethnic' theme dorms, preferential admissions and financial-aid policies, a proportionate number of faculty of their own group, separate student lounges and campus centers, and so on."[38]

And once we start celebrating and institutionalizing our ethnic divisions, where do we stop? If we have Puerto Rican or Chicano studies, why not Ecuadoran studies? Salvadoran studies? Colombian studies? And aren't all such programs a luxury that universities, in times of tight budgets, can no longer afford?

Constructing a group around a perceived grievance is an American tradition—that was, after all, how a group of colonists got together to dump tea into Boston Harbor, around the grievance of taxation without representation. But students in today's ethnic-studies programs have even less likelihood than those colonists in 1773 thought they had of forming a sovereign constituency, and few of them really want to. Some may fall under the spell of extreme cultural nationalists on the faculty or from off campus, just as a couple of generations ago some embraced millenarian Marxism. That is part of the turmoil of growing up, the sort of thing you invite when you expose people—especially energetic young people—to new ideas which they are impatient to see carried to a practical conclusion. But the countervailing forces are strong. After all, many Hispanic students have jobs that expose them to other people and other realities of hierarchy, while on campus they are taking other courses and dealing with other students and know full well they will have to function in a predominantly non-Latino world when they leave campus.

Chicano and Puerto Rican and other Latino studies programs were not a gift to minority students but were fought for and won by Latinos for a series of specific aims. Frank Bonilla, director of the Centro de Estudios Puertorriqueños in New York, from its founding in 1974 until his retirement in 1994, spelled out the most important of these in an article on Puerto Rican studies, which could well be applied to all of Latino studies.

Bonilla starts with the aim of "setting the record straight": The history of Puerto Ricans, to the extent that it was recorded and taught at all, reached the sons and daughters of Puerto Ricans in the United States in distorted and demeaning form. Puerto Rican studies programs have documented the other stories, of resistance to Spanish and later to U.S. rule, and of resourceful inventions in the arts, politics, and social life, both on the island and in the Puerto Rican diaspora. The same task has been taken on by Chicano studies programs in Texas, California, and New Mexico and now the Cuban Research Institute at Florida International University. (Much of the history of these peoples presented in chapter 4 was uncovered and interpreted by scholars working in the context of Latino studies.)

Another aim has been what Bonilla calls "training and self-reproduction" of a Latino intelligentsia. The project has involved recruiting students from the various communities and sometimes lobbying the administration to create more places for them and guiding and encouraging them through what might otherwise seem an alien and hostile academic world. But it has usually also implied something more, something that may be disturbing to critics like Shelby Steele. Latino (or other ethnic) studies programs almost always aspire to instill a commitment to help the people back in the barrios, and beyond, to the working class and to the disadvantaged generally. That is why prospective Latino "yuppies," whose goals are more personal, generally steer clear of these programs, considering them too ideological.

Finally, Bonilla lists "a Puerto Rican contribution to social science."[39] He argues that the discipline is enriched by scholars who bring different cultural assumptions to their work and who therefore can see things—sometimes in the same body of data— that were previously obscure. Bonilla's own work as a political economist illustrates this phenomenon. Using the same macroeconomic data available to all but putting together different strands that others had not thought of as related, he has argued convincingly that Puerto Rico has not been a beneficiary of federal largesse but on the contrary, a net exporter of capital to the United States.[40]

Bonilla speaks here of "Puerto Rican studies," but he has been one of the initiators of a broader alliance among the Latino scholars of different communities. The Inter-University Program for Latino Research, founded in 1988, now includes the Centro de Estudios Puertorriqueños (Hunter College, City University of New York), the Center for Mexican American Studies (University of Texas at Austin), the Chicano Studies Research Center (UCLA), the Stanford Center for Chicano Research (Stanford), the Cuban Research Institute (Florida International University), and other smaller programs in Arizona and New Mexico. The consortium coordinates and seeks funds for nationwide research projects and symposia.

Many of the other programs operating at the level of a single university have also broadened their agendas to respond to more diverse Spanish-speaking populations. Thus, Puerto Rican Studies at Rutgers University has changed its name and curriculum to Puerto Rican and Hispanic Caribbean Studies, and other programs are simply called "Latino Studies," which obliges them to consider a much broader "Latino" or "Hispanic" agenda.

In the Latin American societies that many of the Latino students came from and to which some of them were looking for models, the concept of an intellectual has had a much broader sense than in the United States. There, as Mexican political scientist Jorge Castañeda observes, almost anyone who writes, paints, acts, teaches, and speaks out, or even sings, becomes 'an intellectual.'"[41]

Similarly, the Latino ethnic studies departments have generally made room for artists. Writers, painters, actors, filmmakers, and musicians have been able to find not only an audience but in some cases studio space, technical assistance, and funding with the assistance of these programs. The programs' publications almost always include some identity-affirming art—poetry, illustrations, a music or dance review, for example—along with their sociological or political articles.

The Latino academic intellectuals who engage current political and social issues in language accessible to the masses—scholars like Américo Paredes in Texas; Frank Bonilla, Juan José Torres, and Juan Flores in New York; Mario Barrera and Renato Rosaldo in California; and others—do so mainly in specialized publications like the *Revista Chicano-Riqueña*, *Latino Studies Journal*, the bilingual *Centro*, journal of the Centro de Estudios Puertorriqueños, and so on, or in Op-Ed pieces in the Spanish language dailies *La Opinión* (Los Angeles), *El Herald* (Miami), or *El Diario/La Prensa* (New York).

That Latino "public intellectuals" in academia are not as visible to the (English-speaking) public at large as are some of the black academics—such as Cornel West, Henry Louis Gates Jr., Toni Morrison, Stanley Crouch, Glenn Loury, Stephen Carter, and Shelby Steele—is partly due to this practice of addressing their communities in Spanish and partly to the more active role in public debate of others who are intellectuals in the broader Latin American sense—journalists, novelists, poets, performance artists, visual artists, and songwriters. A large part of the work of Latino academics has been to foster and develop these other kinds of intellectuals and to provide the underpinnings for their understandings of the world.

## The Post-Modern Visualizations

Postmodernism has been described as the "flattening of history in one eternal present that contains all pasts and futures,"[42] meaning that anything may be combined with anything from any imaginary world. In the United States in the 1970s, Hispanic visual artists were already uninhibitedly ransacking the past for striking images plucked from context, making strange collages of Zapata's mustaches or Albizu Campos's famous frown, the thorn-pierced Sacred Heart, watch-chain-swinging *pachucos*, and Mexican *calacas* (skeletons) mixed with contemporary and private references. Of course, like the writers, the visual artists also return frequently to childhood memories. But by far the richest source of imagery for Hispanic visual artists has been the iconography of Catholicism and other religions, like Afro-Caribbean Santería and the ancient religions of indigenous America, that have come into contact with and partially blended with Catholicism in this hemisphere.

Two non-Hispanic curators discovered how difficult it was to represent such diversity when they undertook to produce an exhibition called "Hispanic Art in the United States: Thirty Contemporary Painters and Sculptors." Conceived in 1983, the show opened at the Museum of Fine Arts, Houston in 1987. It was then, they write, that "we discovered that no artist in it was familiar with all, or even half, of the other artists in the show. This again reflects the fact that we were exploring not a single culture, but a set of related ones. Similarly, the Hispanic community arts organizations in various cities tended to know their own scene thoroughly, but not to have a national focus."[43]

The museum director is quite candid about his reasons for wanting the exhibit: The museum needed to boost its attendance if it was to survive and be well funded, and the best way to do that was to bring the programming "closer to the diverse Hispanic communities that make up the city's population." The show drew approximately 150,000 visitors, considered very good by Houston standards, and approximately 30 percent of them were Hispanic, according to sample audience surveys. From the museum-marketing standpoint it was a success.

A committee of fifty Hispanic community leaders was created to help with outreach and publicity, and after the exhibition closed in Houston, this committee was kept alive to help the museum's Education Department recruit Hispanic docents and to carry art education into the Hispanic communities via church groups, schools, and other organizations. Through all these efforts, the museum also established relationships with Hispanic businesses and other organizations that have continued. "In short," the museum director writes, "the exhibition was a small but important step forward in bringing the general art museum and the Hispanic peoples of Houston closer together."[44]

It is apparent, then, that as recently as 1987 there was no clamor from the artists themselves for such an exhibition. Few if any of them yet thought of themselves as Hispanic or Latino. If they did not know of one another's work, it was because it had never occurred to most of them that what another group of artists was doing in a distant city might have anything to do with them just because they all happened to have Hispanic surnames. The non-Hispanic curators, who describe their own motive as an "open-minded exploration," and the museum director, who wanted a broader audience, contributed to creating a dialogue that they imagined was already under way but which, in fact, was not.

According to a Chicano critic, what the Houston curators missed, being Anglos, was the whole political context of the works displayed, particularly the importance of the Chicano movement of the sixties in stimulating protest art.[45] To remedy this defect, he was one of those collaborating in a more explicitly political show, "*Chicano Art: Resistance and Affirmation* (CARA), *1965–1985*," which can be seen as a kind of "answer" to Houston's "*Hispanic Art.*"

In the CARA catalog, this same critic, Tomás Ybarra-Frausto, expatiates on his concept of *rascuachismo*, a Chicano "secret weapon." *Rascuache*, a word supposedly of Nahuatl origin, he defines as an "outsider viewpoint...a funky, irreverent stance that debunks convention and spoofs protocol...a bawdy, spunky consciousness seeking to subvert and turn ruling paradigms upside down....To be rasquache [sic] is to be down but not out—*fregado pero no jodido.*"[46]

Chicano art does have some special emphases—a greater frequency of images of *pachucos* and of striking farmworkers, for example—but one of the things CARA demonstrated, despite itself, was how much in common Chicano art has with other Hispanic art. The perhaps ethnically naive but artistically sophisticated curators of the Houston show had been on to something when they unwittingly invented "Hispanic art."

Besides reciprocal borrowings (there are Chicano paintings with the Puerto Rican flag, for example, to demonstrate solidarity, and Puerto Ricans and other Latino artists liberally borrow whatever they feel they need from the rich Mexican imagery), there are two art forms that are especially common in the art of all the Hispanic groups in the United States. One is the didactic mural, usually telling the story of a people or a community, painted as dramatically as possible in a place as visible as possible to the people whose story is being told. The other is the more intimate composition using religious imagery, often in nonreligious or even antireligious ways, typified by the "home altar."

One Latino artist using religious imagery to subvert traditional religious assumptions is Yolanda López, a Chicana from San Francisco. In her wonderfully joyous "Guadalupe Triptych," for example, the centerpiece is "Portrait of the Artist as the Virgin of Guadalupe" (1978). The grinning young woman with well-muscled thighs, wearing a loose pink dress and clutching in one hand the star-clustered cloak of Mexico's most famous virgin and in the other the snake that in Aztec culture stands for many kinds of power (sexual, cerebral, spiritual), springs forth from a sunburst. The two side panels portray her mother and grandmother, also arrayed with the cloak of stars and sunburst of the Virgin of Guadalupe.

López has said that Chicanos "have to be visually literate. It's a survival skill." To encourage them to think critically of their own imagery, she has done many works based on the familiar Mexican symbol of the "Brown Virgin" of Guadalupe, often interpreting her in modern dress. This recontextualizing of a popular religious figure can be very disturbing to some viewers. Critic Lucy Lippard reports that "when she did a cover for the Mexican feminist magazine *Fem* showing the Guadalupe in short skirt and high heels, its office received bomb threats.[47] In Lopez's more recent work, La Lupita is presented as a Chicana heroine, representing, according to Lippard, "the female force paralleling male heroes like Emiliano Zapata and Diego Rivera."[48]

By far the most notorious use of religious imagery by a Hispanic artist is "Piss Christ" by Andrés Serrano. This is the photograph that brought down the wrath of Jesse Helms and threatened the funding of the entire National Endowment of the Arts, which had helped to pay for an exhibit that included the work.

"I am drawn to subjects that border on the unacceptable," Serrano has said, "because I lived an unacceptable life for so long."[49]

His "unacceptable life" included early abandonment by his father, "a merchant marine who had three other families living in his native Honduras," his upbringing in Brooklyn by his African-

Cuban mother, who spoke no English and had psychotic episodes, and a period of drug dealing and drug addiction after he dropped out of high school.[50]

Serrano's lusciously colored photographs include "Cabeza de Vaca"—the name of an early Spanish explorer of North America—as a literal, severed cow's head; formally arresting close-ups of the dead in a New York morgue; portraits of masked and hooded Ku Klux Klansmen and a Klanswoman; various objects—statuettes, a cross, etc.—immersed in or dripping blood; semen glowing in its trajectory across a dark background, and most famously, "Piss Christ," a plastic crucifix made luminous by immersion in urine. It is a visually striking work, made provocative only by Serrano's insistence on telling us just what it is that gives it that yellow glow. He seems to be literalizing—or coming as close as he could and still make a pretty picture—the common Spanish expletive *"¡Me cago en Dios!"*—literally, "I shit on God," but used so frequently it has about the force of "Gosh darn!" The phrase, like Serrano's work, demonstrates the extreme ambivalence many Hispanic Catholics feel toward their symbols.

Then this and the other works in the series make another point: In a world of AIDS and other plagues, we would all be better off if we demystified these natural human fluids so that we could deal with them rationally.

Artists also reach into older, pre-Hispanic and non-Catholic religious traditions for symbols. Yolanda López did that with her snake in the hand of her "Virgin." In the Caribbean area, the most important non-Catholic imagery comes from Santería, based on religious practices of West Africa and only slightly on Catholicism.

One who used such images was Ana Mendieta, who died in an accident in 1985 just as her work was beginning to be more widely shown. When she was twelve years old, shortly after the Cuban revolution, her parents put her on a plane to the United States to save her from communism. She ended up in an Iowa orphanage where she felt miserable and abandoned. Longing for parents and homeland, she treated the earth, the very soil and rock, as her symbolic mother. In one of her early performance pieces, this vivacious, intense, tiny woman smeared her naked body with chicken blood and rolled in feathers to become the magical white cock of Santería. When she was finally able to return to Cuba in 1980, she traveled to some of the most rugged, rural regions that help mystical significance for her to create impressions of her body on the earth and her homeland, summoning African and indigenous spirits.[51]

At the Museum of Contemporary Hispanic Art in New York in 1985, Jorge Rodríguez and Charles Abramson installed garish and hard-edged composition of cut-out steel angels and zigzag stripes, multicolored ribbons, and organic materials used in Santería for their *Orisha/Santos*, a tribute to "the Seven African Powers." Abramson is an African-American *santero*, a priest of Santería, and Rodríguez is a Puerto Rican sculptor who had been making steel versions of *santos*, the Puerto Rican saint sculptures that are endowed with magical powers.[52] The installation obeys strict ritual requirements about the types of objects and their placement

In contrast, the typical home altar is highly idiosyncratic, a mix of personal mementos and religiously charged figures and images that works as both an evolving spiritual scrapbook and a guardian in homes throughout the Hispanic world. This popular tradition has inspired works by many artists, including Amalia Mesa-Bains's art-deco dressing table *Altar for Dolores del Río*, 1988.[53] Mesa-Bains associates altars with feminism and says that they "became the most political of statements. They were the outgrowth of the individualized oppression in the most private places of the domestic chamber, the bedroom and the kitchen."

Some altars are still used for their original and private magical purposes and are not meant for display. Chicana writer Gloria Anzaldúa keeps one on top of her computer monitor as a kind of muse, "with the *Virgin de Coatlalopeuh* candle and copal incense burning…while I ponder the ways metaphor and symbol concretize the spirit and etherealize the body…[54] María Hinojosa, the National Public Radio reporter, updates her ever-growing home altar with small objects that have magic significance to her and her husband.

Another ironic play on the altar form included in the CARA exhibition was by the Royal Chicano Air Force (RCAF), an art *grupo* (collective)in Sacramento, one of several that emerged from the Chicano movement. The work of the RCAF tends to be as whimsical as its name—advanced members are called "pilots" and guide the young "cadets" in their work. One imaginary flight squadron constructed an exuberantly *rascuache* houselike structure. Upon entering, the viewer would see a strange miniature exhibit with many little compartments and smaller installations, almost like becoming a part of a phantasmagorical Chicano home altar.

Besides working in groups and training new cadres, artists transmit their message of *nosotros* in displays in public spaces, especially murals. Inspired at the outset by the work of the big three muralists of Mexico—José Clemente Orozco, Diego Rivera, and David Alfaro Siqueiros—the mural as public protest art has spread from the Mexican-American communities of Los Angeles and Chicago across the country. Puerto Ricans in New York have adopted the form enthusiastically.

One of the most spectacular of all American public murals is the vast work directed by Judith Baca called *The Great Wall of Los Angeles*. Painted on the sides of the freeway that split the Los Angeles Chicano community in two—the same one that was tearing apart the territory of the protagonist of Danny Santiago's *Famous All Over Town*—the mural depicts the history of Mexican Americans from pre-Columbian days to the near present. In Lippard's description, "the mural is factual, but often witty, as when Rosie the Riveter is vacuumed into a TV to become a housewife after the men return from World War II or when the swooping bodies of Japanese-American soldiers from the heroic 442d Battalion emerge from—or merge with—the stripes in the American flag."[55]

Exhibits like CARA, murals like the Great Wall of Los Angeles, and the provocations of Andrés Serrano show that something of the rebellious, insolent spirit of the sixties and seventies lives on. The berets, the marches, and all the shouting of that period served to establish a new presence—on walls and in galleries and even in the minds of museum directors. More importantly, the struggles of those days and their artistic legacy have established the authority of *nosotros*, the more confident *nosotros* that no longer needs to believe in Aztlán or imminent world upheaval in order to believe in itself. As the Royal Chicano Air Force declares in one of its conceptual bombing runs, *"Aquí estamos, y no nos vamos"* (Here we are, and here we stay.)

## The Nuyorican Poets Café

One artist who has thought a great deal about the evolution of identities is poet, professor, and impresario Miguel Algarín. His poetry, in English, Spanish, and mixed English and Spanish, is widely known from its appearance in many anthologies. He is also known as one of the little group of three that came up with the term "Nuyorican" to describe an identity that wasn't quite Puerto Rican, as in "grown up on the island," but was a special Puerto Ricanish way to be a New Yorker. To students at Rutgers, he is known as a professor of English, with a specialization in Shakespeare. But to lots of other poets, playwrights, and performance artists he is big daddy—the founder, owner, and benevolent manager of the Nuyorican Poets Café, a *rascuache* sort of place deep in Loisaida, the Lower East Side.

As he tells it, Nuyorican literature and the cafe were both christened in 1975. He had first heard the word "Nuyorican" in Puerto Rico the year before, when island Puerto Ricans used it disparagingly to describe New York Puerto Ricans who, by implication, could not speak proper Spanish. It was a put-down, like the Mexican term *pocho*. "When I heard that, I of course instantly knew what they meant, and I knew the schizophrenia of the island linguistically. They all want to be able to say, 'We're Spanish speaking,' but their economy happens in English. And when you can't buy your underwear or your socks in the language that is national or mother tongue to you, you're in trouble. Schizophrenia."

So when he got back, he and his friend playwright Miguel Piñero began to collect the poetry being written in a mix of Spanish and English in New York, "and we decided that, hey, this is Nuyorican poetry."

Algarín and a couple of friends opened the Nuyorican Poets Café that summer. Miguel Piñero, who had already written his prize-winning play *Short Eyes*, was "one of the stars of the place," but the name "Nuyorican" was not meant to exclude anybody. "The space was there. Anyone with work could come and work, you know?"

Allen Ginsberg, then living nearby on Twelfth Street would come by with William Burroughs, Gregory Corso, and Lawrence

Ferlinghetti. Then, to Algarín's surprise, the presence of these famous old beatniks drew European visitors because "Europeans were into the Beats, but also because of Piñero. The Germans and the Italians were doing shows in the cafe, interviewing him. But to their surprise, they'd discover this incredible resource of talent that was up for grabs, free."

Japanese culture vultures got wind of the place, too.

"Until one day, we had this incredible actress, Japanese actress, classical actress, arrive at the cafe, with an entourage of people and incredibly elaborate camera work coming in to do her thing at the Nuyorican Poets Café, you know, for Tokyo. And here there was an audience of poor Nuyoricans, and this Japanese woman is arriving with an entourage and a camera-work team that must have been in the hundreds of thousands of dollars."[56]

In 1992, the quincentennial of Columbus's arrival in the Caribbean, Algarín orchestrated a celebration of the event to counter what he saw as all the "angst" of the many people of color who were condemning Columbus and portraying themselves as victims of the European encounter. Algarín, although a brown Puerto Rican, refused to see himself as a victim, because in the "four hundred years my people have developed on the island of Puerto Rico, the evolution has been complex, to say the least," the mingling of cultures producing as many good things as bad. In his eyes, rather than a victim he had been privileged to be "part of one of the biggest, most extraordinary human experiments that's ever happened...."

The celebration he arranged was a dramatic reading by an all-star cast of poets of various colors of the poem "Paterson," by William Carols Williams. To Algarín, Williams—whose father was Anglo and whose mother was Puerto Rican—exemplifies the success of that extraordinary human experiment of culture mixing.

The cafe is still going strong and still getting attention from foreign visitors and from the media. "Poetry slams" have become part of the routine, and readings and performances are broadcast on Saturday nights over WBAI. It's a place where artists can try out new plays or give a new twist to a play or a poem that wasn't working, and sometimes the stuff is not really ready for prime time, but that's the point. Like America itself, or Puerto Rico, it's a meeting ground for people and experimental ideas from all places and an incubator of the new.

**Revenge Through Laughter**

Within the dominant culture the minority images that circulate emphasize the minority's exoticism, its otherness. Hispanics are viewed as a source of menace, cheap labor, and *salsa* (literally and figuratively). For the Hispanics themselves, finding an autonomous identity means breaking free of the clichés by which the majority assures itself of its centrality. To do this they must continually reappropriate, reinvigorate, or invent their images. And because the collective images are also self-images, everybody who identifies as a Hispanic (or Latino, Chicano, Nuyorican, or any other permutation) has an intimate stake in the process of image production. And because of that, art that presents itself or is presented as Hispanic, Latino, or whatever is not just a matter of personal taste but is of communal concern. This is why every such exhibit, publication, or recording can arouse nationalist passions that may seem far removed from art.

If the artists fail to seize the imagery of their own community, their whole structure of meanings will inevitably succumb to folklorization, cultural eccentricities that the majority deems interesting, possibly charming, and utterly harmless. Their culture will be treated that way in any case, of course: Taco Bells and their pseudo-Mexican menus, statuettes of sleeping peons under big sombreros, pictures of musicians in frilly *rumbero* shirts and other "Latin" kitsch are absorbed to add variety to strips or malls. Such images, though usually inspired by authentic practices from someplace, sometime, in Latin America, are extracted from their original contexts and meanings and are appropriated to suit Anglo-American tastes, idealized or caricatured like those earlier syncretisms, wieners or chop suey or Polish sausage or French fries.

The process cannot be stopped and probably shouldn't be: folklorization and the production of kitsch provide livelihoods for countless minority craftsmen and restaurant owners in the folklore and tourist industries. But it can be subverted, and is subverted, *con gusto* (with pleasure) by the sly satirists in Hispanolandia. As Sigmund Freud noted,

> Humour has in it a *liberating* element. But it has also something fine and elevating....Obviously, what is fine about it is the triumph of narcissism, the ego's victorious assertion of its own invulnerability. It refuses to be hurt by the arrows of reality or to be compelled to suffer....Humour is not resigned; it is rebellious."[57]

When Puerto Rican poet Pedro Pietri, with a ponytail of hair so coarse it could have belonged to a real pony, mustaches forming a sharp-angled wicket over his protruding jaw and lower lip, dressed in black baggy pants, black shirt, and black jacket, with a wide-brimmed, flat-crowned black hat, lurches and bounces onto the stage like a combination of Zorro and Charlie Chaplin and solemnly unfolds a big artwork portfolio with the words pasted on in big white letters, "Spanglish National Anthem"; when the Colombian-born John Leguízamo comes onstage in *Mambo Mouth*, or as any of the outrageous characters he has created for his television series *House of Buggin*; when Los Angeleno comedian Paul Rodríguez cracks jokes in East L.A. Chicano Spanglish; or when Mexican-born Guillermo Peña-Gómez comes onstage decked out as the "Border Brujo," they are signifying the triumph of the collective ego. It's a *rascuache*, Spanglish, punch-drunk ego, but it's still defiant, and it makes Hispanics laugh at themselves and their dilemmas and unites them, at least for that moment, in one strong *nosotros*.

# 8

# American Identities

ONE OF PAINTER JUDY BACA'S SMALLER WORKS, infinitesimal beside her Great Wall of Los Angeles mural, is a triptych called *The Three Marías*, a familiar reference to Catholics. On the right panel is a life-size painting of the maternal María, a modern Chicana version of the Virgin Mother. On the left is the wanton María, heavily lipsticked, her clothing and posture sexually provocative, in a Chicana version of Mary Magdalene. In the center is a mirror. A photograph in Lippard's book shows Judy Baca herself reflected in that middle panel, completing the trio. But obviously this triptych works differently for different viewers. When I stepped up to it at the CARA exhibition, I saw a middle-aged white guy with a beard. What was he doing in this picture?

And why has somebody like me, a Midwesterner of northwest European stock who never even heard much Spanish until after college, written a book like this? But the fact is we all have multiple selves. And at some moment when I was twenty-two or twenty-three, I discovered some of mine had become Hispanic. Or at least I had stopped being a gringo.

One recent evening my wife, an Argentine of fair coloring, and I sat at a banquet closing the meetings of the Association of Puerto Rican Studies, of which I am a founding member. A New York Puerto Rican woman joined us at the table and, after introductions, looked at us quizzically and asked, with a friendly but puzzled smile, "So what brings two gringos to an event like this?"

My wife just laughed. In Argentina, *gringos* are Italian or

223

Eastern European immigrants, and she, having been born on the pampas, could hardly imagine herself as one. But I must have felt just a bit offended, because I replied, "I haven't been a gringo for many years."

Maybe I was being too touchy, but then people tend to be touchy about identities that are hard-won, as distinct from those that are inherited. By telling this story, I hope to illustrate something about how identity shifts occur. It may also help explain why a dark-skinned Chicana reporter from the *Phoenix Sun* found herself, to her surprise and dismay, called *gringa* when she visited Chihuahua.

But first some etymology. I have heard both Americans and Mexicans repeat the psychologically improbable story, which probably comes from an old movie, that the word *gringo* was picked up by Mexicans from the ballad "Green grow the rushes, O...," sung by U.S. soldiers as they invaded Mexico in 1846. Could the Mexicans have been so charmed by their invaders that they named them for a love song?

If so, it must have been because the phrase reminded them of an insult they already knew. Spaniards had been calling foreigners *gringos* since at least 1765. Originally the word meant the gibberish that foreigners spoke and then the people who spoke it. *Gringo* is a jocular alteration of the word *griego* (Greek).[1] The word may actually be older; across the channel, Shakespeare and his sixteenth-century audience already understood "Greek" to stand for something incomprehensible when he had Casca say of a speech, "It was Greek to me" (*Julius Caesar* Act 1, Scene 2). In short, a *gringo* was, and still is in much of Latin America, a foreigner who cannot clearly speak the local language. In Mexico these people are usually North Americans.

Not speaking the language, or not speaking it well, also means that one is missing other signals in the culture and may very well be making a fool of oneself. *Gringos* are cultural incompetents, like *pochos*. The opposite of the *gringo* is the *criollo*, the "one from here."

When I first got to Venezuela in 1963, right after graduating from college, I was an absolute *gringo*—although the Venezuelans in those days were using another word, "*musiú*." I had no more than four words of Spanish—*caballo*, *pistola*, *sombrero*, and *mujer* (which I must have picked up from the movies)—and, apart from one Chicano classmate at Harvard, had never known any Latin Americans or Latinos.

Like a lot of other young Americans in that idealistic moment, I went abroad to save the world and have adventures. I was part of one of the early contingents of an American-founded, privately operated community-development program called *Acción* (Action), still in existence, that at the time was sending young Americans and Venezuelans into the *barrios* to organize self-help projects. In Venezuela *barrios* connotes "slums" or "shantytowns," and before I left, a year and a half later, I had lived in three of them, part of the time in a cardboard house, and in a number of other hovels in the city proper. These were rough places where outsiders were suspect, so I had a strong incentive to blend in as quickly as possible.

Since I have much lighter skin and hair than most Venezuelans and even more unusual blue eyes, inconspicuousness was going to be a challenge. My solution was to wear dark glasses and to imitate everything. I imitated voices, stances, walks, gestures, the way people puckered their lips to point to something or used hand signals, and so on. I wore what my neighbors in the *barrio* were wearing, only less flashy. Within a couple of months I was passing as a *criollo*, at least in brief encounters. My mimicry was so precise that some people claimed they could tell not only that I was a native *caraqueño* but which barrio I came from. They called me *catire*, "blond" (my hair is actually brown, but that was close enough), and assumed I was the son of northern Italian or Spanish immigrants, of whom there were a good many in the country. If the encounter lasted a little longer, though, the other party would begin to suspect something; I had all the right gestures, but I didn't always use them appropriately, because despite my good accent I did not have the vocabulary or the cultural background to understand everything that was being said.

I was learning scripts, playing the part of a *criollo*. Faking it, if you will. But if you fake something long enough and well enough, it becomes less fake. This playacting was changing me in at least two ways. First, the gestures and speech patterns were becoming habits, as comfortable and easy to reproduce without thinking as my older, gringo speech patterns and gestures had been.

Second, I was learning the language. Not just how to imitate the sounds but the way those sounds went together to create meanings, the structure, the inner logic, of the language. Now I sometimes had to stop to think which self to be when I went from one social world to another, as happened occasionally when a bunch of Americans would get together. The real challenge was when I was in a mixed gathering with Americans and Venezuelans, where I often had to act as an interpreter. Because each language was linked to a different concept of self, the constant switching was emotionally draining.

In Spanish thoughts were occurring to me that certainly would not have occurred to me in English, partly because of the sounds of the words and partly because of the different ways they were associated. And this was affecting cultural attitudes I hadn't even known I had. For example, phrases such as *una trigueñita preciosa* (a lovely, dark-skinned girl), accompanied by a gentle opening of a hand, a smile, or some other sign of satisfaction, made me aware of how much more natural it was in the *barrio* than it ever had been at home to associate dark skin with beauty.

Learning the whole complex vocabulary in use in Venezuela for various racial combinations made it impossible for me to fall back easily into the American system of "black" and "white" even after I got home. I could readily understand why Hispanics, especially those from the multiracial Caribbean societies, felt that this American insistence that everyone be black, white, or something altogether different, rather than some specific mix, was totally inadequate to describe them. It angered and frustrated them, as it would later anger and frustrate my young son Alex.

There were other discoveries. One afternoon I joined a group of new Venezuelan recruits to *Acción* whom I was meeting for the first time. I was in my *barrio* clothes, and I was calling myself Edmundo (from my middle name) at the time; in short, I was in full *criollo* drag, and I let them assume I was just another Venezuelan. They were talking about the odd and sometimes disturbing behaviors of the Americans they were supposed to work with, and finding it hard to explain just what it was that bothered them, one of them turned to me as a more experienced hand and said, "Well, you know how the Americans are." Yes, I said, I did.

In fact, I didn't. That is, I could only imagine, from my newly emerging bicultural perspective, what a Venezuelan might think was wrong with Americans. Perceived American aloofness and clannishness, I guess, was part of it. A certain stiffness of gesture or posture when certain subjects were brought up, such as sex or (a common topic among these Venezuelan males) human excretions. An insistence on precise, clock-timed punctuality overriding the sovereign whims of the spirit. A clumsy obviousness in jokes, verbal or practical—often due to inadequacy in the language rather than to lack of subtlety on the part of the Americans. I had to stop and think what it was that people like the person I had been only a few months earlier did that offended or put off people like the one I was, at least partially, becoming.

I left Venezuela with a deep tan, a rapid-fire *barrio* Spanish, and a lot of questions regarding culture and class. I enrolled in graduate school at Northwestern University, just north of Chicago, where I worked in the summer as an organizer in the Puerto Rican community around Division Street on the north side. Then I had an opportunity to go to Puerto Rico to direct a research project and while there met and married a Puerto Rican woman who, like me, was teaching at the University of Puerto Rico. She had a son whom I adopted, and we soon had another son, and our family extended all over the western half of the island. My research also required me to interview people in towns and *barrios* all over the island. From all these contacts and relationships, I developed a second Spanish-speaking *persona*, this one with a Puerto Rican accent, a more dignified vocabulary for teaching political sociology, and a more common one for joking around with my in-laws.

In the following years I was constantly dealing with other Spanish-speaking people, picking up more gestures and expressions and friendships. Besides Puerto Ricans, I became especially well acquainted with Cubans, Chileans, Mexicans, and later Argentines, in their own countries and in the United States, and made briefer work-related visits to Panama, Nicaragua, and Peru.

My Latin American personae have long since ceased to be an actor's studied, self-conscious roles. They are simply among my selves. Rather, to state this a little more carefully, they constitute an alternative identity into which I slip whenever it seems to fit. This is very much like the dual identity that Latin Americans develop after living in the United States for a time, which is why we understand each other so readily. I just started the other way around, from *anglo* to *hispano*. I did not cease being an "Anglo." I just became somebody else as well.

## Selves and Identities

Anyone who goes through such a cultural passage—and many millions of us have, and more do every day, in every part of the world—tends to look for ways to stabilize his or her identity. Just switching from one language to another, or even from one sort of interaction to another within the same language, makes us feel differently about ourselves and behave in a different style, and doing it too often or too quickly can be dizzying. Stabilizing our identity is of the utmost practical importance not just for our own tranquility but also so that others will know how to repond to us.[2]

And if identities can be shifted that easily, how deep and important can they be? What is the relationship between my identities and my "self"? Or are they the same thing?

A classic tradition in sociology is that the "self" is a concept developed in interaction with others, worked out by trial and error as one tries to "be" a certain way; either others go along with it and reinforce it or they do not, in which case one has to try to "be" in a somewhat different way until settling on a self that works.[3] It would seem, then, that people who move between different cultures and subcultures will need to develop several working selves, moving from one to another according to the context. But what is it that is doing the trying, the thing or force conducting all those little experiments before the self is developed?

According to philosopher Daniel Dennett, what we experience as the self, the "me"-ness of our lives, is simply the point within all our sensations and brain impulses from which any one of us is viewing and recounting events at any given moment.[4] He calls it "the center of narrative gravity." It is not a fixed place in the brain (or in the body or in experience or anywhere) but a point of view that shifts according to what sort of story we are constructing (for ourselves or others) at that precise moment. There are always many possible centers of narrative gravity, each activating a different area of the brain, and several different narratives in progress. The "I," or the self, moves among these narrative points, picking up this story for a while, then leaving it to tell another.

This idea is also implicit in the Spanish word for self, "*el yo*," literally "the I." The self is the "I" who tells the story. "Identity" is one of the stories we tell in an attempt to describe that self. It is not a story we can just make up, though, the way we might write a short story—not if we want others to believe it and help us return to that narrative point to tell the story again.

We construct this narrative of our identity by asserting our loyalties to particular communities. As Simmel pointed out long ago, each of these affiliations restricts us by its rules and code of honor. But in a modern society we can be simultaneously affiliated to so many different communties, ranging from established organizations, such as clubs, parties, or churches, to vaguer groupings, such as liberals or conservatives, people of goodwill, or feminists, that we have great freedom to choose to be governed by one set of rules in one instance and another in another.

In contemporary America, ethnic identity is to a large extent another voluntary affiliation. Physical appearance, accent, or some other ineradicable mark may set a person apart and cause him or her to be labeled as Latino or whatever, but the label does not become an identity until it is embraced by the holder. Calling oneself a Latino, Hispanic, Chicano, Boricua, or whatever is a statement of affiliation, of loyalty to and solidarity with that group's rules and codes. One may have multiple affiliations, which become active in different situations. Thus, it is not surprising that a study found that Mexicans and Puerto Ricans in Chicago shifted from describing themselves as Mexicans or Puerto Ricans to calling themselves Latinos when they wanted to create a coalition to demand jobs. Then, when they were back in their respective *barrios*, they became Mexicans and Puerto Ricans once again. Their ethnic identities were "situational."[5]

Innumerable experiences and ideas and the familiarity of particular contexts may keep us returning to the same "self," the same center of narrative gravity.[6] Similarly identity—the guise in which the self presents itself—is sustained by repeated reminders of one's social affiliations. If one's identity as, for example, a Latino *seems* stable, it is not because the self is constant but because it keeps returning to tell its story that way. What makes us return to familiar stories includes all the reminders—from one's picture on a driver's license to the reactions of friends and strangers—of the stories we have told in the past.

## Gains and Losses

Like many of my Latin American friends who have made adjustments to living in the United States, I sometimes pondered what had been gained and what if anything lost in this process of acquiring my new affiliations and my new selves. For me, in going from Anglo into Hispanic culture, several gains were obvious: Access, through the language, to all of Spanish literature; a greater ease of gesture and physical contact; a new ability to talk my way into or out of a range of situations I wouldn't even have known existed; a greater openness to making new friends, and a familiarity with spicier food and music.

By my calculations, there were no losses. I had shed some things, but I was glad to be rid of them. One of those was a certain awkwardness around "people of color," that is, any color other than pink. Another was some typically Anglo middle-class inhibitions about sex—the notion that sexual desire was somehow embarrassing.

But there were other things in Latin American culture that I did not want to adopt and did not feel compelled to. Most important of these was the complex of attitudes of male dominance for which English has borrowed the Spanish word "*machismo*," although it is by no means an exclusively Hispanic phenomenon.[7] In courtship, it implies viewing the woman courted less as a person valued for her own sake than as a mere *ficha*, or game piece, to be captured so as to have something to boast about to one's male friends. In marriage or other long-term, intimate relationships, it often manifests itself as male tyranny, the macho's demand to subject the woman to his will. These attitudes are certainly not universal among Hispanic men; there is a contrary concept of *lo varonil*, manliness, which puts more stress on the male's responsibility *toward* others, as breadwinner and protector, than on his power *over* them. But *machismo* is widespread, shared and reinforced even by many women, especially mothers who insist that their sons do only "manly" tasks and leave the household drudgery to their sisters.

Many Latin Americans and Latinos, and especially Latinas, are able to free themselves from such attitudes only when they enter a new culture. Not all of them make that choice, of course; the conflict between men's insistence on their home-country patterns of male dominance while their wives and daughters are discovering their independence has been one of the great themes of Hispanic American literature, from *Pocho* to *When I Was Puerto Rican*. Latinos, like other migrants, seek to adopt those aspects of the new culture that seem to help them get on with their lives in the ways they want to live them and reject the others, and they don't all make the same choices. It is the ability to choose that is experienced as liberating, in the same way my contact with Latin American culture was liberating for me.

## Tropicalizations

In Salman Rushdie's great novel of cultural dislocation and immigrant ingenuity, *Satanic Verses*, the Archangel Gibreel (formerly Bombay movie star Gibreel Farishta) contemplates staid, ambiguous London.

"...O most slippery, most devilish of cities!—In which...stark, imperative oppositions were drowned beneath an endless drizzle of greys."

Hovering angelically above the city, he decides that the solution is to tropicalize, that is, to Indianize its weather. The expected benefits:

> increased moral definition, institution of a national siesta, development of vivid and expansive patterns of behaviour among the populace, higher quality popular music, new birds in the trees...Improved street-life, outrageously coloured flowers (magenta, vermilion, neon-green), spider-monkeys in the oaks....Religious fervour, political ferment, renewal of interest in the intelligentsia. No more British reserve; hot-water bottles to be banished forever, replaced in the foetid nights by the making of slow and odorous love.

The increased heat and sun will also induce

> new social values: friends to commence dropping in on one

another without making appointments, closure of old folks'
homes, emphasis on the extended family. Spicier food; the
use of water as well as paper in English toilets; the joy of
running fully dressed through the first rains of the monsoon.
   Disadvantages: cholera, typhoid, legionnaires' disease,
cockroaches, dust, noise, a culture of excess.[8]

As Rushdie, Hanif Kureishi, and other artists have shown us,
the immigrants from the outer reaches of what was once the British
Empire are already working these transformations on London, even
without the climate change.[9] And so Algerians and black Africans
have transformed Belleville in Paris, and Turks and Yugoslavs have
refashioned certain neighborhoods in Germany, and so on around
the world, in a process of urban transformation that has only just
begun.[10] In the United States, the newcomers arrive from all those
places, but especially from what was once the periphery of the
Spanish Empire but whose metropolis is now the English-speaking
land to their north. And they, too, are working their
transformations.

As I jog through Loisaida from my home at Broadway and
Fourth Street in Manhattan to the East River, it is easy to see the
signs. Pronounced "lo-ee-SI-da," the name itself is a bilingual pun
that claims the area for the Puerto Ricans, an alteration of "Lower
East Side" that makes it sound almost like the real Puerto Rican
town Loisa Aldea. It was named by one of its sons, the late New
York Puerto Rican playwright and poet Bittman John "Bimbo"
Rivas, in an ode in 1974, heyday of Puerto Rican expression in the
neighborhood, when the Nuyorican Poets Café was just getting
going on East Sixth Street and the Young Lords were organizing,
agitating, and publishing out of a building on East Third.[11]

The low-rent, crowded Lower East Side that was home to
German and later to poor, mostly Jewish immigrants from all over
Europe now has an even more diverse population. There still are
bakeries with signs in Yiddish plus a big Ukrainian Uniate church
and a whole cluster of Ukrainian organizations and buildings,
Polish restaurants, and other restaurants and stores run by people
speaking the languages of India and Bangladesh or in the accents
of the English Caribbean. There are also two supranational tribes,
the Anarchists (concentrated around Tompkins Square Park) and
Yuppies. In the blocks around and including the Lillian Wald

Housing Projects next to the FDR Drive and the river it is the Puerto Ricans, few of whom are anarchists and fewer still are yuppies, who have asserted their claim most forcefully, and their renaming of this area has remained quasi-official. The signs on Avenue C at Fourth and Third streets still read "Loisaida Avenue."[12]

I trot east past hopeful little stores with proud signs, groceries displaying the bright-yellow-and-red cans of Café Bustelo or Pilón and bins of green and yellow plantains, fibrous ñames and craggy yautías, delis with exotic beers, and a few shops with East Indian or West Indian foods and spices. There are shops of magic herbs and religious trinkets, from any religion and all religions, including Santería. Older established churches have signs welcoming parishioners in English and in Spanish, and there are many smaller churches in storefronts or converted townhouses—Pentecostal, mostly—that don't bother with English in their signage.

As I approach Avenue C, the complex stench, made up of souring food and fabric discarded in the street and the sweeter, suffocating fumes of cars and buses, gives way briefly to smells of bubbling vegetable oil and *masa* of frying *empanaditas, pastelillos, bacalaítos,* and *alcapurrias* from a corner shop advertising *cuchifritos*—Puerto Rican snack food—served with sweet *café* and warmed milk. In and around the big housing projects over near the river, between Avenue D and the FDR Drive, children squeal and run on the sidewalks and in the playgrounds, men stand around joking or tinker under cars, and women stroll and watch the territory. Their skin colors range from slightly tawny to very dark, their hair from wavy like Gypsies to tight coils like Africans, and like working-class people everywhere, they all move comfortably in their bodies no matter what their shapes. They greet each other and joke in the soft, almost "s"-less working-class accent, with its "l" and "r" switches and the aspirated double "rr," of the people who call themselves *lo' pueltojjiqueño'*.

In the blocks just west of the projects, Loisaida is a gallery of spectacular street art, much of it of collective authorship and often marked specifically as Puerto Rican—by subject matter, color, style, or to erase all doubt, the implanting of the three-barred red, white, and blue flag. Murals appear wherever there is a large wall, many of them signed "Chico." A smaller sign by Chico, as large as the space would allow in one of the little gardens between buildings, commemorates one Cano, R.I.P., with a crude, vigorous drawing of a young Latino's face.

Some of those little gardens, supported by small grants, nominal membership fees, and much volunteer labor, are formal compositions of flora, pathways, and tiny pools, sometimes with a picnic table and barbecue pit. There's one on Fourth Street between C and D labeled *Tranquilidad*. There a little plaque by the gate informs us, "Here stood Synagogue Cheva Bikin, Chalin B'nai Israel, Anshei Baranov, Built 1887." (Across the street is a building still standing from the 1880s, now painted white with brown trim on its vaulted door and windows and labeled in elaborate signage, San Isidoro y San Leandro, Orthodox Catholic Church of the Hispanic Rite.)

The most characteristic artistic appropriation of vacant lots in Loisaida includes a *casita*, a little wooden house brightly painted and set back in the lot. The land in front is treated as a *batey*—the open space before a Puerto Rican house which is to the suburban front lawn as the paved *plaza* of a Spanish American town is to the landscaped park stretching out before a town hall in New England. That is, the *batey* of a house in Puerto Rico is an open place for all manner of spontaneous human activity rather than for quiet viewing or strolls through the horticulture. The *batey* before the Loisaida *casitas*, however, is symbolic, so crowded with personal mementos that there is scarcely room for spontaneous activity. It is more like an eclectic home altar, often with dolls and carefully placed toys mixed with religious and Puerto Rican patriotic images.

On Third Street between B and C, right across from the present location of Miguel Algarín's Nuyorican Poets Café, is a *casita con batey* called Brisas del Caribe, carefully built up over the years by its creator, a laborer pensioned because of a back injury, that each spring includes tropical plantings that—as he well knows—will only begin to germinate before first frost destroys them. A hand-lettered sign on the fence announces: "Se Venden Pasteles, Se Hacen Maquinas Para Moler Berduras—a misspelled invitation to buy a Puerto Rican delicacy, *pasteles*, and vegetable grinders—with a street and apartment number but no telephone. The casita here and another one nearby named Jardín los Amigos are just big enough for four men to sit inside and play dominoes, but they rarely do. The *casita* is really a mixed-media sculpture, the centerpiece of the altar of the pseudo *batey*. The real *batey*, where men set up their domino tables and women and men gather to banter and kids to play, is the sidewalk.

The other type of appropriation of vacant lots is the collective sculpture of junk or found objects, making no pretension of reproducing rural life on the island but celebrating instead the machine culture of the city. An especially impressive one is on the corner of Avenue C (Loisaida Avenue) at Second Street, where the lot has been completely occupied by a strange monster of steel, fiberglass, and other materials, part of which towers giddily in the outer corner, like a turret or warrior defending the space. Its cornerstones include a motorcycle that looks as though it had survived the eruption at Pompeii and an iron safe, its heavy door gaping open toward the viewer on the street.

Meanwhile, on the other coast, Mexicans and Mexican Americans, Salvadorans, Hondurans, and other Latinos have appropriated and transformed their spaces in East Los Angeles. The homes and streets that were designed by and for an Anglo white middle class thirty and forty years ago have been redefined with movable props, alterations to the houses, paint on the walls, and the active street life of its current Latino residents. Tables for domino games—as in New York—transform sidewalks into a public plaza, and canopies convert abandoned gas stations into restaurants. Here, unlike Loisaida and most of New York, houses have front yards, intended by their original designers to run one into another as a continuous, decorative front lawn. These have been enclosed and individualized with statuary and knickknacks, their walls low enough to permit viewing of the display and elbow-leaning in conversations with passersby. Murals of community struggles claim the walls and the spaces they enclose, the red, white, and green of the Mexican flag serving as a marker of ownership as clearly as the Puerto Rican red, white and blue in eastern *barrios*. Low-rider competitions, strolling mariachis and loud *banda* music blaring from radios, street vending, conversations on the street, and the food smells of tortillas and chile, comino and culantro, "Latinize" the area, reminding Los Angeles that it still is no more and no less than a favored outpost of the northern Mexico desert.[13]

These and other groups are Latinizing, or in some cases re-

Latinizing, American cities throughout the Southwest, the Southeast, the Northeast, and the Midwest as thoroughly as Gibreel
Farishta hoped to tropicalize London. What is happening in the
United States today is a kind of coassimilation: one more cultural
exchange, like the many this country has experienced before, in
which each side learns from the other and together they create a
new cultural synthesis.

## The Language as a National Flag

Many Anglo writers and politicians have voiced fears that bilingual
education and other public uses of Spanish will foment ethnic
separatism and "Balkanize" this country. But that is not what the
struggle for language rights is all about.

Hispanics fight for bilingual education and other language
rights in part for practical reasons, to protect the interests of
themselves and their children. In today's world, as international
communications become ever easier and more rapid, preserving
Spanish is a way of hedging one's bets. While English is still the
most important language of business and technology worldwide,
there is a whole immense region outside and a large population
inside the United States where markets, contacts, and opportunities are mainly in Spanish. Even Richard Rodriguez, the
California writer who has not always been sure he wanted to
consider himself Hispanic, keeps going back to recover his once-
abandoned Spanish.

Whether bilingual education is good pedagogically obviously
depends on how well it's done. It may help a child comprehend
first lessons and better equip him or her for adult life with the
wider resources of a bilingual culture. Or, if done clumsily or with
a narrow ideological agenda, it may delay the child's learning or
turn him or her off from school—although culturally insensitive
monolingual schooling is even more likely to do that. If done well,
such programs are potentially beneficial to us all, since there can
be no doubt that knowing two or more languages is better than
knowing one. But these technical and pedagogical issues, as
important as they are in themselves for our children's growth and
happiness, are beside the point in a discussion of identity.

The main reason U.S. Hispanics defend their right to use

Spanish in public discourse and to maintain it through their children's education is that they want to be able to continue thinking of themselves as "Hispanic." And since the Hispanics have so little else in common—they are not a single race and do not have a single religion or even a single cuisine—the Spanish language becomes the one thing they can use to identify the members of the group. Many of those who defend bilingual education and the right to speak Spanish at work and to have ballots printed in Spanish are not themselves comfortable speaking or reading the language, but that doesn't matter. The language is their flag, which they cannot surrender without giving up a part of themselves.

## Hispanic Nation—Made in the U.S.A.

A recent book by British-born American journalist Peter Brimelow is provocatively titled *Alien Nation*. It has the virtue of stating clearly the fears that many English-speaking Americans feel regarding the rapid growth of the Hispanic nation and other non-European immigrant groups. Its thesis is that the United States is letting in too many people, and more importantly, they are the wrong kinds of people. The nonwhite newcomers and even whites from as alien a region as Latin America, he argues, cannot or will not sustain the Anglo-American traditions that have made this country great.[14]

There are many problems with Brimelow's discussion, beginning with the highly speculative bases for his claim that immigrants cost more than they contribute to the native-born who are themselves children of native-born—that is, to the people who would be living in this country if the present immigrants had not come.

The problem here is not just the difficulty of guessing what would have happened in the economy absent immigration, including which industries would have suffered and which benefited, and so on. The more serious problem is that it is a pointless question. One cannot, as Brimelow proposes, promote American prosperity by stemming immigration from the poorer countries, because the two phenomena are tied together as parts of the same system. U.S. prosperity is in part dependent on foreign investment by U.S. corporations to create large-scale export industries in poorer countries; these new or enlarged enterprises destabilize the local economies, forcing smaller local enterprises to fold and displacing their entrepreneurs and workers and, by their effects on farm and land prices or their consolidation of larger landholdings, also displace formerly self-supporting peasants. Since the new foreign-based enterprises do not have room for or cannot use the skills of all these displaced entrepreneurs, workers, and peasants, those people join a growing pool of potential emigrants. At the same time, entrepreneurs based in the United States, especially in the electronics, clothing-manufacturing, and other industries, are continually creating low-paid entry-level jobs here which absorb some immigrant labor and encourage further immigration.[15] Thus, no drastic slowdown of immigration to the United States is likely without a collapse of the U.S. economy.

Brimelow's other major argument is that the types of immigrants the United States is receiving are turning it into an "alien nation," a nation of aliens. He means that the large numbers of nonwhites and of whites who do not come directly from Europe— that is, Hispanics—threaten to destroy the special character of the United States because "the American nation has always had a specific ethnic core. And that core has been white."[16] A nation to him is not an imaginary and voluntary construct, agreed upon by its members, but "an *ethnocultural community*" that "intrinsically implies a link by blood" and is fundamentally "an extended family."[17] Non-Europeans, he insists, can never fully join the American family even as adoptees because they cannot comprehend and do not respect this country's ancestral traditions.

This is a peculiarly un-American way of viewing America, one that was explicitly repudiated in our Declaration of Independence. That document breaks with the old reverence for blood linkages to speak of a nation *formed* by men, consciously and for specific purposes—namely, life, liberty, and the pursuit of happiness.

As for that "white ethnic core," what has been at the center of this country's history is not any one ethnic group but the struggle over rights. The forming of the American nation did not end with the English settlers at Jamestown and Plymouth; it has been a very violent and conflictive process in which people of all the races that make up this country played parts. Very large parts of our country's present territory, the whole Southwest and the Southeast, were once Spanish, and their populations were already mixed with indigenous nations and with African Americans by the time they were incorporated into the United States. The Brown Berets and Young Lords of the 1960s, the striking farmworkers and miners of the 1920s, 1930s, 1940s, and beyond, and all those who are still lobbying, marching, protesting, or otherwise demanding to be heard were and are acting in a truly American tradition, the tradition of struggle for full participation by any means necessary that goes back at least to the Boston Tea Party of 1773 and Nat Tyler's rebellion. Americans of every color, accent, and religion have taken this to be their right.

People from the Hispanic tradition may, like Brimelow, also think of the nation as an extended family, but a family of the Hispanic type. In such families the members need not be related by "blood" but may be *hijos e hijas de crianza*, sons and daughters by virtue of their being taken in and cared for by the other family members. It is the only kind of family that America can be.

But most important, we must understand that the Hispanic nation is not in any way *alien*. It is something that is being made right here in the United States, right now. The Hispanic nation is American not only because the ancestors of many of its members were established here before there was a United States. It is American because the whole idea of "Hispanicness" or of a "Latino community" is a home-grown response to problems of discrimination. It is not an ethnic identity that Spanish-speaking people bring with them when they arrive but something they create in response to conditions here in this country and is shaped by U.S. institutions ranging from the structure of the telecommunications industry to the practices of art galleries and museums.

It is also an emulation of an old American tradition: the creation of a solidarity group based on partly invented, partly real ethnic distinctions as a way to confront perceived injustice or simply to get ahead. Such ethnic movements, based on pragmatic alliances that may have only dubious historical precedent, have been formed often in American history for similar reasons. Thus, Tuscans and Lombards and Calabrese and others muted their rivalries to become "Italians" and then "Italian Americans." German-speaking immigrants of Jewish ancestry eventually (but only after years of resistance) joined forces with Yiddish-speaking Eastern Europeans to assert a common pride in being "Jewish." Other German speakers from Austria, Switzerland, and the various German states—who had not always been particularly friendly to one another back home—in the United States formed associations (*Bunds*) and a press addressed to "Germans" or sometimes "German Americans." Some spoke fervently of creating a *Deutschtum* (Germandom) on U.S. soil to preserve their language and traditions. The Germans' insistence on using and teaching their language in communities across the United States aroused Anglo fears much like those being voiced by the "English Only" movement today.

Yet even though some 58 million Americans claim German descent—more than those of any other ancestry—the *Deutschtum* dream has simply evaporated, and the threat of a Germanization of American culture—once taken very seriously by Anglo publicists—has passed.[18] Less and less Italian is heard in Little Italy, less and less Greek in Greektown. It may not have seemed so to any of these groups at the time, but their assertion of a separate ethnic identity, with national costumes and festivals and eventually political caucuses, was a move leading to their assimilation into an expanded American culture. Their resistance to premature assimilation was what allowed them to negotiate the terms of their acceptance of the laws and customs of the new home. Thus, they were contributing while they were adapting to our common culture. That is, they ultimately assimilated into an America that they had helped change.

Mexican Americans, Puerto Ricans, Cubans, Dominicans, Colombians, Salvadorans, and all the others from the Spanish cultures are trying to do the same thing. Being a public, even ostentatious Hispanic is not so different from wearing a button saying "Kiss me—I'm Italian" or "*Erin go bragh!*" These are all ways of saying, Yes, I'm an American, and part of being American is having the freedom to be a little different!

Many Hispanics are people who could never become "Americans" if the racial criteria proposed by some were to prevail, even if they dropped their Spanish surnames. Because of their skin color and hair texture, they would forever remain no more than *pochos*, "tailless ones," or socially inferior beings. Others who are white enough to pass could do so only by abandoning their darker friends and relatives. And this is something most of them do not want to do. Becoming "Hispanic," then, is the only way open to them to be Americans, real authentic Americans with dignity.

They are beginning to embrace the new and less precise categories of Hispanic or Latino so that they can be part of a larger and more influential group and thereby negotiate better terms of assimilation. When they call themselves Hispanics or Latinos, they are not declaring allegiance to any foreign place, but just the opposite. Declaring onself "Hispanic" is a step back from allegiance to Mexico, Cuba, Puerto Rico, the Dominican Republic, or some other land and a step toward joining America.

# Notes

## 1. Imagining a Nation

1. Virgil P. Elizondo, *"Mestizaje* as a Locus of Theological Reflection," in *Frontiers of Hispanic Theology in the United States*, eds. Allan Figueroa, Deck and S. J. Maryknoll (New York: Orbis Books, 1992), 109.

2. James Baldwin, *Notes of a Native Son*, 1984 ed. (Boston: Beacon Press, 1955), "Autobiographical Notes," 8.

3. Anthony Appiah, But would that still be me? Notes on gender, "race," ethnicity, as sources of "identity." Paper presented at symposium, Gender, Race, Ethnicity: Sources of Identity; special issue, Eighty-seventh Annual Meeting, American Philosophical Association, Eastern Division, *Journal of Philosophy* 87 (10 October 1990): 497. Cf. also Ramona H. Edelin et al., "Afro-American or Black: What's in a Name? Prominent Blacks and-or African Americans Express Their Views," *Ebony*, July 1989, 76.

4. Benedict Anderson, *Imagined Communities: Reflections on the Origin and Spread of Nationalism* (London: Verso, 1991), 5–6.

5. Cf. Eric Hobsbawm, "Introduction: Inventing Traditions," in *The Invention of Tradition*, eds. Eric Hobsbawm and Terence Ranger (Cambridge: Cambridge University Press, 1983), 1–14.

6. Anderson, *Communities*.

7. "Sociedad natural de hombres a los que la unidad de territorio, de origen, de historia, de lengua y de cultura, inclina a la comunidad de vida y crea la conciencia de un destino común," in *El pequeño Larrousse ilustrado* (Paris: Librairie Larrousse, 1989); my translation.

8. "'Or l'essence d'une nation est que tous les individus aient beaucoup de choses en commun, et aussi que tous aient oublié bien des choses.'" Ernest Renan, "Qu'est-ce qu'une nation?" in *Œuvres Complètes*, 1, p. 892, cited in Anderson, 1991: 6.

9. Joshua Meyrowitz, *No Sense of Place: The Impact of Electronic Media on Social Behavior* (New York: Oxford University Press, 1985), 57.

10. G. Gómez-Peña, *Warrior for Gringostroika* (St. Paul, Minn.: Graywolf Press, 1993), 71.

11. Richard Dawkins, "Selfish Genes and Selfish Memes," in *The Mind's I: Fantasies and Reflections on Self and Soul*, eds. Douglas R. Hofstadter and Daniel C. Dennett (New York: Basic Books, 1981), 143.

12. Geoffrey Fox, "Lucha y decepción del libertador," *Areíto* 9 (1983): 22–25 and "Liberty and People: Ideological Analysis of the Political Writings of Simón Bolívar," unpublished paper submitted to Primera Bienal Internacional de Ensayo "Simon Bolívar," Caracas, 1983.

13. Miguel Rojas Mix has cataloged much of this phenomenon. See his

243

"Bilbao y el hallazgo de América latina: Unión continental, socialista y libertaria...." *C.M.H.L.B. Caravelle* 46 (1986): 35–47; and Miguel Rojas Mix, "Reinventing Identity," *NACLA Report on the Americas* 34 (1991): 29–33. "Latino Net" is one of several Internet fora for propagating this meme. Throughout 1994 and to this writing, Subcomandante Marcos and the Zapatista National Liberation Army of Chiapas, Mexico, have easily evaded Mexican government censorship by transmitting their messages on the Internet.

14. Rodolfo O. de la Garza, et al., *Latino Voices: Mexican, Puerto Rican, and Cuban Perspectives on American Politics* (Boulder, Colo.: Westview Press, 1992).

15. *Los Angeles Times*, February 6, 1970; quoted in David J. Weber, ed. *Foreigners in Their Native Land: Historical Roots of the Mexican Americans* (Albuquerque, N.M.: University of New Mexico Press, 1973), 9. Salazar was killed by Los Angeles County sheriff's deputies while covering a Chicano antiwar rally in 1970.

16. The origin and intention of this term is discussed in chapter 5.

17. Miguel Rojas Mix, "Bilbao y el hallazgo de América latina: Unión continental, socialista y libertaria...," *C.M.H.L.B. Caravelle* 46 (1986): 35–47.

18. De la Garza, et al., *Latino Voices*.

19. Georg Simmel, "The Web of Group Affiliations," in *Conflict and the Web of Group Affiliations* (New York: Free Press, 1955), 125–195.

20. Lawrence H. Fuchs, *The American Kaleidoscope: Race, Ethnicity and the Civic Culture* (Middleton, Conn.: Wesleyan, 1990), 330.

## 2. Counting

1. Elizabeth Kadetsky, " 'Save Our State' Initiative: Bashing Illegals in California," *Nation*, October 17, 1994, 418.

2. Marc Cooper, "The War Against Illegal Immigrants Heats Up," *Village Voice*, October 4, 1994, 34.

3. Alurista. "El Pan Espiritual de Aztlán," in *Aztlán: Essays on the Chicano Homeland*, eds. Rudolfo A. Anaya and Francisco A. Lomelí (Albuquerque, N.M.: Academia/El Norte Publications, 1989).

4. Cooper, "Illegal Immigrants."

5. Ibid.

6. U.S. Census Bureau, "Current Population Reports: Population Projections for States, by Age, Sex, Race and Hispanic Origin 1993-2020," Washington, D.C., 1993.

7. Cf. quotes in Sam Roberts, "Hispanic Population Outnumbers Blacks in Four Major Cities as Demographics Shift," *New York Times*, October 9, 1994, 34.

8. Ron K. Unz, "How to Grab the Immigration Issue," *Wall Street Journal*, May 20, 1994, A10. The author is described as "a Palo Alto businessman...challenging Gov. Pete Wilson in California's June 7 Republican primary." The challenge failed.

9. *Hispanic Link Weekly Report* (April 25, 1994): 5.

10. Tom Smith, "Ethnic Survey," in *GSS Topical Report Number 19*, National Opinion Research Center (Chicago: University of Chicago, 1990); cited in Roberto O. de la Garza et al., *Latino Voices: Mexican, Puerto Rican, and Cuban Perspectives on American Politics* (Boulder, Colo.: Westview Press, 1992).

11. De la Garza, *Latino Voices*, 13.

12. Earl Shorris, *Latinos: A Biography of the People* (New York: W. W. Norton & Company, 1992), 13.

13. U.S. Bureau of the Census, *Twenty Censuses: Population and Housing Questions, 1790–1980* (Washington, D.C.: U.S. Government Printing Office, 1979), quoted in Yen Le Espiritu, *Asian American Panethnicity: Bridging Institutions and Identities* (Philadelphia: Temple University Press, 1992).

14. Yen Le Espiritu, "Asian American History and Culture," in *Asian American Panethnicity: Bridging Institutions and Identities*, ed. Sucheng Chan (Philadelphia: Temple University Press, 1992), 113.

15. Lawrence Wright, "One Drop of Blood," *New Yorker*, July 25, 1994, p. 46.

16. Ibid., p. 52.

17. Espiritu, *Panethnicity*, 113.

18. Ibid., 131.

19. Ibid., 114.

20. Jacob S. Siegel interview, November 11, 1994.

21. Espiritu, *Panethnicity*, 117.

22. María Elena Diéguez, head of research for Univisión, interview, May 12, 1992.

23. Jorge del Pinal interview, July 8, 1994.

24. Steven A. Holmes, "Census Officials Plan Big Changes in Gathering Data," *New York Times*, May 16, 1994, 1, 13.

25. Patricia A. Montgomery, *The Hispanic Population in the United States: March 1993*, Current Population Reports, Series P-20-475, issued May 1994 by the U.S. Bureau of the Census.

26. Interview, June 29, 1992.

27. Calvin Veltman, "The Status of the Spanish Language in the United States at the Beginning of the 21st Century," *International Migration Review* 24 (1990): 111.

28. Ibid., 122.

29. *Hispanic Link* 12 (September 12, 1994).

30. Arthur M. Schlesinger Jr., *The Disuniting of America* (New York: W. W. Norton & Company, 1992), 109–10; cf. Lawrence H. Fuchs, *The American Kaleidoscope: Race, Ethnicity and the Civic Culture* (Middleton, Conn.: Wesleyan, 1990), 458–73.

31. Ibid. If a common language could do that, there would be no war in what was Yugoslavia.

32. Thomas Weyr, *Hispanic U.S.A.: Breaking the Melting Pot* (New York: Harper & Row, 1988), 74–75.

33. "Sería una locura—comenta una pedagoga cubana—negar a nuestros hijos los beneficios del inglés que es, no sólo el idioma de la promoción y el ascenso en América, sino también el del comercio internacional y las nuevas technologías. El hablar solamente español surge, tantas veces, como un refugio contra la suficiencia, el desprecio anglo." Alberto Moncada, *Norteamérica con accento hispano* (Madrid: Instituto de Cooperación Iberoamericana, 1989), 97–98.

34. Bernard Braem, "Bilinguisme et biculturalisme dans la communauté hispanique aux États-Unis," in *Les minorités hispaniques en Amérique du Nord (1960–1980): Conflits idéologiques et échanges culturels*, ed. Jean Cazemajou (Bordeaux: Presses Universitaires de Bordeaux, 1985): 50.

35. Moncada, *Norteamérica*.
36. Frank René Solano, "Societal Predictors of Spanish Language Use Among Hispanics at Home," Ph.D. diss., Yeshiva University, 1992.

## 3. The Image Machine

1. Lawrence H. Fuchs, *The American Kaleidoscope: Race, Ethnicity and the Civic Culture* (Middleton, Conn.: Wesleyan, 1990), 29.
2. Jane H. Lii, "Dateline: Chinatown," *New York Times*, January 6, 1995, 4. Chinese-language television programming in the New York area consists of five hours a week on cable, most of it entertainment.
3. Arnoldo De León, *The Tejano Community, 1836–1900* (Albuquerque: University of New Mexico Press, 1982); also cf. chapter 4, below.
4. Bernardo Vega, *Memoirs of Bernardo Vega: A Contribution to the History of the Puerto Rican Community in New York*, trans. Juan Flores, ed. César Andreu Iglesias (New York: Monthly Review Press, 1984).
5. *"80 años de historia (1913–1993),"* Suplemento de aniversario de El Diario/La Prensa, 1993.
6. Michael Parenti, *Inventing Reality: The Politics of the Mass Media*. (New York: St. Martin's Press, 1986).
7. "El campeón de los hispanos." This continues to be the slogan of the combined *El Diario/La Prensa*.
8. *"80 años de historia (1913–1993)."*
9. Enrique Fernández, "Premios en la prensa hispana," *Más*, Julio–Agosto 1991, 68.
10. "Harnessing the Power of Hispanic Radio," *Broadcasting*, Apr. 30, 1990, 56.
11. Carlos Agudelo, "De nuevo en sintonía con Paco Navarro," *Más*, Enero–Febrero 1992, 55.
12. Ana Veciana-Suárez, *Hispanic Media: Impact and Influence* (Washington, D.C.: Media Institute, 1990).
12a. Currently (May 1996), is owned 50 percent by Televisa, 25 percent Perenchio, and 25 percent Venevisión. The division Univision Television is owned 25 percent by Televisa, 12.5 percent by each of the other partners.
13. Steven Beschloss, "The Missing Pot of Gold: Saul Steinberg and Bill Grimes Got Into Spanish-language TV Believing the Big Money Would Come. They're Still Waiting," *Channels*, July 16, 1990, 30.
14. NOTIMEX/Miami, 1992.
15. Veciana-Suárez, *Hispanic Media*, 26–27.
16. Ibid.; cf. also "Publishers Shout Over the Din; Future Gains by Hispanic Print Hinges on Quality—in Either Language," *Advertising Age*, Feb. 12, 1990, S12.
17. Cf. "Hispanic Broadcasting Comes of Age," *Broadcasting*, Apr. 3, 1989, 37.
18. "...acostúmbrese usted y escríbalo como quiera."
19. "...y se llama GRAMATICA," *El Diario/La Prensa*, 1992.
20. M. L. Stein, "Concerned About Diversity," *Editor & Publisher* 125 (May 9, 1992): 22; M. L. Stein, "Newspapers Are Trying to Diversify," *Editor & Publisher* 125 (May 9, 1992): 23.
21. Veciana-Suárez, *Hispanic Media*, 19.
22. Aside from religious communities of Amish in Pennsylvania, Stearns County in Minnesota and Amana in Iowa are probably the best-known examples.

23. Lawrence H. Fuchs, *The American Kaleidoscope: Race, Ethnicity and the Civic Culture* (Middleton, Conn.: Wesleyan, 1990), 29.

## 4. The Peoples Within the Image

1. Some Hispanic historians make rather too much of David Glasgow Farragut's Spanish ancestry. As his middle name shows, he had other reference points. Born in Tennessee in 1801 and a U.S. Navy midshipman from the age of nine, he could not have had much exposure to anything Spanish. For the Farragut quote and certain other historical details I have relied on James Trager's invaluable reference work *The People's Chronology: A Year-by-Year Record of Human Events from Prehistory to the Present* (New York: Henry Holt, 1992).

2. L. H. Gann and Peter J. Duignan, *The Hispanics in the United States: A History* (Boulder, Colo.: Westview Press, 1986), 11.

3. Roger L. Parks, "Crypto-Jewish Tradition in the American Southwest" (downloaded from a CompuServe library in 1992); cf. Roger L. Parks. "'El leñador y los enanitos': A crypto-Jewish version of a Spanish folktale." *Romance Philology* 46 (1992): 1.

4. Cf. the oral history collected in Américo Paredes, *Uncle Remus con Chile* (Houston: Arte Público Press, 1993), 26.

5. D. A. Brading, *The Origins of Mexican Nationalism* (Cambridge: Cambridge University Press, 1985), 110.

6. Gann and Duignan, *Hispanics*, 15–17.

7. Cf. the words of a Mexican villager who had crossed it: "...but what a river that Bravo is. Why, it's gobbled up a lot of Mexicans....The water goes like this in a pure whirlpool, and wherever a whirlpool grabs a person, it grabs him and he doesn't get out, it takes him down under." James D. Cockcroft, *Outlaws in the Promised Land: Mexican Immigrant Workers and America's Future* (New York: Grove Press, 1986), 33–34; statement by Isauro Reyes, age fifty-six, from the village of La Purísima, Michoacán.

8. Manuel A. Machado Jr., *Listen Chicano! An Informal History of the Mexican American* (Chicago: Nelson Hall, 1978), 49.

9. Cockcroft, *Outlaws*, 48.

10. Interview of José G. Solárez Jr. in the Ayuntamiento (town hall) de Guadalupe, Arizona, June 21, 1991. On the Yaqui rebellion and its origins, see José Mancisidor, *Historia de la revolución mexicana* (Mexico: Libro Mex Editores, 1959), 74–76.

11. Cockcroft, *Outlaws*, 53.

12. Cf. George J. Sánchez, (New York: Oxford University Press, 1993), 19ff.

13. Telemundo broadcast, July 3, 1994.

14. J. A. Villarreal, *Pocho* (New York: Anchor Books, 1959), 150.

15. For a sympathetic discussion of the *pachucos* and their mythic role in Chicanismo, cf. Marcos Sánchez-Tranquilino and John Tagg. "The Pachuco's Flayed Hide: The Museum, Identity, and Buenas Garras," in *Chicano Art: Resistance and Affirmation, 1965–1985*, eds. Richard Griswold del Castillo, Teresa McKenna, and Yvonne Yarbro-Bejarano (Los Angeles: Wight Art Gallery, UCLA, 1991), 97–108.

16. On the ANMA, see Mario T. García, "American Labor and the Left: The Asociación Nacional México-Americana, 1949–1954," in John A. García et al.,

eds., *The Chicano Struggle: Analyses of Past and Present Efforts* (Binghamton, N.Y.: Bilingual Press/Editorial Bilingüe, 1984); cf. article on Virginia Chacón, one of the participants and the widow of Juan Chacón, a strike leader who also starred in the movie: Patricia Gonzales and Roberto Rodríguez, "Heroine Recalls Epic Strike," *Hispanic Link*, December 5, 1994, 4.

17. Héctor Morales, interview, Phoenix, Arizona, August 19, 1993.

18. "Cuba y Puerto Rico son / de un pájaro las dos alas; / reciben flores y balas / en el mismo corazón."

19. Bernardo Vega, *Memoirs of Bernardo Vega: A Contribution to the History of the Puerto Rican Community in New York*, trans. Juan Flores, ed. César Andreu Iglesias (New York: Monthly Review Press, 1984).

20. John J. Johnson, *Latin America in Caricature* (Austin: University of Texas Press, 1980), 81, 85.

21. Vega, *Memoirs*.

22. Oscar Hijuelos, *The Mambo Kings Play Songs of Love* (New York: Farrar, Straus & Giroux, 1989).

23. Interview, May 6, 1993.

24. Richard Santillan, "Latino Politics in the Midwestern United States: 1915–1986, in *Latinos and the Political System*, ed. F. Chris García (South Bend, Ind.: University of Notre Dame Press, 1988), 107.

## 5. Coming Together

1. For a description of the efficiency of Cuba's G-2, or military intelligence, see Jorge G. Castañeda, *Utopia Unarmed: The Latin American Left After the Cold War* (New York: Knopf, 1993).

2. Rieff also lists equally capricious interventions of Fidel in fields as diverse as medical research, cattle breeding, and even meteorology in *The Exile: Cuba in the Heart of Miami* (New York: Simon & Schuster, 1993), 106.

3. At the time the U.S. government was dispersing the new arrivals from Miami, which is why they happened to arrive in Chicago.

4. Geoffrey Fox, "Honor, Shame, and Women's Liberation in Cuba: Views of Working-Class Emigré Men," in *Female and Male in Latin America: Essays*, ed. Ann Pescatello (London: University of Pittsburgh Press, 1973), 273–90.

5. Geoffrey Fox, "Cuban Workers in Exile," *Trans-Action (Society)* 8 (1971): 21–30; "Race, Sex, and Revolution in Cuba," in *Interracial Marriage: Expectations and Realities*, eds. I. R. Stuart and L. E. Abt. 293–308. (New York: Grossman, 1973); and *Working Class Emigrés from Cuba* (Palo Alto, Calif.: R&E Research Publications, 1979).

6. Americas Watch, "Dangerous Dialogue: Attacks on Freedom of Expression in Miami's Cuban Exile Community." (Washington, D.C.: Human Rights Watch, 1992), and "Dangerous Dialogue Revisited: Threats to Freedom of Expression Continue in Miami's Cuban Exile Community." (Washington, D.C.: Human Rights Watch, 1994).

7. Rieff, *Exile* 119.

8. Americas Watch, "Dangerous Dialogue."

9. M. Torres, "Beyond the Rupture: Reconciling With Our Enemies, Reconciling With Ourselves," *Michigan Quarterly Review* 33 (1994): 425.

10. Interviews, María de los Angeles Torres, March 27, 1985, and subse-

quently; cf. Geoffrey Fox, "Chicago: Mayor's Actions Reflect New Political Balance," *Hispanic Monitor* 2 (April 1985): 1–2.

11. Interview of Rev. Daniel Alvarez, March 22, 1994.

12. Mirtha Natacha Quintanales, "The Political Radicalization of Cuban Youth in Exile: A Study of Identity Change in Bicultural Context," Ph.D. diss., Ohio State University, 1987.

13. Americas Watch, "Dangerous Dialogue."

14. In issue no. 3, for example, dated October 1974 (and published in New York), the main story is about Cuban youth in Puerto Rico, but almost as much space is given to fiction by Lourdes Casal and poetry by Guillermo González, Juan Rodríguez, and Eduardo de Zayas.

15. "Entrevista a Lourdes Casal: Dos semanas en Cuba," *Areíto* 1 (1974), reprinted in *Areíto*'s tenth anniversary issue, 9:9.

16. *Areíto* 9 (1984): 74; Americas Watch, "Dangerous Dialogue."

17. Mark Day, *Forty Acres: Cesar Chavez and the Farm Workers* (New York: Praeger, 1971).

18. Manuel A. Machado Jr., *Listen, Chicano! An Informal History of the Mexican American* (Chicago: Nelson Hall, 1978).

19. Day, *Forty Acres*, 64.

20. All these charges, and more, are in Machado, *Chicano!*

21. Arturo Vázquez, interview, Chicago, March 22, 1994.

22. Yet another hypothesis is that it is a combination of *chihuahuense*, or native of Chihuahua, where many Chicanos came from, and *mexicano*.

23. Carlos Muñoz Jr. and Mario Barrera, "La Raza Unida Party and the Chicano Student Movement in California," in *Latinos and the Political System*, ed. F. Chris García (South Bend, Ind.: University of Notre Dame Press, 1988), 213–35.

24. J. A. Villarreal, *Pocho* (New York: Anchor Books, 1959).

25. See derivation of "race" in the *Oxford English Dictionary*; also cf. Joan Corominas, *Breve diccionario etimológico de la lengua castellana* (Madrid: Editional Gredos, 1987), for the derivation of *raza* in Spanish, which appears to be native to Iberia.

26. José de la Isla, "Richard Nixon's Hispanic Legacy Still Shrouded," *Hispanic Link Weekly* (May 2, 1994), 3.

27. Muñoz and Barrera, "La Raza," 232.

28. Luis Antonio Cardona, *Contributions of the Hispanics to the United States of America* (Rockville, Md.: Carreta Press, 1991), 38.

29. Luis J. Rodríguez, *Always Running: La Vida Loca: Gang Days in L.A.* (Willimantic, Conn.: Curbstone Press, 1993).

30. Carlos Montes, interview, November 17, 1994.

31. E. J. Hobsbawm, *Primitive Rebels: Studies in Archaic Forms of Social Movement in the 19th and 20th Centuries*, 1965 ed. (New York: W. W. Norton & Company, 1959), 3.

32. Ibid., 32.

33. On the active and violent participation of girls in street gangs, cf. Joan Moore, James Diego Vigil, and Josh Levy, "Huisas of the Street: Chicana Gang Members," *Latino Studies Journal* 6 (1995): 27–48.

34. T. S. Kuhn, *The Structure of Scientific Revolutions*, 2nd ed. (New York, 1969).

35. Cf. Joshua Meyrowitz, *No Sense of Place: The Impact of Electronic Media on Social Behavior* (New York: Oxford University Press, 1985), 133 footnote.

36. This, of course, was true not only of Latinos. Martin Luther King Jr. in his last speeches asserted a Christian argument against the Vietnam War, at least partly prompted by the challenges of radical groups such as the Black Panthers.

37. Arturo Vázquez, interview, Chicago, March 22, 1994.

38. This eliminated literacy tests and the poll tax and required that there be bilingual ballots where a linguistic minority had over 5 percent of the vote, thus enfranchising the many Spanish-speaking citizens of the United States in the Southwest.

## 6. Forging the National Agenda

1. U.S. Department of Commerce, Bureau of the Census, "1990 Census Profile," no. 2, June 1991.

2. The phrase "charismatic authority" was introduced by the German sociologist Max Weber in the 1890s. "Charisma" alone is of course a much older term, which Weber borrowed from early Christian theology. See *From Max Weber: Essays in Sociology*, trans. H. H. Gerth and C. Wright Mills, eds. H. H. Gerth and C. Wright Mills (New York: Oxford University Press, 1958).

3. If documentation is needed, cf. Eric Hobsbawm, *The Age of Extremes: A History of the World*, 1914–1991 (New York: Pantheon, 1994).

4. On Perón's charismatic relationship with his followers, see Geoffrey Fox, *The Land and People of Argentina* (New York: HarperCollins, 1990).

5. Pablo Guzmán, "La vida pura: A Lord of the Barrio," *Village Voice*, March 21, 1995, 24–31.

6. COINTELPRO, described by FBI director J. Edgar Hoover in a later-revealed memo of March 3, 1968, targeted what Hoover called Black Nationalist Hate-Groups, including the Black Panther party and even that advocate of brotherly love Martin Luther King Jr.

7. Guillermo Torres, "Where's the Fire in Our Bellies?" *Hispanic Link* 12 (June 6, 1994): 3.

8. *Hispanic Link* 12 (April 11, 1994): 1–2.

9. See discussion below. Bert N. Corona, "Chicano Scholars and Public Issues in the United States in the Eighties," in *History, Culture, and Society: Chicano Studies in the 1980s; National Association for Chicano Studies*, eds. Mario T. García et al. (Ypsilanti, Mich.: Bilingual Press/Editorial Bilingüe, 1983), 11–18.

10. *Hispanic Link* 12 (April 11, 1994)1–2.

11. Cf. Yen Le Espiritu, *Asian American Panethnicity: Bridging Institutions and Identities* (Philadelphia: Temple University Press, 1992). Espiritu's husband is Filipino, which explains why this Chinese-American woman has a Spanish surname in what must be described as an Asian-American panethnic household.

12. Interview, March 22, 1994.

13. Cynthia E. Orozco, "The Origins of the League of United Latin American Citizens (LULAC) and the Mexican American Civil Rights Movement in Texas With an Analysis of Women's Political Participation in a Gendered Context, 1910–1929," Ph.D. diss., University of California, Los Angeles, 1992.

14. Mario Barrera, "The Historical Evolution of Chicano Ethnic Goals: A Bibliographic Essay." *Sage Race Relations Abstracts* 10 (1985): 1–48.

15. *Hispanic Monitor*, March 1985, 6.

16. For a detailed and coherent interpretation of how the "War on Poverty" evolved and its impact on one city, Chicago, see Nicholas Lemann, *The Promised Land: The Great Black Migration and How It Changed America* (New York: Knopf, 1991).

17. Linda Chávez, *Out of the Barrio: Toward a New Politics of Hispanic Assimilation* (New York: Basic Books, 1991), 80.

18. Interview, February 22, 1993.

19. Interview, March 22, 1994.

20. See Geoffrey Fox, "Organizing the New Immigrants: The Hispanic Trade Unionists' Perspective" (New York: New York Research Program in Inter-American Affairs, New York University, 1983) and "Hispanic Organizers and Business Agents in the New York Apparel Unions" (New York: New York Research Program in Inter-American Affairs, New York University, 1984).

21. Corona, "Chicano Scholars."

22. Rick Mendosa, "Power to the People," *Hispanic Link* 13 (February 20, 1995):4.

23. "On Chávez Anniversary, Foundation Support Still Weak," *Hispanic Link* (April 18, 1925):1.

24. Colman J. Barry, *The Catholic Church and German Americans* (Milwaukee: Bruce Publishing Co., 1953).

25. Interview, August 19, 1993.

26. A related group is the National Hispanic Leadership Agenda, a coalition of twenty-eight national associations and community leaders.

27. *Hispanic Monitor* 1 (February 1994), 1–2.

28. *Hispanic Monitor* 1 (May 1984), 1.

29. Guillermo J. Grenier et al., *Latinos in the 1990 Elections Project: The Case of Miami* (Miami: Latino National Policy Survey, 1991), 57.

30. *Hispanic Link*, (March 14, 1994): 1, 5.

31. Twenty-one states now have such commissions, with few paid staff. (Massachusetts, Oklahoma, Rhode Island, and Wisconsin have none—all commission work is done by unpaid commissioners; Washington, D.C., has the most paid staff, with thirteen.) *Hispanic Link* 12 (July 25, 1994).

32. Phil Duncan, ed. *Politics in America: 1994, the 103rd Congress* (Washington, D.C.: Congressional Quarterly, 1993).

33. Kay Bárbaro (pseudonym), *Hispanic Link* (March 21, 1994):3.

34. Lawrence H. Fuchs, "The Secrets of Citizenship," *New Republic*, March 23, 1992, 39.

35. Cockcroft, 188–89.

36. De la Garza, 385–86.

37. Richard Rodriguez, *Days of Obligation: An Argument With My Mexican Father* (New York: Penguin, 1992), 69.

38. Ibid.

39. *Hispanic Link* (July 18, 1994): 3.

40. *Hispanic Link* (April 11, 1994): 4.

41. See *Hispanic Link* (July 11, 1994): 1.

42. *Hispanic Link* (May 23, 1994): 3.

43. *Hispanic Link* (November 8): 3; (November 29): 3.

44. Melita Marie Garza, *Hispanic Link Weekly Report* (July 25 and August 1, 1994): 1–2; reprinted from the *Chicago Tribune*. Garza suggested that Chavis might have more sensitivity to Latino issues than most African American spokesmen, since he is married to "an Afro-Hispanic from the Dominican Republic" and he and his children speak fluent Spanish.

45. Garza, *Weekly Report*.

46. All quotes from Garza, *Weekly Report*.

47. Guillermo J. Grenier, et al., *Latinos in the 1990 Elections Project: The Case of Miami* (Miami Latino National Policy Survey, 1991), 26.

48. Ibid., 39.

49. Torres, "Fire."

## 7. Image Makers

1. Joan Arce Bello, executive director of the Association of Hispanic Arts (AHA), quoted in *El Diario/La Prensa*, May 7, 1993, 4.

2. James Baldwin, *Notes of a Native Son*, 1984 ed. (Boston: Beacon Press, 1955), 8; José Antonio Villarreal, *Pocho* (New York: Anchor Books, 1959); Piri Thomas, *Down These Mean Streets* (New York: Knopf, 1967); Richard Rodriguez, *Hunger of Memory: The Education of Richard Rodriguez* (New York: Godine, 1982).

3. Enrique Fernández, "Spitfires, Latin Lovers, Mambo Kings," *New York Times*, April 19, 1992, 30.

4. Clara E. Rodríguez, *Puerto Ricans: Born in the U.S.A.* (Boston: Unwin Hyman, 1989), 164.

5. In the nationalist movements of nineteenth-century Europe, the growth of the vernacular press was accompanied by "the vernacularization of another form of printed page: the score. After Dobrovsk'y came Smetana, Dvorak, and Janácek; after Aasen, Grieg; after Kazinczy, Béla Bártok; and so on well into our century." Benedict Anderson, *Imagined Communities: Reflections on the Origin and Spread of Nationalism* (London: Verso, 1991), 75.

6. As Panamanian singer and songwriter Rubén Blades demonstrates in a 1994 video shown on public television, *En Clave*.

7. Jimmy Santiago Baca, *Working in the Dark: Reflections of a Poet of the Barrio* (Santa Fe, N.M.: Red Crane Books, 1992), 11.

8. For example, the architect César Pelli, born and educated in Argentina, known among other things for Battery Park City and the high-rise addition to the Museum of Modern Art in New York City; Susana Torre, another architect born and educated in Argentina, designer of prize-winning homes and public buildings and author of works on American architectural history and urban design; the photographer and essayist Camilo José Vergara, from Chile, whose recent work has focused on urban decay and the resourcefulness of the poor in American cities; and, of couorse, the clothing designer Oscar de la Renta, from the Dominican Republic.

9. As American philosopher George Herbert Mead wrote, "We speak of the past as final and irrevocable. There is nothing that is less so, when we consider it as the pictured extension which each generation has spread behind itself. One past displaces and abrogates another as inexorably as the rising generation

buries the old. How many different Caesars have crossed the Rubicon since 1800?" Or how many Pancho Villas have crossed the Río Bravo since 1916? He adds, "the past is a working hypothesis that has validity in the present within which it works but has no other validity....And the novelty of every future demands a novel past." George Herbert Mead, *On Social Psychology: Selected Papers*, Anselm Strauss (Chicago: University of Chicago Press, 1956), 322–23, 337.

10. "BARRIO, 949, del ár. *barr* 'afueras (de una ciudad)' o más precisamente del derivado árabe *barrî* 'exterior', en árabe vulgar bárri." Joan Corominas. *Breve diccionario etimológico de la lengua castellana* (Madrid: Editorial Gredos, 1987).

11. Susana Torre, "En busca de una identidad regional: evolución de los estilos misionero y neocolonial hispano en California entre 1880 y 1930," in *Arquitectura neocolonial: América Latina, Caribe, Estados Unidos*, ed. Aracy Amaral (Mexico: Fondo de Cultura Económica, S.A. de C.V., 1994), 47–60.

12. George Hadley-García, *Hispanic Hollywood: The Latins in Motion Pictures* (New York: Citadel Press, 1990); cf. discussion by Rubén Blades, "The Politics Behind the Latino's Legacy," *New York Times*, April 19, 1992, sec. 2, p. 31.

13. Mirtha Natacha Quintanales, "The Political Radicalization of Cuban Youth in Exile: A Study of Identity Change in Bicultural Context," Ph.D. diss., Ohio State University, 1987, 84–85.

14. Blades, "Legacy."

15. Ilan Stavans discusses this phenomenon in his introduction in Harold Augenbraum and Ilan Stavans, eds., *Growing Up Latino: Memoirs and Stories* (Boston: Houghton Mifflin, 1993), xix.

16. Villarreal, *Pocho*, 165. The derivation of *pocho* is taken from Tom McArthur, ed., *The Oxford Companion to the English Language* (Oxford: Oxford University Press, 1992).

17. Ibid., 100.

18. Ibid, 149. A vignette of violence in a farmworkers' strike, while memorable, is all too brief to satisfy those seeking understanding of the 1930s background to the farmworkers' movements of the sixties, but can be considered a useful supplement to John Steinbeck's *Of Dubious Battle*, which describes the dynamics of those early struggles but focuses more on the Anglo migrant laborers called "Okies."

19. Ramón Saldívar, *Chicano Narrative: The Dialectics of Differences*, The Wisconsin Project on American Writers, ed. Frank Lentricchia (Madison: University of Wisconsin Press, 1990), 65.

20. Rudolfo A. Anaya, *Bless Me, Ultima* (Berkeley, Calif.: Tonatiuh-Quinto Sol International, 1972).

21. Rodriguez, *Hunger of Memory*.

22. Richard Rodriquez, *Days of Obligation: An Argument With My Mexican Father* (New York: Penguin Books, 1992).

23. Saldívar, *Chicano Narrative*, 169–70.

24. Cf. Henry Louis Gates Jr. "'Authenticity,' or the Lesson of Little Tree," *New York Times Book Review*, November 24, 1991, 1.

25. Marcienne V. Rocard, "From Alienation to Self-Assertion in *Famous All Over Town* (1983) by Danny Santiago," in *Les minorités hispaniques en Amérique du Nord (1960–1980): Conflits idéologiques et échanges culturels*, ed. Jean

Cazemajou (Bordeaux: Presses Universitaires de Bordeaux, 1985), 151–62.

26. Dagoberto Gilb, *The Magic of Blood* (New York: Grove Press, 1993).

27. Thomas, *Mean Streets*.

28. Bernardo Vega, *Memoirs of Bernardo Vega: A contribution to the history of the Puerto Rican community in New York*, trans. Juan Flores, ed. César Andreu Iglesias (New York: Monthly Review Press, 1984); Julia de Burgos, *Canción de la verdad sencilla* (San Juan, P.R.: Imprenta Baldrich, 1939); Jesús Colón, *A Puerto Rican in New York, and Other Sketches* (New York: Mainstream Publishers, 1961). Colón wrote for radical Spanish-language papers for many years before beginning an English-language column for the *Daily Worker* in 1955.

29. Esmeralda Santiago, *When I Was Puerto Rican* (New York: Vintage Books, 1994).

30. The book was notable for an additional reason. Her publisher, Vintage, asked her to translate it into Spanish for release in this country as a paperback of identical design, making this one of the first books to be published by a major publisher in Spanish for the U.S. market.

31. Oscar Hijuelos, *The Mambo Kings Sing Songs of Love* (New York: Farrar, Straus & Giroux, 1989).

32. Marifeli Pérez-Stable, "Culture Maker: Oscar Hijuelos." *Culturefront* (Winter 1993), 17–19.

33. Cristina García, *Dreaming in Cuban* (New York: Knopf, 1992).

34. There are several small journals publishing this work in the United States, most of them university based. Some major publishers in the United States, including Knopf and Bantam, and some in Latin America are also putting out books in Spanish by U.S. Hispanics. For a collection of writings in Spanish by Colombians on U.S. life, see Eduardo Márceles Daconte, *Narradores colombianos en U.S.A.: antología* (Bogotá: COCULTURA, Escritores Colombianos en la Diáspora, 1993).

35. Jaime Manrique, *Latin Moon in Manhattan* (New York: St. Martin's Press, 1992).

36. Santayana's works are well known. T. R. Ybarra, the son of a Venezuelan general and a Massachusetts parson's daughter, is today best remembered for his *Young Man of Caracas* (New York: Ives Washburn, Inc., 1942), a lively memoir, and a biography of Venezuela's greatest hero, *The Passionate Warrior: Simón Bolívar.* (New York: Ives Washburn, Inc., 1929).

37. Shelby Steele, "The New Sovereignty: Grievance Groups Have Become Nations Unto Themselves," *Harper's*, July 1992, 47–55.

38. Ibid., 48.

39. Frank Bonilla, "Puerto Rican Studies and the Interdisciplinary Approach," in *Toward a Renaissance of Puerto Rican Studies: Ethnic and Area Studies in University Education*, eds. María E. Sánchez and Antonio M. Stevens-Arroyo (Highland Lakes, N.J.: Atlantic Research Publications, Inc., 1987), 15–20.

40. Frank Bonilla and Rebecca Morales, "Critical Theory and Policy in an Era of Ethnic Diversity: Economic Interdependence and Growing Inequality," in *Latinos in a Changing U.S. Economy: Comparative Perspectives on Growing Inequality*, eds. Rebecca Morales and Frank Bonilla (Newbury Park, Calif.: Sage Publications, 1993), 226–40.

41. Jorge G. Castañeda, *Utopia Unarmed: The Latin American Left After the Cold War* (New York: Knopf, 1993), 177.

42. Celeste Olalquiaga, *Megalopolis: Contemporary Cultural Sensibilities* (Minneapolis: University of Minnesota Press, 1992), xiii.

43. Jane Livingston and John Beardsley, "The Poetics and Politics of Hispanic Art: A New Perspective," in *Exhibiting Cultures: The Poetics and Politics of Museum Display*, eds. Ivan Karp and Steven D. Lavine (Washington, D.C., and London: Smithsonian Institution Press, 1991), 104–20.

44. Peter C. Marzio, "Minorities and Fine-Arts Museums in the United States," in *Exhibiting Cultures: The Poetics and Politics of Museum Display*, eds. Ivan Karp and Steven D. Lavine (Washington, D.C., and London: Smithsonian Institution Press, 1991), 121–27.

45. Tomás Ybarra-Frausto, "The Chicano Movement/The Movement of Chicano Art," in *Exhibiting Cultures: The Poetics and Politics of Museum Display*, eds. Ivan Karp and Steven D. Lavine (Washington, D.C., and London: Smithsonian Institution Press, 1991), 128–50.

46. Tomás Ybarra-Frausto, "*Rasquachismo:* A Chicano Sensibility," in *Chicano Art: Resistance and Affirmation*, 1965–1985, eds. Richard Griswold del Castillo, Teresa McKenna, and Yvonne Yarbro-Bejarano (Los Angeles: Wight Art Gallery, UCLA, 1991), 155–62.

47. Lucy R. Lippard, *Mixed Blessings: New Art in a Multicultural America* (New York: Pantheon, 1990), 42.

48. Ibid.

49. Quoted in Robert Hobbs, "Andres Serrano: The Body Politic," in *Andres Serrano:* Works, 1983–1993, ed. Patrick T. Murphy (Philadelphia: Institute of Contemporary Art, University of Pennsylvania, 1994), 17–43.

50. Hobbs, "Andres Serrano."

51. Lippard, *Mixed Blessings*, 96.

52. Lippard, plate 9.

53. Lippard, plate 16, 82.

54. Gloria Anzaldúa, *The Graywolf Annual Five: Multicultural Literacy*, eds. Rick Simonson and Scott Walker (p. 40); quoted in Lippard, p. 81.

55. Lippard, caption to plate 28.

56. Interview, August 11, 1987.

57. Sigmund Freud, "Humour," in *Character and Culture*, ed. Philip Rieff (New York: Collier, 1963), 263–69.

## 8. American Identities

1. Cf. Joan Corominas, *Breve diccionario etimológico de la lengua castellana*, ed. Dámaso Alonso, 3rd ed., Biblioteca románica hispánica (Madrid: Editorial Gredos, 1987).

2. Erving Goffman, "Embarrassment and Social Organization," in *Interaction Ritual: Essays on Face-to-Face Behavior* (Garden City, N.Y.: Anchor Books, 1967), 97–112.

3. George Herbert Mead, *On Social Psychology: Selected Papers*, ed. Anselm Strauss (Chicago: University of Chicago Press, 1956). Goffman complicates this view somewhat by speaking of "multiple selves" and offers this "double definition": "the self image as an image pieced together from the expressive implications of the full flow of events in an undertaking; and the self as a kind of player in a ritual game who copes honorably or dishonorably, diplomatically or

undiplomatically, with the judgmental contingencies of the situation." Erving Goffman, "On Face Work," in *Interaction Ritual: Essays on Face-to-Face Behavior*, (Garden City, N.Y.: Anchor Books, 1967), 5–46.

4. Daniel C. Dennett, *Consciousness Explained* (Boston: Little, Brown, 1991).

5. Felix M. Padilla, *Latino Ethnic Consciousness: The Case of Mexican Americans and Puerto Ricans in Chicago* (South Bend, Ind.: University of Notre Dame Press, 1985).

6. For an insight into this dynamic, cf. Richard Dawkins, "Viruses of the mind," in *Dennett and His Critics: Demystifying Mind*, ed. Bo Dahlbom (Cambridge, Mass.: Blackwell Publishers, 1993), 13–27.

7. Geoffrey Fox, "Honor, Shame, and Women's Liberation in Cuba: Views of Working-Class Emigré Men," in *Female and Male in Latin America: Essays,* ed. Ann Pescatello (London: University of Pittsburgh Press, 1973, 273–90, and Geoffrey Fox, "Race, Sex, and Revolution in Cuba," in *Interracial Marriage: Expectations and Realities*, eds. I. R. Stuart and L. E. Abt (New York: Grossman, 1973), 293–308.

8. Salman Rushdie, *Satanic Verses* (New York: Viking, 1988), 354–55.

9. For example, in Kureishi's films *Sammy and Rosie Get Laid* and *My Beautiful Laundrette* and his story "With Your Tongue Down My Throat," *Granta* 22 (Autumn 1987): 19–60.

10. Cf. Hans Magnus Enzensberger, "The Great Migration," *Granta* (Winter 1992), 15–51.

11. Cf. *Loisaida* 15 (August 1992); issue dedicated to the memory of Bimbo Rivas.

12. For a description of the area and its evolution, see Janet L. Abu-Lughod, ed., *From Urban Village to East Village: The Battle for New York's Lower East Side* (Cambridge, Mass.: Blackwell Publishers, 1994), especially Mario Maffi, "Appendix: The Other Side of the Coin: Culture in Loisaida."

13. James Thomas Rojas, "The Latino Landscape of East Los Angeles," *NACLA Report on the Americas* 28 (1995): 32–34.

14. Peter Brimelow, *Alien Nation: Common Sense About America's Immigration Disaster* (New York: Random House, 1995).

15. Saskia Sassen, "Why Migration?" NACLA *Report on the Americas* (July 1992): 14–19.

16. Op. cit., 10.

17. Ibid., p. 203.

18. U.S. Census of the Population, 1990.

# Index